# EDUCATOR'S INTERNET FUNDING GUIDE

## *CLASSROOM CONNECT'S* REFERENCE GUIDE FOR TECHNOLOGY FUNDING

By David G. Bauer

and the staff of
*Classroom Connect*

Dorissa Bolinski, Editor

classroom
CONNECT

2221 Rosecrans Blvd., Suite 221, El Segundo, CA 90245
Email: connect@classroom.com
URL:http://www.classroom.com

*Cover Illustration:* Daniel Delis Hill
*Design and Layout:* John Svatek
*Indexer:* Kim Conlin

Copyright © 1998 by Classroom Connect, Inc.

CORPORATE OFFICE
2221 Rosecrans Blvd., Suite 221
El Segundo, CA 90345

URL: www.classroom.com

*Library of Congress Catalog Card Number:* 96-60721

10  9  8  7  6  5  4  3  12  11

ISBN 0-932577-13-X

# CONTENTS

# PREFACE

INTERNET ACCESS is proving to be an invaluable tool in the classroom. Students, teachers, and even whole school districts are benefiting from the easy availability of the Internet's massive amounts of information, but connecting to the Information Superhighway requires funds. This book will serve as a guide for all teachers, principals, school board members, concerned parents, or school technology committee heads who want to avail this resource to their students. You realize the potential gains your students can achieve through the use of the Internet in the classroom, so Internet access for your school becomes your mission. But where do you go from here? Before your school becomes connected, you have to address some important questions. Do you know what equipment, facilities, and training you'll need? How will you get the money to accomplish your goals? Your plan must be guided by a willingness to fully use the great educational opportunities that the Internet and other technological advances can provide to your school.

*This book will guide the reader through the steps necessary to obtain Internet funding from sources other than the school board.*

Finding money to connect schools with the Internet can be a challenge, but you should know that $2 billion may become available to grantseekers during the next five years to finance Internet hookup and other computer technologies for schools. President Clinton is a strong supporter of the Technology Literacy Challenge, an initiative that could begin supplying funds in 1997. In addition, many companies, such as Bell Atlantic, are helping schools get connected. This book will teach you how to tap into these government and corporate dollars.

Whether your school is in Gainesville, Florida or Canberra, Australia, school budgets are being stretched to the breaking point, and new computers and phone lines may not be on your school board's priority list.

So, how do you seek funding from sources other than the school board to initiate access or expand existing resources? Many different methods for obtaining these funds exist. This book will guide the reader through the steps necessary to obtain Internet funding from sources other than the school board.

Raising funds to increase your school's Internet resources can be a challenge, requiring much dedication, but your commitment alone will not be enough. Successful development of technical resources will depend upon your ability to attract others who will also commit to your cause and volunteer their services, donate their funds, and/or help in acquiring resources from others.

Many novice fund-raisers mistakenly believe that they can convince others to "give" simply by conveying their personal conviction, zeal, and commitment to a project. Not only does this approach fail, but overzealous fund-raisers often find that their friends begin to avoid them. Successful fund-raising requires a values-based approach—you must provide potential donors with an exciting opportunity for them to express their personal values through your project.

In order to be successful at raising money for Internet access, you must know why and how access to this resource will appeal to your target donors. Whether you decide to seek funds from foundations and corporations or from the community, your primary focus should always be on why someone else, not you, would support the goal of your project with their, not your, money and/or time.

When considering launching a campaign to raise funds for Internet access, remember that:

- No quick-and-easy techniques for raising money exist.
- The development of technological resources for Internet access requires significant investment, hard work, planning, and follow-through.

Both novice and experienced fund-raisers will appreciate the proven time and cost efficient fund-raising techniques presented in this book and the fund-raising system outlined in the following chapters. The system is based upon the basic tenet that people give money to people they know and trust and for causes in which they believe. Volunteers who believe in and practice ethical fund-raising techniques are the building blocks for this system. In Chapter 2, you will learn how to organize an Internet/Technology Support Group consisting of volunteers who will help you elicit funds for your cause through a variety of means.

Don't be tempted to copy the successful fund-raising techniques of other schools without first analyzing whether these techniques will work for you. Likewise, avoid rushing out to hire a fund-raising professional. Many groups mistakenly think the easiest way to deal with fund-raising is to hire someone else to do it. Before you buy into this way of thinking, read this book and complete the worksheets included in it. In the process you'll learn a great deal, including:

- How to identify the types of fund-raising that your Internet Technology Support Group should consider.
- How to generate your own funding plan.

Professional fund-raisers seldom act independently to raise money for their clients' projects. They can help you get organized; they can assist you in developing a plan; and they can help you facilitate your plan. But they are seldom effective at making calls on donors alone. While you may feel more comfortable when they accompany you on your solicitations, donors will wonder what percentage of their contribution is supporting the fund-raiser and how much is actually going to your school's technology project.

**About this Book** This book explains the basics about grantseeking and other forms of fund-raising. You will learn how to organize an Internet/Technology Support Group; solicit grants from foundations, corporations, and federal and state government; write winning proposals; and organize and implement other successful fund-raising activities. Many chapters contain valuable worksheets to help you organize and plan fund-raising activities. In addition, you will find sample letters to use as guides when contacting potential funding sources. For your convenience, these worksheets and letters are contained on the CD-ROM accompanying this book, so you can easily tailor them to your specific needs. In the appendices to this book, you will find a number of addresses that can link you with funding resources via the Internet. Also included is a list of hundreds of grantmaking foundations and corporations. This list contains information on each organization's name, address, funding focus, geographic focus, contact guidelines, deadlines, funding range, and special interests. The list has been converted into a searchable database on the CD-ROM.

Remember, organization is key to successfully generating money for your Internet/Technology plan. Fund-raising is like baking a cake—before going to the oven, you must first assemble the basic ingredients. This book is designed to help you develop the fund-raising ingredients necessary to produce the best results, whether you are approaching fund-raising from the classroom, building, or school-district level.

**About the author**  As an acknowledged grants expert and lively lecturer, David Bauer has taught successful grantseeking and fund-raising techniques to more than 15,000 individuals. He is the Director of Development for the Center for Educational Accountability and Associate Professor at the University of Alabama, Birmingham School of Education.

In 1981, he created David G. Bauer Associates, a consulting firm that provides educationally based grantseeking and fund-raising seminars and materials. He has also served as the Assistant to the President of the State University of New York, College of Technology and as Director of Extramural Funding and Grants Management at the University of Rochester School of Medicine, Department of Pediatrics.

During his prolific career, Mr. Bauer has written a number of grant and fund-raising books, including: *The Grantseeking Primer for Classroom Leaders*, *The Principal's Guide to Grant Success*, *Successful Grants Program Management*, *The Fund-Raising Primer*, *The How-To Grants Manual*, *The Complete Grants Sourcebook for Higher Education, and Administering Grants, Contracts, and Funds*.

In addition, he has developed two videotape series—*Winning Grants* and *Strategic Fund Raising,* and two software programs—*Winning Links* and *Grant Winner.*

# 1 What Internet Access Means to Your Educational System

THE INTERNET is the fastest growing communications medium ever. This chapter discusses the Internet as an educational tool. In it, you will learn:

- How the Internet can change the current learning environment.
- What the Internet can do for your school.
- How the Internet came into existence.

The most exciting and revolutionary change occurring in education today is the Internet, the world's information superhighway. As the fastest growing communications medium ever, the Internet links more than ten million computers in 160 countries, creating a worldwide communications network that's become home to nearly 100 million people. They constantly communicate with each other, share ideas, and access databases containing the latest information on any topic you can imagine. You can easily understand why the Internet is considered an invaluable tool in the classroom.

Elementary and secondary teachers, media specialists, librarians, administrators, and students are a growing community on the Internet. At last count, more than 65 percent of all schools were connected to the Internet (1996). Several of the states with the most "wired" c;assrooms are: Arkansas, California, Florida, New York, Oregan, Pennsylvania, Tennessee, and Texas.

**Why All the Excitement?** At its most basic level, having access to the Internet brings three dramatic changes to schools:

*Hundreds*

*of thousands of*

*educators get connected*

*to the Internet each*

*month, along with new*

*sources of online*

*information.*

1. The Internet breaks down classroom walls, bringing students and teachers into contact with people and places they would otherwise never have met or visited. This "breaking down of walls" usually occurs when students take their first steps online and send email messages to a class on the other side of the world. Teachers, often isolated in their classrooms, suddenly have immediate access to thousands of colleagues. The classes, and indeed, the schools they attend, suddenly become connected, and the barrier of distance disappears.

2. The Internet dramatically expands classroom resources by making the latest information, graphic images, and software available at the click of a mouse. These resources yield individual and group projects, collaboration, curriculum and lesson plan materials, and an increased level of idea-sharing found only in schools with online access.

3. Internet use encourages independent, autonomous learning, which most educators agree helps students become lifelong learners. And since the Net removes class, race, ability, and disability as factors in communication, it's a natural tool for addressing the needs of all students.

The vibrant, online educational community that's thriving on the Internet has only just begun to take shape. Hundreds of thousands of educators get connected to the Internet each month, along with new sources of online information.

Many of these new online information sites have great educational value that teachers everywhere can integrate into their existing curriculum. Thus, you can easily understand why the Internet has become such a hot topic among educators, students, administrators, and parents around the world!

The Internet is certainly not a fad. It may change dramatically over the next decade—for better or worse—as dynamic forces such as rapid growth, increasing commercialism, and government intervention pervade the system and redefine the Internet paradigm. But a great number of opportunities are emerging—opportunities for teaching and learning in exciting, innovative ways; creating and imagining new worlds; and opening the frontiers of human interaction. Not only will students learn to search, retrieve, collect, and exchange information via the Internet, but they will also learn to analyze, write about, and publish information about any topic. In the near future, not being online will be equivalent to not having an automobile, telephone, or television. Our high-tech, fast-paced, and global society already puts a premium on information, so the sooner your school and its staff get online the better. Today's students will need to be prepared to function and thrive in this new global environment.

Some educators feel that their students are more actively involved, question more, contribute more, work more cooperatively, and initiate learning more often when they use the Internet in the classroom. Others believe that the Internet's ability to allow communication with people all over the world is one of its most important advantages. And still others find that the Internet helps them feel less isolated behind their classroom doors. Some say it enables them to teach their students how to efficiently manage

4

information.

The nature of education is evolving; no longer is the teacher just a dispenser of knowledge. Rather, the teacher acts as a guide in the student's discovery of knowledge. Therefore, the Internet is a timely tool during this stage in education's evolution. Information is the bedrock of knowledge, understanding, and power, so universal access to worldwide databases, up-to-the-minute information, and people-to-people networking provided by the Internet is crucial.

**What Can the Internet Do for My School?**

Here are just a few of the ways schools are using the Internet to reach their educational goals:

- Accessing information—much of it never before available to such a wide audience—in forms such as news bulletins, books, directories, government documents, scientific research, studies, guides, and more.
- Bringing experts from myriad fields into their classrooms, taking students on electronic field trips to the Louvre in France or to the White House in Washington, D.C., and following an explorer as he or she makes new discoveries on a distant continent.
- Downloading hundreds of free lesson plans from sites all over the Internet.
- Collaborating on projects with schools thousands of miles away. Students easily communicate with peers or keypals (email penpals) across the globe. Think how foreign language students would value having access to teachers and students in Europe or Asia! Before too long, schools will be using cutting-edge Internet technology such as CU-SeeMe to use their computers to videoconference with students worldwide.
- Listening to classical or jazz music while learning about its composers, or viewing video clips created by a fourth grade class located thousands of miles away.
- Locating free graphics files, computer programs, and

other free technical material.

Libby Adams, a computer resource teacher in a Kansas City magnet school, believes that the Internet has broken down her classroom walls. When her year-long classroom theme was worldwide communications, her class worked with other students who had visited Mexico via the MayaQuest Project, followed an Arctic team to the North Pole through the International Arctic Project, and compared that expedition with earlier online Antarctic visits. Her class learned how Spring shows its face in many parts of the world, and they tracked the weather from Iceland to Hawaii. Because of the Internet, these distant places were not just dots on a map for her students, but real locales with a human side that could not have been unlocked in textbooks.

**Just What Is the Internet?** The Internet is difficult to define in just a few sentences. Technically, the Net is an interconnected, spider web–like system of millions of computers linked together with telecommunications software and hardware. It's really the sum of all people and organizations who connect their personal computers to other computers with devices called modems. Modems enable computers to communicate through phone lines, linking people from the far reaches of the world.

The Internet began as a global communications network designed by the U.S. military in the mid 1960s that would operate even if one or more links became inoperative. As universities and research laboratories began to do more direct business with the government, they were granted access to the Internet, known then as the ARPANet. For almost two decades the Internet existed for the exclusive use of government, researchers, and higher education institutions. In the early 1990s, the government changed the way it financially supports the Internet, making it easier for individuals to affordably access the network. Within a year, dozens of entrepreneurs formed companies offering low-cost Internet access to individuals, businesses, and schools. Now, almost anyone with a computer and modem can get online and start surfing the Net!

No doubt about it—the Internet is a vital communication tool that should become a permanent fixture in all schools and a part of the teaching process. But connecting schools to the Internet costs money, and finding that money can be a challenge. So the question remains—how can you find funds for Internet access at your school? Finding the funds for Internet connection is possible, but to do so, you must first understand the basics of the Internet and then determine how to make its value apparent to those in control of the funds! Appendix A confronts some of the technical issues involved in connecting your school to the Internet.

So, you realize what the Internet can do for your students and teachers in the classroom. Next, you need to think about organizing an Internet Technology Support Group to help you unearth the money necessary to access this exciting tool. The next chapter will explain just that.

# 2 Developing a Support Group and Linkages to Funding Sources

ATTRACTING support for your Internet access project will be key to its success. This chapter explains how to assemble community volunteers into an Internet Technology Support Group to help raise funds for your Internet access project. It will address:

- How to generate interest for your plan to elicit help from individuals and organizations.
- The best types of people for your support group.
- How to contact potential volunteers.

Before you raise any money for your technology plan, you must develop community support and "buy-in" from key individuals and organizations and develop an Internet Technology Support Group to help in your fund-raising efforts. While you may feel ready to single-handedly write a grant proposal or ask a local millionaire for the money, hold back. Your chances for success increase dramatically when you involve others in your plan. Your support group can include community volunteers, including teachers, school administrators, parents, students, alumni, business persons, area college professionals, senior citizens, and others.

**Getting People to Support Your Plan**

❖

*A visible and involved group that supports your Internet technology educational program will assure potential donors that you will be able to continue to raise the funds necessary to support the equipment, software, and program maintenance that their investment will require.*

❖

You are aware that access to the Internet will enhance teaching and learning in your school. Next, you need to discern what others know about the Internet and why they would care about the Internet opportunity and educational enhancement. Remember, people care about things that get through their coat of armor and touch the values they hold dear. Individuals and organizations likely to support the development of technology resources need to see vivid examples of how Internet access will affect their areas of concern. By identifying how individuals/organizations can relate access to the Internet with their areas of concern, you will accomplish two important steps:

1. You will identify the types of individuals and organizations you need for a support group. Whether you are developing a school district's technology program or just trying to get your building onto the Internet, you will need to form a support group to ensure success. Once the group is formed, you will gain insight into its members' values and motivations and the approach you should take to get them to support your project.

2. By documenting how Internet access will improve education, you can begin the process of developing special projects or appeals. For example, you may want to consider how the advantages of the Internet could be used to help mentally and physically challenged children reach their full potential. In fact, parents of these children are often organized and vocal and could be important supporters to enlist in your cause.

Before you decide to slay the fund-raising dragon, remember that your ability to raise money will depend largely on how well you have documented your support. You will need to demonstrate that you have a strong base of support, whether you locate a government, foundation, or corporate grant source or raise money by implementing a variety of fund-raising activities.

The existence of a visible and involved group that supports your Internet/technology educational program will assure potential donors that you will be able to continue to raise the funds necessary to support the equipment, software, and program maintenance that their investment will require. Federal and state grantors will actually consider the involvement and strength of a prospective grantee's support group when making funding decisions. This area is frequently evaluated and assigned points by reviewers when scoring and ranking proposal applications. In fact, many grantors will want to know when your support group was formed, the number of times it has met, and the length of the meetings. They will then use this information to assess your true commitment to solving the problem you are proposing to address.

Even when raising funds through means other than grantseeking, you need to assure the prospective donor that your support group is committed to ensuring the donor's funds are used to see an Internet/technology/education problem through to the desired end.

**Building Your Support Group**

This book can assist school districts who have yet to initiate a broad-based technology support group, as well as schools within a district who want to access technology quicker than their district technology committee is willing. First, find out if a formal technology committee already exists within your district. Your Internet Technology Support Group can work in tandem with an existing technology committee or work alone if one does not exist. You will also need to learn if any district policies related to the formation and activities of such a committee or group exist. Of course, if you've never heard of your district's technology committee, it probably does not exist, and if it does, it is not doing a very good job! In either case, your district should welcome your group's assistance.

Strong support groups have several attributes that you should consider during the formation and growth of your group.

1. Strong support groups consist of a variety of people who join together to address a particular problem. You do not need special permission to join together to help the youth in your community, but you will need to attract concerned individuals who care about improving your educational system. Don't just gather people who want to "preach to the converted." Likewise, do not fill your support group with computer wizards and Internet surfers. Choose members from a wider base of support. Consider involving individuals from the following categories and groups:

   • *School Officials*—This group includes educators, curriculum experts, technical support staff, learning lab instructors, and administrators.

   • *Volunteer Support Groups*—From the Parent Teacher Association (PTA) to the student council, individuals from these groups should be included in your Internet Technology Support Group.

   • *Alumni*—If your school has an alumni group enlist support from its members, and consider developing one if none exists. In fact, you can develop an alumni group with the explicit purpose of raising funds for technology.

   • *Students*—Yes, ask students to join your group. They will provide a sobering influence to help keep your solutions pragmatic and user-friendly. The students you choose must be excited about the opportunities that technology can provide. They must also want to be involved in its integration into their school and the funding need to do this.

- *Teacher Organizations and Unions*—The efforts of your support group will create change in the classroom by integrating technology into the curriculum. These changes will require teacher retraining and inservice education. Therefore, it is important to immediately acquire the support of these advocates.
- *Business People*—You can raise the level of awareness, concern, and support of the business community by asking a group of interested employers involved with your chamber of commerce to provide you with information on the Internet and technology needs of their companies. Data on the technical entry-level skills needed by their employees will affirm their support of your project. In addition, it will help persuade those who believe education requires no more than the basic "three Rs," a blackboard, and a ruler.
- *College and University Professionals*—Local college and university professionals can provide your Internet Technology Support Group with a wealth of human resources. Individuals from these institutions are often knowledgeable of the community and have access to information on funding sources right at their Internet fingertips. They also know people at their institutions who have experience in grantseeking and organizing grants systems. In addition, they will be happy to work with a group whose efforts will help provide higher education with computer literate high school graduates.
- *Senior Citizens*—Many technology groups hesitate to ask senior citizens for their help because they fear that the seniors will not understand cutting-edge technology. However, senior citizens can play a valuable role in your Internet Technology Support Group if they are correctly cultivated. If you can explain to them how Internet access and technology enhancement will allow their grandchildren to compete and excel in the next century, you can win their undying support.

2. Strong support groups have a cause, a need, and a mission. You will learn how to refine your cause later in this book, but now you need to internalize Chapter 1's message— Internet access and enhanced technological resources will afford your students every opportunity to excel.

3. Strong support groups have structure. Develop a list of the necessary subcommittees and the tasks that must be accomplished to generate the level of change your group desires. Examples of subcommittees include: public relations; accounting and finance; technology equipment; software; education; governance and bylaws; and school board recruitment. Contact a corporation in your area to see if they will lend you their strategic planner to help you organize a structure and a mechanism to develop your goals and objectives.

4. Strong support groups develop their own way of approaching the tasks necessary to function and develop job descriptions that will insure success. Members assess their resources and their management styles and compare their findings with the requirements of the job.

5. Strong support groups consist of movers and shakers. You may have heard the expression, "Give the job to a busy person and they will get it done." Individuals who are organized and motivated will produce the best results for your group.

6. Strong support groups view themselves as winning teams made up of individuals who are able to work together. The individuals are aware of their own work styles and skills, and they bring this knowledge to the group. When organized properly, the group develops a synergism that fulfills the individuals' needs. Individuals work to develop their own sense of achievement, and recognition is important only if it reflects how and what they value and why they got involved.

It may be beneficial to provide your group with a seminar on quality management techniques or work styles to help your group members appreciate their different approaches to task development and completion. Such a workshop will also allow members to discuss how to help each other function most effectively and how to develop a leadership structure that works. This may prevent some common group problems. For example, selecting a leader who repeatedly changes the direction, process, structure, and expectations of the project would not be a wise choice for a group that primarily likes an environment in which the process, quality indicators and deadlines are known and adhered to. To avoid such a selection, however, the group members must understand the group's dynamics.

Use the Support-Group Worksheet on the next page (Figure 2.1) to list key individuals and organizations in your community, why they may be interested in Internet access and the development of technology resources (the advantages to them) for students, and how you can approach them for endorsement of your project and involvement in your support group.

**Resources Required to Raise Money**   In addition to the active support of individuals and organizations in your community, you will need resources. The worksheet on page 15 (Figure 2.2) provides a nonexhaustive list of the resources required to raise money. Use the worksheet to list the individuals or organizations that may be helpful in providing these resources. For instance, I was recently working on a project in which a local printer took a particular interest. He provided all of the printing free of charge. In addition, he solicited a paper supplier to donate all of our paper needs. What resources can you identify and match with a potential donor or donor group?

Do not forget to include the service groups who have expressed concern regarding education or school-to-work transition. Review the list in Figure 2.3 on page 16 of service clubs and organizations and add your own suggestions to the list. (Note: Besides working with your support group

**Figure 2.1**
Support-Group Worksheet

Review the suggested categories of individuals and organizations to include and record the names of potential participants.

**Whom to Invite:**

_____ Parents _____

_____

_____ Corporate leaders _____

_____

_____ Foundation board members _____

_____

_____ College professors and educators _____

_____

_____ Retired teachers _____

_____

_____ Wealthy and influential people _____

_____

_____ Other individuals _____

_____

_____ Organizations _____

_____

**Why They Might Be Interested:**

_____

_____

**Who Will Approach Them and How:**

_____

_____

**Figure 2.2**
Community Resources
Worksheet

Put a check mark next to all
of the resource areas where
you will need assistance. List
the individuals or organizations that could be helpful in
providing these resources.

_____ Evaluation of project _____

_____

_____ Computer programming_____

_____

_____ Computer equipment _____

_____

_____ Printing_____

_____

_____ Layout and design work_____

_____

_____ Budget skills, accounting, cash flow, auditing_____

_____

_____ Purchasing assistance _____

_____

_____ Audiovisual assistance (equipment, videotaping, etc.)

_____

_____ Travel _____

_____

_____ Long-distance telephone calls_____

_____

_____ Searching for funding sources _____

_____

_____ Sales skills _____

_____

_____ Writing and editing skills _____

_____

_____ Other equipment and materials _____

_____

_____ Other _____

_____

and/or providing some of the resources necessary to raise money, Hellenic groups, business groups, service clubs, and membership organizations may be interested in providing grant support for your project. These groups are often approached to support parts of a costly proposal or a matching grant component, or to challenge other organizations to raise an amount equal to their grant.)

**Figure 2.3** Service Clubs and Organizations

| Organization | Contact/Phone | Interests/Values |
|---|---|---|
| Jaycees | _____ | _____ |
| Junior League | _____ | _____ |
| Kiwanis Club | _____ | _____ |
| Knights of Columbus | _____ | _____ |
| Masons | _____ | _____ |
| Church Groups | _____ | _____ |
| | _____ | _____ |
| Fraternal Groups | _____ | _____ |
| | _____ | _____ |
| Other | _____ | _____ |
| | _____ | _____ |

**Getting Your Foot in the Door**

So far you have identified the individuals and organizations you should approach for support and have focused on the reasons they might be interested. Starting with a few volunteers, identify who will contact these individuals and organizations and decide the goal of that contact. Forming a small steering committee of self-starters from your community who are interested in helping develop the structure for a larger Internet Technology Support Group is a good way to begin. You can invite the general public to an open forum or town hall meeting to discuss the formation of an Internet Technology Support Group. However, be aware that a town hall meeting can become unmanageable, especially if a large number of Internet technology critics are present. Instead, you may want to ask some key individuals from your steering committee to invite other persons who are already knowledgeable about the Internet's opportunities to a larger meeting and discuss the formation of your support group. Hold a series of meetings at which you both present your project plan and emphasize the role of the support group.

You will ultimately benefit by developing a support group. For instance, you may be able to capitalize on one of your new advocates who has links to a government agency, a corporate donor, or a foundation. Studies document the following:

- Success increases five times with a foundation or corporate funding source when contact is made by a linkage or mutual friend before the proposal is written.
- Success increases three times with government grantors when preproposal contact is made.

You need to organize your support group now so you can find out whom your members know! As soon as the group is organized, and you feel that its members are ready to "buy into" and work for school change/improvement, begin an inventory of their linkages. A "linkage" is a direct association between one of your support group's members or an indirect association of a member's friends or family with an organization or business that could potentially provide funds or services for your project.

Use the following sample letter (Figure 2.4, on the next page) and the worksheet (Figure 2.5, on pages 20–21) to uncover who knows whom. Have your most prestigious support group member sign the letter and introduce the concept of linkages at one of your group meetings. This will improve the quantity and quality of the linkages divulged.

**Figure 2.4**

Inventory of "Linkages"
Sample Letter

Dear *[Name]*:

There are solutions to the problems/opportunities that we have discussed at our support group meetings, but the implementation of the solutions costs money. We will seek some of this money through grant funds from foundations, corporations, and state and federal sources.

Foundations and corporate sources granted over $16 billion last year, and this figure will climb to $17 billion this year. These funding sources make these awards every year, and every year the funds they distribute will increase. However, these grantors have limited staff and support. In fact, while there are some 40,000 foundations, they employ only 4,000 individuals, and fewer than 1,000 have offices. Considering these factors, we must carefully plan our approach, especially since research indicates that contacting the grantor before writing the proposal increases success by 500 percent.

That's where you come in. We are not soliciting you for money, nor do we want a list of all your wealthy friends. We are asking that you provide us with a list of your friends, associates, and relatives who have a relationship with grantors so that we will know whom to call to help us get our foot in the door.

The attached Foot-in-the-Door Worksheet is aimed at gathering the information we need. This linkage information will help us to know when to ask you for assistance in securing personal or telephone contact with a grantor. Your responses will be kept confidential, and the only person who will have access to this information is *[name of individual]*. While we are a neighborhood school, we can still reach out to a variety of funding sources, and the linkages you provide will help us do so.

When our research indicates that our project is particularly suited to a funder that you know, we will contact you to discuss your assistance. We may just need a foot in the door, or you may want to accompany us on a visit to the potential funding source or even visit them yourself. In any event, we will not contact any of the sources you suggest without your prior approval.

Please review and complete the attached Foot-in-the-Door Worksheet before our next meeting on *[date]* so we can work together to make a difference. If we do not receive the worksheet before this date, please expect us to call you to arrange to pick it up.

Sincerely,


*[Your name]*

Bauer and Ferguson's user-friendly software package provides a way for you to organize and manage your linkages so that you always know who has the ability to get your group's foot in the door of a particular funding source. The program—Winning Links—operates on an IBM or IBM-compatible computer and is available on 5.25″ or 3.5″ disks. If you are interested in obtaining more information about this software program, call (800) 836-0732.

Developing a support group and a system for gathering linkage information will provide the basis for continued investment in your school's technology needs. The Internet opportunities for your children's educational development will change, requiring new equipment, in-service classes for education, and maintenance. Whether you are selecting techniques to raise resources for your initial investment, increase your current level of Internet technology, or maintain and upgrade your existing system, funds will be necessary, and your support group will be ready.

After your support group is assembled, you are ready to begin approaching potential funders. These include foundations, corporations, government agencies, and individuals. The next chapter will explain how to persuade donors to motivate themselves to give.

**Figure 2.5**
Foot-in-the-Door Worksheet

Name and Title: _____

_____

Home Address and Phone (Winter and Summer):

_____

_____

Business Address & Phone:

_____

_____

1. Of what foundation boards are you currently a member?

_____

_____

2. Of what foundation boards are you a past member?

_____

_____

3. On what foundation boards do members of your family serve?

| Name of Relative | Relationship | Name of Foundation |
|---|---|---|
| _____ | _____ | _____ |
| _____ | _____ | _____ |
| _____ | _____ | _____ |

4. On what foundation boards do your friends and associates serve?

_____

_____

5. With what corporations do you have a relationship?

| Name of Corporation | Relationship to Corporation |
|---|---|
| _____ | _____ |
| _____ | _____ |
| _____ | _____ |
| _____ | _____ |

**Figure 2.5**
(continued)

6. What corporate relationships do relatives, friends, and
   associates have?

   *Name*                  *Corporation*          *Relationship to Corporation*
   _____        _____       _____
   _____        _____       _____
   _____        _____       _____
   _____        _____       _____

7. In what federal, state, city/county funding agencies do you
   have contacts?

   *Name of Agency*
   *(Department/Division/Program)*             *Name/Title of Contact*
   _____        _____
   _____        _____
   _____        _____

8. What contacts do you have with federal, state, and city or
   county elected officials who could influence education-
   related appropriations? If the federal official is a senator or
   representative, indicate what state he or she represents.

   Name & Title: _____

   Federal/State/City/County: _____

   Which State: _____

   Which City, County: _____

   Name & Title: _____

   Federal/State/City/County: _____

   Which State: _____

   Which City, County: _____

9. Are you a member of or do you have a consulting, advisory,
   or other relationship with other groups or organizations?

   *Name of Organization*                  *Nature of Your Relationship*
   _____        _____
   _____        _____

# 3 Why Individuals and Organizations Should Fund Your Technology Program

Your Internet Technology Support Group will need to know how to present its project to potential donors. This chapter will help you organize the information you need before approaching donors for money to fund your Internet access project. You will learn:

- How to get donors to motivate themselves to give money to your program.
- How to document that your students' and teachers' level of achievement would increase with Internet access and better technology.
- How to create a draft of your plan by outlining your project and summarizing important aspects.

Now that your Internet Technology Support Group is in place, you must decide how to present your project so others will give. Describing the "cause" or the reason to give is the first step in successful fund-raising.

When asked why individuals should donate to increasing a school's technology, most novice fund-raisers would document the lack of equipment, reduced access to computers and the Internet, the age of their existing technology base, and/or difficulties with the current equipment. The basic problem with these types of responses is that they center on physical equipment and prevent the donor from focusing on the real issue.

**Getting the Donor to Give**

Your "cause" is not to increase the quality and quantity of educationally based equipment and technology at your school. Donors do not give because equipment is over-utilized, old, or nonexistent. They give because they perceive what you could do for education with better technology. In other words, the Internet and the necessary technical equipment are a means to an end. Access to the Internet for each classroom, student, and teacher is not an "end"—it is a means to change what exists now in your school.

Focusing on that "end" will provide motivation for the donor to give. Your group must clearly define what an increase in technology will enable your school and its students, teachers, and administrators to accomplish. For example, how is your request for increased technology and Internet access related to:

- Increasing achievement scores.
- Preparing students for future employment opportunities.
- Promoting individualized instruction.
- Addressing the challenges of special needs' students.
- Maintaining student interest.
- Tracking student profiles to provide feedback to parents.

Be sure to explain how the community could benefit from your project—a superior school system breeds a larger pool of well-trained and prepared future employees.

To talk knowledgeably about your school's technology needs, you must complete an inventory of your school's existing equipment and current capacity to support Internet technology. The following technology inventory worksheet (Figure 3.1) will help you identify the areas of need in your school. Be careful not to waste time collecting this information if it has already been collected. Therefore, contact the technology department of your school or school district to find out:

- If there are other groups concerned with this issue.
- If your school has a standing committee on technology or a subcommittee that deals solely with the Internet.
- If there are technology-related district goals and objectives already in place.
- If there are rules you must follow in raising funds for technology.

If you cannot locate an existing technology inventory, volunteers from your support group can work with students, teachers, and administrators to prepare one. The Technology Inventory Worksheet does not need to be completed by a technology, communications, or computer expert. But recruiting knowledgeable volunteers from the business community (phone company, power company, etc.) to help you perform the inventory will raise your community stakeholders' awareness of your school's situation. (See Chapter 2).

..............................................................................................................

**Figure 3.1**
Technology Inventory
Worksheet

**Complete this worksheet for each target group or project.**

School building: _____

Number of instructional areas: _____

Number of computers: _____

*(continued)*

**Figure 3.1**
Technology Inventory
Worksheet *(continued)*

| *Hardware Specs (e.g., RAM)* | *Year Purchased* | *Software Location (e.g., computer lab)* |
| --- | --- | --- |
| _____ | _____ | _____ |
| _____ | _____ | _____ |
| _____ | _____ | _____ |

Special technology-related equipment and software:

_____

_____

Network communication (LANs, ISPs, SLIPs, PPPs, etc.):

_____

_____

Number of electrical outlets per classroom or instructional area:

_____

_____

Number of classrooms or instructional areas with telephone capabilities:

_____

_____

Type of wiring:

_____

_____

Other important physical characteristics:

_____

**Figure 3.1** **Current Instructional Tech Capability**
*(continued)*

- Computer Usage (Number Hours/Week): _____

- Lab Usage (Number Hours/Week): _____

- Specialized Uses: _____

  Teleconferencing (Number Hours/Week): _____

  Internet (Number Hours/Week): _____

  Extended Classroom (Number Hours/Week): _____

  Used Where: _____

  Used By whom: _____

  For what purpose: _____

**Teacher Training in Educational Technology:** Conduct a survey to find out the number of teachers with computers and their current experience base.

**Administrative Usage of Computers:** Conduct a survey to find out the current experience base of your administration.

Percentage of students/staff with access to home computers: ___

Hours per week that student/staff spend doing homework on personal computers: _____

Percentage of students/staff with Internet connection: _____

*(continued)*

**Figure 3.1**
Technology Inventory
Worksheet *(continued)*

Hours per week students/staff spend on the Internet: _____

How the Internet is being used by students/staff: _____

_____

Does the school have a computer club? _____

Who maintains the existing computers and network? _____

Who makes purchasing decisions (i.e., hardware, software, upgrades)? _____

*If you are proposing that the Internet and increased technology will increase subject competency and student scores, you must clearly document the levels at which your students and technology currently operate.*

Once you have completed your school's physical inventory and surveyed your students, faculty, and administration, you will know what facilities exist to support your school's Internet capability. When soliciting funding sources, you will claim that Internet access and increased communications technology can increase student achievement and promote positive changes in your instructional delivery. To prove this, you must document that a gap exists between your student's current achievement level and the level of achievement that could be attained through increased and more current technology (Figure 3.2). Your school's guidance office and officials can help your group document the left side of Figure 3.2, which illustrates your students' current knowledge and skill levels in basic subject areas and on standardized tests. Your technology inventory worksheet provides the data on existing access and usage of the Internet and technology enhanced instruction. If you are proposing that the Internet and increased technology will increase subject competency and student scores, you must clearly document the levels at which your students and technology currently operate.

**Figure 3.2**
Knowledge and Skills Gap

| What Exists Now | What Could Be |
|---|---|
| Current achievement level | Increased achievement and skills |
| Test scores (e.g., math, reading) | Projected increase in test scores |

In order to establish the goals on the right side of Figure 3.2 (what your students' knowledge and skill level could be), consult teachers and administrators. By focusing on the changes in student achievement that are most likely to be influenced by access to the Internet and communications technology, you can establish goals for your school. Once you commit to these goals, you will be able to:

- Develop a motivating and compelling case or need. (The motivation is to close the gap or, in other words, reduce the disparity between what the current situation is and what it could be.)
- Outline a plan to close the gap, describing what access and equipment will be needed and how the sequence of events to effect change will occur.
- Establish measurable objectives and time frames so that everyone knows how, when, and what will be measured.

Your next step is to document the gap in technology, equipment, and software. (See Figure 3.3.) Use the physical information collected on your Technology Inventory Worksheet to develop a concise picture of your technology gap. For example, your school may supply only one computer for every 100 students, and your classrooms may be equipped with only three 110 volt electric outlets and have no phone or cable access. Likewise, there may be only a few classes with Internet access, benefiting only a small portion of your student body. You need to show what the situation is like now and what it could be. For instance, you might

**Figure 3.3**
Technology, Equipment, and
Software Gap

| What Exists Now | What Could Be |
| --- | --- |
| Hardware, software | Number of computers |
| Number of students with computer access | Number of students with computer access |
| Number of classrooms with computer access | Number of classrooms to be computer accessible |

mention that you plan on making one computer available for every five students and equipping every classroom with multiple outlets and phone and cable access.

Now that you have both the knowledge and skills gap and the technology, equipment, and software gap clearly focused, you are ready to develop a draft of your plan for bridging the void between what is and what could be. The following spreadsheet (Figure 3.4), known as a Project Planner, will help you outline your project and summarize several important aspects, including:

1. The staffing necessary to complete your tasks.
2. The prescribed activities that will occur and how they relate to cost and the attainment of the objectives.
3. A framework in which to evaluate the tasks performed by consultants.
4. A detailed analysis of the materials, supplies, and equipment related to each objective.
5. A budget and cash forecast.
6. A way to document in-kind or matching contributions.

**Guidelines for Completing a Project Planner**

There are many ways to complete a Project Planner, but you will find the following general guidelines helpful. Just remember that the key is to make your Project Planner work for you as you plan and implement your project. If you are not familiar with spreadsheets, the Project Planner can seem a bit overwhelming. But, the only real mistakes you can

**Figure 3.4**  Project Planner Worksheet

# PROJECT PLANNER™

© David G. Bauer Associates, Inc.
(800) 836-0732

PROJECT TITLE: _____

Proposal Developed for _____

PROJECT DIRECTOR: _____

Proposal starting date _____

Proposal Year _____

Sheet ____ of ____

A. List Project objectives or outcomes A. B.
B. List Methods to accomplish each objective as A-1, A-2, A-3 ... B1, B-2 ...

| MONTH | | PROJECT PERSONNEL | TIME | PERSONNEL COSTS | | | | CONSULTANTS • CONTRACT SERVICES | | | | NON-PERSONNEL RESOURCES NEEDED SUPPLIES • EQUIPMENT • MATERIALS | | | | | SUB-TOTAL COST FOR ACTIVITY | | MILESTONES PROGRESS INDICATORS | |
|---|---|---|---|---|---|---|---|---|---|---|---|---|---|---|---|---|---|---|---|---|
| BEGIN | END | | | SALARIES & WAGES | FRINGE BENEFITS | TOTAL | | TIME | COST/WEEK | | TOTAL | ITEM | COST/WEEK | QUANTITY | TOT. COST | | TOTAL I.L.P | | ITEM | DATE |
| C / D | E | F | | G | H | I | | J | K | | L | M | N | O | P | | Q | | R | S |

TOTAL DIRECT COSTS OR COSTS REQUESTED FROM FUNDER ▶

MATCHING FUNDS, IN-KIND CONTRIBUTIONS, OR DONATED COSTS ▶

TOTAL COSTS ▶

T

% OF TOTAL

100%

▼   ▼   ▼

make when completing it are mathematical, such as incorrect addition, multiplication, etc.

*Column A/B: Objectives and Methods*

List your project objectives and label each; for example, Objective A, Objective B, Objective C, etc. List the methods you will use to accomplish each of the objectives. Think of the methods as the tasks or activities you will use to meet the need. Label each of the methods under its appropriate objective; for example, A-1, B-1, C-1, etc.

*Column C/D: Month*

Record the month you will begin each activity or task and the month you will end each activity or task. For example, 1/4 means you intend to begin the first month after you receive funding and perform the activities over four months (16 weeks). If you know the start-up month, you can use it.

*Column E: Time*

Record the number of person hours, weeks, or months needed to accomplish each task listed in column A/B.

*Column F: Project Personnel*

List the names of the key personnel who will spend a measurable or significant amount of time on each listed task or activity and on the accomplishment of each objective. (You have already recorded the time under column E.)

*Columns G–I: Personnel Costs*

Column G lists salaries and wages, column H the fringe benefits, and column I the totals. If you are approaching your fund-raising plan from the district level, remember to provide an estimate of the salary, wage, and fringe benefits for each key person listed in column F. Be sure to analyze whose services will be donated (volunteers). Add an asterisk to all personnel donations; remember that their fringes *and* their wages will be donated.

*Columns J–L: Consultants and Contract Services*

Column J lists consultants' and contractors' time worked. Column K lists the cost per week. Column L lists the total. These three columns refer to individuals who are not in your normal employ and to services not normally provided by someone in your school. (Note: No fringe benefits are paid to these individuals.)

*Columns M–P:*
*Materials and Supplies*

Column M lists the item. Column N lists the cost per item. Column O lists the quantity. Column P lists the total cost. Use these four columns to list the supplies, equipment, and materials needed to complete each activity and to itemize the associated costs. Do not underestimate the resources needed to achieve your objectives. Ask yourself and your key personnel what is needed to complete each activity. Again, designate donated items with an asterisk.

*Column Q:*
*Subtotal Cost for Activity*

Column Q is derived by adding together Columns I, L, and P—the total for personnel costs, consultant and contract services, and nonpersonnel resources. You can do this either for each individual activity or for each objective. If you do this for each objective, you will have to add together the subtotals for all of the activities under that objective.

*Column R–S: Milestones*
*and Progress Indicators*

Column R lists how you inform funding sources of your progress in accomplishing your objectives (e.g., quarterly report). Think of these as milestones or progress indicators. Column S records the dates the funding source will receive the listed milestones or progress indicators.

**What to Do with a**
**Complete Project Planner**

With the gap between what is and what could be clearly defined and a draft of your plan in hand, you are now ready to elicit "buy in" from donors. This step is crucial, since individuals who "buy in" to solving a problem end up investing their time and money.

With documentation in hand, you are now ready to intelligently approach potential donors. In the next chapter, you will learn where the money is so you can close the gap between what your educational system is and what it could be with more technical resources!

# 4 The Marketplace

How much do you know about the funding market-place? This chapter provides some enlightening questions and answers. In it you will learn:

- How much money is given to nonprofits each year.
- What source allots the most private funding dollars.
- How much money the federal government grants to nonprofits.
- What percentage of federal grants is available for Internet access/technology enhancement in schools.

Please take a guess at each of the following questions. By comparing your guesses to the correct answers you will discover that you may have some misconceptions that must be changed in order to develop a successful fund-raising strategy. It is a mistake to go to a specific funding source just because you *think* it has the money you need. Base your approach on *knowing* where the money is.

**Quiz Your Support Group**    Administer this quiz to your support group. Assure them that they do not have to sign it and that no one will know what they guess. Ask that they give each question a try even if they have no idea of the correct answer.

QUIZ   1. Approximately how much money do private (i.e., nongovernmental) sources give each year to the 598,000 nonprofit organizations in the United States?
a. $ 25 billion
b. $ 75 billion
c. $100 billion
d. $130 billion

2. What percent of private funding is derived from each of the following sources?

| | |
|---|---|
| Foundation grants | _____% |
| Corporate grants | _____% |
| Individual donations | _____% |
| Bequests (wills) | _____% |
| | 100% |

3. Approximately how much money does the federal government grant to nonprofits each year?
a. $ 50 billion
b. $ 75 billion
c. $100 billion
d. $125 billion

4. What percentage of federal grants is available for developing access to the Internet and to technology enhancement in elementary and secondary schools?
a. $ 2 billion
b. $ 5 billion
c. $ 10 billion
d. Unknown

❖

*The first rule*

*of fund-raising is*

*to know where the*

*money is!*

❖

After you have collected the quizzes and tabulated the answers, display the distribution of guesses for the group to see and compare them to the correct answers. Incorporate Figure 4.1 (1994 Contributions) into your presentation. It is important to tell your group the correct answers so they can base their fund-raising strategy on marketplace facts, not fiction. The first rule of fund-raising is to know where the money is!

QUESTION 1   *Approximately how much money do private (nongovernmental) sources award each year to the 598,000 nonprofit organizations in the United States?*

$130 billion is given away by private sources annually to nonprofit organizations, and this figure is growing. The amount has risen each year since records have been kept, and for only three years, the increase did not exceed the rate of inflation.

**Figure 4.1**
1994 Contributions

Total Giving
$129.88 billion

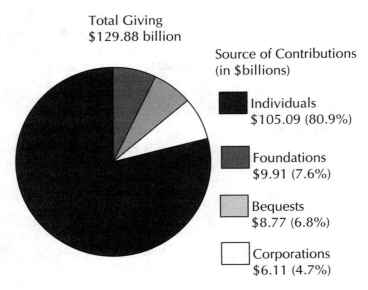

Source of Contributions
(in $billions)

Individuals
$105.09 (80.9%)

Foundations
$9.91 (7.6%)

Bequests
$8.77 (6.8%)

Corporations
$6.11 (4.7%)

QUESTION 2   *What percentage of private funding is derived from various sources?*
   Of the $130 billion awarded, foundations grant 7.6% or $9.91 billion; corporations award 4.7% or $6.1 billion; individuals give 80.9% or $105.09 billion; and bequests (wills) award 6.8% or $8.77 billion. (Review Figure 4.1.)

*Foundations and Corporations*   Most support groups will think (and wish) that the percentage from foundations and corporations is larger than it is. They would like to believe that all they need to do is write a grant to the Smith Foundation or the Jones Company, and the money will come rolling in.

Although this is not exactly true, it is heartening to know that the largest percentage of the more than $16 - billion in corporate and foundation grants is available for education, with elementary and secondary education receiving a growing percentage of these funds each year. Therefore, your group will probably be able to raise some support from foundations and corporations. In addition, it is the easiest marketplace to contact first for two reasons: first, most members of your support group will believe it is the best place to go, and second, few resources are required to generate results. In fact, most of the billions granted from foundations and corporations are made from applications that consist of one- or two-page letter proposals! (Chapter 5 explains this process in detail.)

*Individual Donations*   Figure 4.1 clearly illustrates that your best bet for raising funds is through individual donations. This source of contributions accounts for more than $100 billion and is growing each year. Even when the amount of money given to religiously affiliated organizations is subtracted from total individual giving, more than $50 billion is still distributed to other types of nonprofit groups.

Your support group members will begin to perspire when you provide them with this information—they may wonder if you will ask them to solicit their friends and family for money. The truth is you will, but not just yet. First develop a group plan to approach foundations and corporations and then state and federal grantors. The group will be open to the idea of getting money from others by writing letter proposals and submitting applications; then by the time these easier funding options are exhausted, they will be committed enough to your project to address the individual giving marketplace.

*Bequests*  Wills account for approximately $9 billion of the $130 billion contributed annually to nonprofit organizations. Do not abandon this marketplace simply because you need immediate access to money. Remember, most Americans do not have a will. It is especially important that parents with children have one to help keep their children together if they should meet an untimely death. Your school should actually help parents establish a will and while doing so, suggest that they set aside a percentage of their estate for your school to meet the technology challenge of the future.

This subject is discussed again in Chapter 10, but remember—your group needs to anticipate funding for technology on both a short- and long-term basis.

QUESTION 3  *Approximately how much money does the federal government grant to nonprofits each year?*

The federal government grants approximately $75 billion to nonprofits each year. Determining how much of this goes to elementary and secondary education is difficult. The 1995–96 changes in Congress, the budget impasse, and the support for allowing states to choose how to spend their education money, have made these estimates more difficult to determine. However, we know that the bulk of grants from the Department of Education goes to elementary and secondary schools, either by direct grants to schools or the ever-popular block grants that send the funds to a designated state agency to distribute (usually the State Department of Education or the Governor's designated recipient). Therefore, conservative estimates are that $20 to $25 billion in federal grants funds are in some way related to K–12 programs. Chapter 7 explains more about the federal grants marketplace.

QUESTION 4 *What percentage of federal grants is available for developing access to the Internet and to technology enhancement in elementary and secondary schools?*

The answer to this question is unknown. The amount of federal money available for your school's technology needs and in particular, Internet access, depends on how you plan to use the Internet in education and what target groups will benefit. Many programs will support the inclusion of the Internet as part of a proposal to deal with a particular problem. For example, if your project requires you to use Internet access and educational programs for students with substance abuse problems, funds designated for substance abuse could be available. In the same fashion, if you linked your Internet access project to the environment, Native Americans, at-risk students, etc., you could take advantage of grant funds designated to those areas, as well. The amount of federal grant funds available to you really depends on your creativity.

Currently, support exists for the federal government to provide Internet-access assistance to schools. During the next five years, grantseekers may gain access to $2 billion to finance Internet hookup and other computer technologies for schools. President Clinton has asked Congress to create the Technology Literacy Challenge Fund for education technology grants for states. While unveiling the program at a junior high school in New Jersey, President Clinton said: "When we complete the work of bringing the information superhighway to all education . . . it will empower everybody." If the program is approved, either it will be included under an existing education program listed in the Catalogue of Federal Domestic Assistance, or a new program will be created. The Education Department would begin distributing funds in 1997, based on a formula that may include the number of students in each state. Does this news mean your support group should wait for the federal government to provide you with a grant? No! Start putting your plans into effect to develop a secure funding base for the future. Between political changes and battles, the money may never get to your school. Even if it does, it will not pay for everything. Chapter 7 shows you on how to stay abreast of newly emerging federal opportunities.

Considering the facts alone, individual giving provides your greatest dollar potential, but you should go to the grants marketplace first. This follows the second rule of fund-raising—get the money from the most accessible marketplace first!

Make your support group feel at ease by telling them that you will leave no stone unturned in your grants' quest, but be realistic and conservative in your estimates of funds expected and make sure they know that grants represent only a small fraction of your fund-raising potential.

Also let them know that money for any shortfall in realizing your technology plan needs to come from individuals and through fund-raising activities and that you will need to raise funds continually to maintain your system and keep up with changes. Grantseeking and proposal preparation help create the commitment and enthusiasm necessary for individual fund-raising—the strategy that will push your project to its goal. Once your group understands the basics of fund-raising from individuals, they will be amazed at how unfounded their fears were.

Having assessed the funding marketplace and assembled your support group, you are ready to initiate your fund-raising effort. In the next chapter, you will learn how to approach foundations with your Internet technology plan.

❖

*The second rule of fund-raising is get the money from the most accessible marketplace first!*

❖

# 5 Using Foundation Grants to Obtain or Enhance Internet Access

FOUNDATIONS allot billions of dollars annually. How can your group tap into foundation dollars set aside for education? This chapter will help you build a strategy for winning foundation grants. You will discover:

- The different types of foundations.
- The best approaches to use to interest each type of foundation in your project.
- How to research your best foundation prospects.
- How to contact the foundations you select.
- How to write a winning proposal.

**Foundations** Some 40,000 private grantmaking foundations are active in the United States today. Foundation grants total approximately $10 billion annually. Every year elementary and secondary schools make significant inroads to capturing more and more of the foundation grant dollars dedicated to education. Although K–12 education still receives a smaller portion than colleges and universities, it is important to keep in mind that being the primary recipient of these funds is not as important as sharing in them. This can be successfully done by understanding the preferences of foundations—including their preferred recipient, grant type, and grant size.

Many grantseekers mistakenly believe that all foundations are large, have sizable staffs, and make big grants. In reality, only 1,000 of the 40,000 foundations have an actual office, and they employ less than 4,000 individuals. In terms of grant size, only 70,000 grants awarded more than $10,000 annually to the more than 598,000 nonprofits in the United States. While most of us have heard of the large million dollar foundation grants, we seldom hear about the hundreds of thousands of foundation grants for less than $10,000!

*Four Types of Foundations*

There are four basic types of foundations, and each type will view your technology project from its own perspective. Your school has the potential to attract foundation grant funding for technology, but only if you are knowledgeable about the opportunity.

1. National General-Purpose Foundations

These are large, well-known foundations. While they number fewer than 100 of the total 40,000 foundations, they have hundreds of millions of dollars in assets. Of the $10 billion in grants awarded each year by foundations, national general-purpose foundations represent the largest contributor.

These foundations employ staff. Most of the 4,000 individuals employed by foundations work for this group. National general-purpose foundations fund a wide variety of projects locally and nationally, and, in some instances, internationally. They often have an interest in educational innovation and in the economic concerns of education. They spend a good deal of time reviewing proposals and sometimes consult experts in the field. They meet more often than smaller foundations, and often have staff available for preproposal contact. Examples in this group include the Ford and Rockefeller Foundations.

National general-purpose foundations are interested in funding model or demonstration projects that serve as examples of what can be done. Many are interested in technology and how Internet access and usage can increase learning. But to fund your project, they must see that your school's technology needs are similar to others and that your solution can be used in other geographic areas. They also like to fund applicants with known project personnel in the field and projects that can validate the models through certain evaluation components.

National general-purpose foundations seldom fund schools to replicate what another school has already undertaken as a model project. To secure funding from this type of foundation, you will have to generate a unique, new, and creative approach to an education problem that utilizes the Internet to change education outcomes in your school.

2. Special-Purpose Foundations

These foundations support a relatively narrow range of grant interests. Numbering only a few hundred, they still constitute a major influence in their fields of choice. They have directors and staff and, similar to the large national general-purpose foundations, meet more often. In addition, they spend more time reading proposals than other types of foundations.

This group contains many technology-related educationally based grantors. The Exxon Education Trust and the Annenberg Foundation are just two examples of those who are interested in technology, the Internet, and educational improvements.

The boards of special-purpose foundations and the outside readers they may employ to review proposals have extensive knowledge in their own narrow field of education and technology. To acquire resources from this group, you will have to demonstrate that your school has worked as a team with experts in the field. For example, they will view your proposal as a more efficient or useful model to promote the changes they desire in education if you collaborate with a college or university. Even though your school may not have a core of experts in the field, the expertise of your support group's members may provide the extra advantage you need to succeed.

Special-purpose foundations like to fund projects that advance their special field of interest or serve a specific constituency. For example, a special-purpose foundation may define their purpose as furthering a specific subject area such as science, math, or social studies; or a constituency group such as women, the handicapped, the economically disadvantaged, or the gifted. Your support group should review the usefulness of technology—and specifically Internet access—and brainstorm how your school could increase scholastic achievement in the populations or areas where these special-purpose foundations direct their interest and grant dollars.

**3. Community Foundations**

This is the fastest-growing type of foundation in terms of numbers and assets. The name refers to the geographic area they serve. There are currently more than 300 community foundations in the United States. Some have full- or part-time staff, and the composition of their boards normally reflects the community they seek to enhance. Their funds are usually generated from bequests, and their grants must benefit the community in which they are located. Examples include the Cleveland and Chicago Foundations.

Community foundations can be found in cities of all sizes. From San Diego, California to Utica, New York, community foundations are a great source of support for education and an excellent source for small grants as well. They can be very helpful in providing matching funds or resources for needs assessment when you establish your technology plan.

4. Family Foundations   Family foundations account for approximately 80 percent of all foundations. However, they award less than 20 percent of all foundation grants. Only the largest of the 35,000 family foundations have a director, and few have staff or peer review. Family foundations normally award smaller grants. Their boards usually meet only one or two times a year for an average length of three hours. Therefore, decisions are made quickly, and there is little opportunity for discussion with prospective grantees, either before or after the deadlines.

To better understand family foundations, consider this— 68,495 grants of more than $10,000 were awarded in 1994. However, these grants totaled only $5.6 billion, or approximately one-half of the $9.9 billion total in foundation grants. The other $4.3 billion–plus constituted hundreds of thousands of grants for less than $10,000, and most of these smaller grants came from family foundations. The smaller grants were awarded to approximately 598,000 tax-exempt groups, but education garnered only a small percentage, and only a portion of those allotted to education went to the estimated 71,887 elementary and middle schools in the United States.

*What Foundations Fund*   Many novice grantseekers mistakenly believe that foundations make a lot of grants for bricks and mortar, and will buy computer equipment. Guess again, or better yet, look at Figure 5.1 which illustrates the percent of foundation grant dollars by type of project.

To attract foundation grant support for technology and Internet access, you should refer to your project as program development or research on how to improve scholastic achievement within a specific target population. As you can see from Figure 5.1 on the next page, describing your proposal as an equipment grant is the kiss of death. Remember, the goal of your project is to improve, enhance, and change education. Foundations will buy cable, wire, computers,

| Type of Support | Percent of Total | |
|---|---|---|
| **General support** | 12.3 | |
| General operating | | 11.5 |
| Annual campaigns | | 0.8 |
| **Capital support** | 22.4 | |
| Capital campaigns | | 2.5 |
| Building and renovation | | 11.7 |
| Equipment | | 1.9 |
| Computer systems and equipment | | 1.0 |
| Land acquisition | | 0.3 |
| Endowments | | 3.3 |
| Debt reduction | | 0.2 |
| Collections acquisition | | 1.7 |
| **Program support** | 44.5 | |
| Program development | | 31.0 |
| Conferences and seminars | | 1.5 |
| Faculty and staff development | | 2.7 |
| Professorships | | 1.0 |
| Film, video, and radio | | 1.0 |
| Publication | | 1.3 |
| Seed money | | 2.3 |
| Curriculum development | | 2.6 |
| Performance and productions | | 0.5 |
| Exhibitions | | 0.6 |
| **Research** | 10.5 | |
| **Student aid funds** | 5.8 | |
| Student aid | | 0.5 |
| Fellowships | | 2.8 |
| Internships | | 0.2 |
| Scholarships | | 2.3 |
| **Other** | 0.8 | |
| Technical assistance | | 0.7 |
| Emergency funds | | 0.1 |
| **Not specified** | 20.0 | |

*Source:* The Foundation Grants Index, *1994. Based on a sample of 1,020 larger foundations.*

modems, and telephone access as long as these items are a means to an end. The end results come from the use of these items, not from their installation.

*Searching for the Best Foundations*

Most foundations give where they live; however, some give on a broader regional and/or a national level. Those which give regionally or nationally to support technology in schools and Internet access, in particular, are listed in Appendix C. This is a good place to begin your search for prospective funders, but be aware that many other foundations exist that give locally for educational technology. Many resources exist to help you find potential funders. The following is a summary of the most popular, basic research tools.

**Foundation Research Tools**

The Foundation Center, an independent national service organization, is the best source for information on foundations and the grants they make. The Center operates five National Reference Collections—in New York City, Washington, D.C., Atlanta, Cleveland, and San Francisco. The Center has also organized *Cooperating Collections* to help nonprofits that are unable to access the National Collections. Cooperative Collections have been established in libraries, community foundations, and even some nonprofit agencies throughout the United States. The organizations are not paid to house the Cooperating Collections, although they do receive the publications for free. Use the information in Appendix D to locate the Cooperating Collection nearest you, and take advantage of its many reference books on foundation funding—including your state's directory of foundations. The reference books can be used at no charge.

The Foundation Center publishes several popular grants reference materials that are national in scope, including *The Foundation Directory*. Available at your Cooperative Collection, this yearly publication is the most important single reference work on grantmaking foundations in the

United States. The 1996 edition is the 18th. To be included in the Directory, a foundation must either have assets of at least $2 million or make grants in excess of $200,000 annually. More than 7,500 of the existing 40,000 foundations have met at least one of these criteria and are included in the Directory.

*The Foundation Directory, Part 2: A Guide to Grant Programs $50,000 to $200,000* is also a very important publication, describing more than 4,900 mid-sized foundations that make annual grants of $50,000 to $200,000. Both *The Foundation Directory* and *The Foundation Directory, Part 2* are indexed according to the following:

- *Foundation Name*—If you already know the name of a foundation that may be interested in technology and/or Internet access, you can locate it in the Directories using this index. The index entry will provide you with a crucial piece of information—the state in which the foundation is registered. You need to know this to locate the foundation in the Directories, since the entries are in alphabetical order by state.
- *Subject Field*—This index will help you locate the foundations that are interested in funding your particular area. Technology is becoming increasingly popular as a funding subject.
- *Donors, Trustees, and Officers*—This index provides information that may help you develop linkages with foundations.
- *Geographic Region*—Foundations are listed under the state in which they are located. Foundations in boldface type make grants on a national, regional, or international basis. The others generally limit giving to the city or state in which they are located.

All of the indexes refer to the foundations by a four-digit number that can be found above the foundation's name. As mentioned previously, the foundations are arranged in alphabetical order according to the state in which they are incorporated. The Foundation Center's World Wide Web site is http://fdncenter.org. On the following pages, Figure 5.2 presents a fictitious entry as it would appear in *The Foundation Directory*.

*The Foundation Grants Index* is another popular Foundation Center publication. Published annually, this Index lists more than 72,000 grants made by 1,000 of the largest foundations. The 24th edition (1996) indexes grant awards of $10,000 and larger. The *Index* is divided into seven sections: grants listings, grant recipients, subject, type of support/geographic, recipient category index, index to grants by foundation, and foundation. Figure 5.3 (on page 53) presents a fictitious example of an entry in Section 1 of the *Index*.

In addition to having many excellent books on foundation funding, your Foundation Center Regional Library also has three other tools to help you research foundations with which you should be familiar.

- *The 990 Internal Revenue Service Foundation Tax Returns.* The Internal Revenue Service requires private foundations to file income tax returns each year. The 990-PF returns provide fiscal details on receipts and expenditures, compensation of officers, capital gains or losses, and other financial matters. Form 990-AR provides information on foundation managers, assets, and grants paid and/or committed for future payment. Reviewing the income tax returns of your "best" prospects will help you validate your approach and develop tailored proposals. The Foundation Center's National Collections in New York City, Washington, D.C., Atlanta, Cleveland, and San Francisco have the past three years of tax returns for all private foundations on microfiche. Each Cooperating Collection has returns for private foundations located in its state and sometimes in surrounding states.

**Figure 5.2**
Sample entry, *The*
*Foundation Directory*

## The Foundation Directory 2762

The Jessica Vastell Foundation
1651 North Broadway
Chicago 60604
312-896–9700

Incorporated in 1926 in Illinois.

| | |
|---|---|
| **Donor(s):** | Sabastian Vastell, Mrs. Jessica Vastell |
| **Foundation type:** | Independent |
| **Financial data (year ended 6/30/95):** | Assets, $150,444,176 (M); expenditures, $6,488,200 including $4,488,200 for 126 grants (high $300,000, low: $200; average: $10,000–$50,000), employee matching gifts: $85,200 for 65 and $1,200,200 for 7 foundation-administered programs. |
| **Purpose and activities:** | Dedicated to enhancing the humane dimensions of life through activities that emphasize the theme of improving the quality of teaching and learning. Serves precollegiate education through grantmaking and program activities in elementary and secondary public education. |
| **Fields of interest:** | Elementary and secondary public education, teaching, social services, child welfare. |
| **Types of support:** | Consulting services, technical assistance, special projects. Limitations: No support for colleges and universities (except for projects in elementary and secondary education). No grants to individuals, or for building or endowment funds, or operating budgets; no loans. |
| **Publications:** | Annual report, informational brochure (including application guidelines), financial statement, grants list. |
| **Application information:** | Grant proposals for higher education not accepted; fellowship applications available only through participating universities. |
| **Application form:** | Not required |
| **Initial approach:** | Letter |
| **Copies of proposal:** | 1 |
| **Deadline(s):** | None |
| **Board meeting date(s):** | May and Nov. and as required |
| **Final notification:** | 4 weeks |
| **Write:** | Dr. Andrew Brown, President |

**Figure 5.2**
(continued)

| | |
|---|---|
| **Officers:** | Sabastian Vastell, Chair; Jessica Vastell, Vice-Chairman and Secretary; Andrew Brown, President; Winifred L. Bower, Vice President; Franz Kirshbaumer, Treasurer; Bilal Ali, Program Director |
| **Trustees:** | John R. Lige, Virginia S. Smith, Donald C. Crowne, Jr., Charles Ludwig, George L. Sloan, P. John Cassidy. |
| **Number of staff:** | 4 full-time professionals; 1 part-time professional; 4 full-time support. |
| **Employer Identification Number:** | 679014579 |

**Figure 5.3**
Sample Entry—Section 1
*Foundation Grants Index*

## Education; Elementary and Secondary; Illinois. Vastell Foundation, Jessica, The.

**2713.** *Association of Indiana School Administrators, South Bend, IN. $28,000, 1995.* For reorganization of schools project. 9/14/95.

**2714.** *Association of Michigan School Administrators, Detroit, MI. $10,000, 1995.* For Consortium for Schools of the Future. 10/21/95.

**2715.** *Hazelnut School District, Hazelnut, MO. $11,000, 1995.* For individualized computer programs for at-risk students. 6/9/95.

**2716.** *Kids in Between, Kansas City, MO. $15,000, 1995.* For educational program for teachers working with children of divorce. 10/15/95.

**2717.** *Platterton School District, Agnes Middle School, Alexandria, VA. $13,000, 1995.* For staff development activities related to increased technological resources project. 7/15/95.

- *Grant Guides*. Published by the Foundation Center, these computer-produced guides to foundation giving are available in 30 different subject areas. Each of the guides has three indexes—by subject, geographic location, and recipient.
- *Online Information*. The Foundation Center maintains two databases—one providing information on grant-makers and the other on the grants they distribute. Access to these databases is through DIALOG (files 26 and 27). Contact DIALOG at 800-334-2564 for more information.

*Developing Key Search Words*

As you can see, many standard grants resources have subject indexes which list by subject all the funding sources included in the resource that have an expressed interest in that subject. Subject areas such as computer sciences, science and technology, elementary education, and secondary education can be used as key words to help you search for potential funding sources.

When you begin your search for the best funding source for your project, start by determining the key words that can be related to your project. Some examples may include: disadvantaged education, drug-free schools, physical fitness, computer learning, humanities education, international education, etc. Also, think of ways you could change or adapt your project to relate to more key words or subject areas. The object is not merely to relate your project or idea to as many key words as possible, but to determine the ways your project could be related to various funders' interests. In addition, consider redefining your project in a way that it could be considered a model or demonstration project and/or a tool to reach out to other geographic areas such as the state, the nation, rural areas, urban areas, and even other countries.

For example, how would you need to change your Internet access project to make it international in scope? First, you should check with your local government to see if it has already identified a "sister city" for your town in Europe, Asia, Africa, or South America. If it has, your mayor's office or chamber of commerce has probably already made a commitment to develop access to and promote understanding with this city. Therefore, you could easily redefine your school or classroom Internet project in light of this commitment, as one aimed at promoting communication, language acquisition, and appreciation of other cultures by connecting to your sister city.

Dennis M. Norris, a grant writer for the Metropolitan School District in Perry Township, Indianapolis, Indiana, used the redefinition model to brainstorm unique ways that telecommunications could expose his landlocked students to the ocean. Through brainstorming, he and several of his district's middle school teachers came up with the idea of forming a partnership with the U.S. Coast Guard's icebreaking vessel, the *Polar Star*. Further redefinition of this unique project revealed that it could be made more attractive to a greater number of potential funding sources by focusing on increasing the number of females in science, math, and engineering. This focus proved quite successful in boosting the project's "fundability."

You can also achieve similar results by brainstorming ways your project could be redefined and expanding your number of key search words. Figure 5.4 on the following page lists many of the key words found in reference books and computer-assisted retrieval systems. Review the list and circle any of the words that are relevant to your project. You may find it helpful to make a brief notation of any significant ways you could change your solution to make it relate to a particular key word.

*Using the Internet to Search for Foundations*

Many grant foundations have an Internet presence and have created their own World Wide Web pages to offer quick access to general information about the foundation, their guidelines and deadlines for grant proposals, annual reports, and even instructions for email grant submissions.

**Figure 5.4**
Key Words Worksheet for
Foundation Grantseeking

Adult/Continuing Education
Alternative Modes/Nontraditional Study
Arts Education Programs
Bicultural/Bilingual Education Programs
Biological Sciences Education Programs
Business Education Programs
Career Education Programs
Children/Youth
Cognition/Information Processing
Communications Education Programs
Computer Science Education Programs
Computer Sciences
Computer-assisted Instruction
Conference Support
Early Childhood/Preschool Education
Educational Counseling/Guidance
Educational Reform
Educational Studies—Developing Countries
Educational Testing/Measurement
Educational Values
Elementary Education
Employment Opportunity Programs
Employment/Labor Studies
Energy Education Programs
English Education Programs
Environmental Studies Education Programs
Fine Arts Education Programs
Foreign Language Education Programs
Foreign Scholars
Gifted Children
Handicapped Education Services
Handicapped Vocational Services
Handicapped/Special Education Programs
Health Education Programs
Humanities Education Programs
Illiteracy
Information Dissemination

**Figure 5.4** International Studies Education Programs
(continued)  Journalism Education Programs
Learning Disorders/Dyslexia
Mathematics Education Programs
Minority Education Programs
Music Education Programs
Nutrition Education Programs
Opportunities Abroad
Parental Involvement in Education
Philosophy
Philosophy of Education
Physical Education Programs
Physical Sciences Education
Precollegiate Education—Arts Education Programs
Precollegiate Education—Bilingual Education Programs
Precollegiate Education—Economics Education Programs
Precollegiate Education—Humanities Education Programs
Precollegiate Education—Professional Development
Precollegiate Education—Science/Math
Education Programs
Prizes/Awards
Professional Development
Professional/Faculty Development
Reading Education Programs
Remedial Education
Rural Education
Rural Services
Rural Studies
Science and Technology
Secondary Education
Teacher Education
Telecommunications—Education Materials
Vocational/Technical Education
Women's Education Programs—Business Management
Women's Education Programs— Science/Engineering
Women's Studies Education Programs

The following is a list of several foundations that support education and their Web addresses:

*The Alfred P. Sloan Foundation,* www.sloan.org

*AT&T Foundation,* att.com/foundation

*Bell South,* www.bfs.org/bfs

*Heinz Endowments,* www.heinz.org/menu.html

*Intel,* www.intel.com/intel/smithso/innov/communit.html

*George Lucas Educational Foundation,* glef.org

*MCI,* www.mci.com/about/friends/home.shtml

*Sun Microsystems,* www.sun.com:80/corporateview/
corporateaffairs/grants.html

*Westinghouse Electric Corp.,* www.westinghouse.com/
ca/ca_hp.html

*Autodesk Foundation,* www.autodesk.com/compinfo/
found/found.html

*IBM,* www.ibm.com/IBM/IBMGives/

*Pew Charitable Trusts,* www.pewtrusts.com

In addition, several nonprofits have created electronic grants databases that compile fund information related to their specific cause or mission. For example, if you have defined your project as beneficial to children at risk for substance abuse you may want to check out Join Together, which provides funding information on foundation sources that are interested in substance abuse. You can reach Join Together at http://www.jointogether.org/jointogether.html.

The GrantsWeb site is a good place for first-time Internet users to begin mining the Net for grants resources. It provides links to private and public grant sources and allows grantseekers to access databases such as ED's Education Resource Information Center (ERIC). GrantsWeb can be reached at http://cavern.uark.edu/rsspinfo/grantweb.html.

The World Wide Web site linked to the Duke University School of Engineering's home page also contains several good links and resources for grantseekers. The page offers access to philanthropic foundations, publications, and research. To get there, point your Web browser to http://www.acpub.duke.edu/~ptavern/Pete.Philanthropic.html.

Refer to Appendix B for more information and the addresses of funding resources located on the Internet.

**Developing a Foundation Grants Plan**  Your task now is to develop a system for approaching foundations that appear to be your best opportunities for funding. Success depends on developing a tailored approach for each of your prospects. By completing the following Foundation Strategy Worksheet (Figure 5.5), you will begin to develop a prioritized list of foundations with the information you need to initiate your plan of action.

**Figure 5.5**
Foundation Strategy Worksheet

| Foundation Deadline | Need | Approach | Contact | $ |
|---|---|---|---|---|
| | | | | |

List the foundations you have chosen to approach and their deadlines under column A of the worksheet. In column B, identify the needs that will be outlined for the prospective grantor. In column C, briefly describe the solution that your research has proven to be most interesting and acceptable to the foundation. In column D, indicate the individual(s) responsible for making contact and preparing the proposal. In column E, place the likely range or probable amount that is appropriate to request based upon your research. Review the completed worksheet and set the order in which the foundations will be contacted under column A. You might also want to indicate the likelihood of funding from each prospect (e.g., excellent, good, fair, long shot, and so on).

**How to Contact the Foundations You Select**

Many of the large foundations will mail you general information concerning their grants program, including grant application guidelines, annual reports, and newsletters. Use the Sample Letter to a Foundation Requesting Information and Guidelines in Figure 5.6 as a guide for contacting only those that have stated, as found in your research, that application guidelines or other information is available. Foundations that provide guidelines usually have a director and a staff to respond to your request.

*Sending for Information and Guidelines*

Please note that this is an inquiry letter for information only. It is not a proposal to the foundation. Use this letter for foundations that do not have a Web site.

*Telephoning Foundations*

Send an inquiry letter first, and if you get no response, you are justified in telephoning the foundation. However, be aware that with fewer than 1,000 of the 40,000 foundations occupying offices, successful telephone contact is limited. Many of the entries in foundation-resource directories do not list telephone numbers. Even if a phone number is listed in an entry or on an IRS tax return, do not call the foundation if the information clearly states that there should be no contact except by letter.

In general, if you are not aware of any rules or instructions that discourage phone contact, you should telephone the foundation. Of course, the optimum approach is to arrange a personal visit. If a face-to-face meeting is not possible, try to gather the same information you would in a visit via the telephone.

.......................................................................................................................................................................

*Date*

**Figure 5.6**
Sample Letter to a
Foundation Requesting
Information and Guidelines

*Name*
*Title*
*Address*

Dear *[contact person]*:

My research on *[foundation]* indicates that you provide application guidelines to prospective grantees. I am developing a proposal in the area of *[topic]*, and I would appreciate receiving these guidelines at your earliest convenience.

I would also appreciate any other information you may have that could help us prepare a successful, quality proposal. Please add us to your mailing list for annual reports, newsletters, priority statements, and program statements.

Since both of our organizations are committed to [*subject area*] I believe you will find the ideas we plan to propose interesting. *[Mention any linkage relative to the foundation. Also, the linkage could jointly sign the letter or send it himself.]*

Sincerely,

*Name/Title*
*Phone Number*

The best way for you to initiate contact with a foundation is through a mutual friend or linkage that your school or support group may have with one of the staff or board members of the foundation. Review the section in Chapter 2 on linkages to help you get your foot in the door with foundation grantors.

When you talk to the foundation official to discuss your approaches to solving the problem, ask him or her if you can fax a one-page summary of your ideas, and call back to discuss them. Try to arrange a mutually agreeable time to talk.

*Contacting Foundations before Sending a Proposal*

1. If appropriate, phone the contact person. Your purpose for calling is to validate the information you have already collected. Your questions should reflect your knowledge of the foundation's granting pattern and priorities and elicit their interest in your approaches to solving a problem or increasing educational opportunities in your school. Introduce yourself and state the purpose of the call. (You may find it helpful to review your needs data before calling.) Remember, you are not calling for yourself; you are calling for your students, your school, and the field of education. Do not initiate the conversation by stating, "We need. . ." or by mentioning Internet access. Reference the need for students to develop skills or scholastic achievement.

2. If you reach a secretary or administrative assistant, ask to talk to the foundation director or to the staff person best able to answer your questions.

3. Demonstrate that you are different from other grantseekers. Show that you purposefully have selected their foundation by making a statement that reflects your research. For example, "I am contacting the _____ Foundation because you have demonstrated a desire to _____ . My research shows that 40 percent of your funds in recent years were committed to this area."

4. Tell them what you want. For example, state, "I would appreciate five minutes of your time to determine which of the approaches I have developed for the XYZ School would appeal to your board and elicit your foundation's greatest support." Note that you may use the fax approach here to maintain their interest. Remember, you are presenting the funder with an opportunity to meet their needs. They are looking for good programs to support. You are not begging. So get them excited about your project!

5. My place or yours? Your first choice is to meet with the funder. Tell them you would like to meet to discuss your grant approaches. You can try to visit them, or they may be interested in coming to visit your school. By visiting you, they could observe your students and see the actual needs population or problem firsthand. The funder will expect to pay their own way if they visit you and conversely will also expect you to pay your way if you visit them.

6. Who should be your representative(s)? Whether you visit the funder or they come to you, your team should be small—usually no larger than two. You could select an active and concerned volunteer from your support group who is donating his or her time to your proposed project. The other person could be either yourself or a paid school representative.

7. What should the team wear? The rule of thumb is to dress in a manner similar to the way that the foundation official dresses. Although many individuals from the world of education are offended by the notion that people are judged by their clothes, you might want to take a look at *New Dress for Success* by John T. Malloy. In short, you are judged by what you wear, so dress accordingly. Your project and students are worth your best effort to project a good image to the prospective funding source.

8. What should the representative(s) take to the meeting? What you take with you is extremely important. Focus on your objective. You expect to accomplish the following in a person-to-person visit with the potential grantor:

- Agreement about the need or problem to be addressed.
- A discussion of the prospective funder's interest in your proposed solution.
- Information on the grants decision process so you can tailor your approach.
- Validation of your research and estimate on the amount of your grant request. You can avoid the common mistake of proceeding directly to the money issue by bringing material that solidifies agreement on the need or the problem. In many cases, the grantor has difficulty envisioning the problem through the eyes of a student or an educator.

Use the following techniques to help the funder gain insight into the problem. Your materials should educate the grantor, not try to convince him or her.

- *Videotapes*—Make a short (three to five minutes) videotape that demonstrates the problem. A student-made tape can be very moving. Both elementary and junior high school students can make a short video as a class or school project. A videotape tells a compelling story because it enables the funder to see what the actual need is.
- *Slides and Audiotapes*—A professional-looking and sounding program created by students and volunteers is another effective means of enabling a potential grantor to clearly understand the need.
- *Picture Book*—A picture book that documents the need may provide the starting point for a discussion of how the funder views the problem.

Again, the objective of the meeting is to establish agreement on the need for a project; to ascertain the funding source's interests; and to discuss several approaches or solutions to the problem.

*The Foundation Has No Staff, but You Have a Linkage to a Board Member*

This opportunity occurs more often than does an actual visit to a foundation office. The steps are the same because the goal is the same. You should try to meet at your school. If such a meeting is not possible, meet at the board member's office or home, or as the last choice, at a restaurant for lunch, breakfast, or coffee.

*Recording Your Research and Preproposal Contact*

Preproposal contact can validate your research on the funding source and add to your body of knowledge so that you can develop a grant-winning strategy. Your research should be organized and make use of every possible time-saving technique.

If you haven't already done so, establish an alphabetical file for each of the grantors you are considering. This will be a great start in organizing your grants effort.

Generate foundation research worksheets, such as the one in Figure 5.7 on the next page, for the grantors you believe are the most likely prospects for funding, based on your research. Use each worksheet to keep a record of the information you have gathered to date. Update the worksheet as you obtain additional information and materials. Also use the worksheet to log all contact made with the foundation including face-to-face, telephone, and written contact.

In addition to information on a particular foundation, you also need to collect as much information as you can on individual foundation officers, board members, and trustees. This information can help you determine how to deal with any preferences and biases you may encounter and to locate other possible linkages between the foundation, your school, a volunteer on your support group, etc.

Use the foundation funding staff history worksheet (Figure 5.8, page 68) to record the information you collect. Store the worksheet in the appropriate foundation's file.

**Figure 5.7**

Foundation Research
Worksheet

Foundation: _____

Deadline Date(s): _____

Create a file for each foundation you are researching and place all the information in this file. Use this research worksheet to:

- Keep a record of the information you have gathered,
- Maintain a log of all telephone and face-to-face contact with the foundation, and
- Log all correspondence to and from the grantor.

Address: _____

Name of Contact Person: _____

Telephone Number: _____

Title of Contact Person: _____

Fax Number: _____

Place a check mark next to the information you have gathered and placed in the file for the foundation.

_____ Description of the granting program

      Note Source _____

_____ Information on past grants

      Note Source _____

_____ Application Information/Guidelines

_____ Sent for      _____ Received

_____ Annual Report

**Figure 5.7**  \_\_\_\_\_ Sent for  \_\_\_\_\_ Received
(continued)

\_\_\_\_\_ Newsletters/Other Reports

\_\_\_\_\_ Sent for  \_\_\_\_\_ Received

\_\_\_\_\_ Funding Staff History

\_\_\_\_\_ Written Summary of Each Contact Made

\_\_\_\_\_ Grantor Strategy Worksheet

\_\_\_\_\_ List of Board Members/Officers

\_\_\_\_\_ 990 IRS Tax Return

## Record of Face-to-Face and Telephone Contact

| Date | Contacted by | Foundation Contact | Results/Action |
|------|--------------|--------------------|----------------|
|      |              |                    |                |

## Record of All Correspondence Sent and Received

| Date/Correspondence | Purpose/Correspondence | Results/Action |
|---------------------|------------------------|----------------|
|                     |                        |                |

**Figure 5.8**
Foundation Funding Staff
History Worksheet

Foundation: _____

1. Name of Foundation Contact: _____

2. Title: _____

3. Residence Address: _____

   Phone: _____

   Email: _____

4. Business Address: _____

   Phone: _____

   Email: _____

5. Linkages/Contacts: _____

_____

_____

_____

_____

_____

List any data you have uncovered that might help you:

- Determine ways to deal with any of contact's preferences and biases
- Locate other possible linkages between this individual and you, your school, and a volunteer on your support group, etc.

**Figure 5.8**
(continued)

6. Birth date: _____ Birthplace: _____

7. Marital Status: _____ Children: _____

8. Employer: _____ Job Title: _____

9. College/University: _____ Degree(s): _____

10. Military Service: _____

11. Clubs/Affiliations: _____

12. Interests/Hobbies: _____

13. Other Board Memberships: _____

14. Other Philanthropic Activities: _____

15. Awards/Honors: _____

16. Other: _____

**Notes:**

_____

_____

_____

_____

_____

_____

_____

**Writing Foundation Proposals**

Private granting sources utilize a variety of terms to refer to the format in which proposals must be submitted. Foundations may ask that you request a grant by writing a:

- Letter of inquiry.
- Letter proposal.
- Concept paper.
- Preproposal or preliminary letter.

Regardless of the terminology, you must develop a distinctly different proposal for each foundation. Although you will encounter only a few private funders with application requirements that rival the federal government's, it is imperative that you follow any instructions provided by the foundation. For example, limitations on number of pages and attachments must be observed.

The foundation grants marketplace is very different from the federal grants arena. Because private grantors have few office workers and few paid reviewers, they seldom have a predetermined scoring system for proposal evaluation. Some of the larger foundations have a specified proposal format and hire experts in the field to review proposals, but they are relatively rare. In general, proposals submitted to foundations are read by board members or trustees who have a limited amount of time to spend reviewing hundreds of proposals. Many of these foundation decision makers are not experts in the areas funded by the organization and few are professional reviewers. They know what their foundation is looking for, and they answer only to their fellow trustees or board members. They prefer short, clear proposals that can be read rapidly. A proposal must immediately stimulate their interest and sustain it. Demonstrating that you have purposefully selected their organization and have constructed a tailored approach based upon their needs is an indication that you respect the reader's time.

Never use the "shotgun," one-proposal-fits-all approach. The reader can see at a glance that the same proposal has been "shotgunned" to a list of prospective funders. The

❖

*Never use the*

*"shotgun,"*

*one-proposal-fits-all*

*approach.*

❖

"shotgun" approach tells the funding source that their foundation was lumped together with others and that their individual values and needs were ignored for the convenience of the grantwriter. The results of the "shotgun" approach are worse than disappointing. Not only will its 99 percent rejection rate cost you the backing of your support group, but you will also negatively position your project and school with those foundations forever. The forethought and effort you have invested thus far in studying the proactive grants process means that you will not be shotgunning but using a telescopic lens to focus on your most likely funder. Remember, you are striving for a 40–50 percent success rate. Your foundation proposal is not a direct-mail fund-raising piece on which you can expect a 1 percent return—the grantors you solicit should represent one of the most prestigious groups of potential supporters for your school's technology project. You must present them with your best effort, not the most convenient or easiest.

*The Letter Proposal* The most common type of proposal to a foundation is written as a letter and submitted on the applicant's stationery or letterhead. Most private funders limit letter proposals to two or three pages and do not allow attachments. The main components of a letter proposal include:

1. An introductory paragraph with your reason for writing.
2. A paragraph describing why you selected this particular grantor.
3. A needs paragraph.
4. A solution paragraph.
5. A request for funds paragraph.
6. A uniqueness paragraph indicating why your school should receive the grant instead of another school.
7. A closing paragraph.
8. Signatures.
9. Attachments (if allowed).
10. Required additional information.

*Sections of a Letter Proposal*

Outlined below are detailed descriptions of the various sections of a typical foundation grant proposal.

1. Introduction

In this section refer to any linkages or friends who have already talked to the foundation board members/trustees on your behalf. For example: "Emily Rogan suggested that I contact the Jones Foundation with an exciting project that deals with technological enhancement, an area in which our school and your board share an interest." Avoid focusing on yourself. Do not begin with: "We are writing to you because we need . . ." The funding source knows you are writing to them, and what you need is not their primary concern.

2. Why You Selected Them

Demonstrate that you have done your homework by showing off your knowledge of the foundation. Analyze your foundation research. For example, by closely examining a foundation's IRS tax return you may be able to develop an interesting fact or statistic that is not obvious and does not appear in a foundation resource publication. You could also site an outstanding grant recipient or program previously funded by the foundation to demonstrate your familiarity with their granting pattern and history. For instance, if a foundation's tax return indicates that approximately 20 percent of their grants are related to increasing the math and science skills of K–12 students, you could add two years together and say something like, "My research indicates that in a recent two-year period, the Smith Foundation made X grants totaling over $X for projects focusing on increasing the math and science skills of children in grades K–12. Your granting pattern has prompted us to submit this proposal focusing on enhancing our students' skills in these areas by increasing their access to technology."

This section of your letter proposal should make the funder realize that:

- You did your homework—you researched them and know their interests.

- You believe they are special and unique, and worth the time to research.
- They should keep reading because they may learn more about themselves and how you have tailored your proposal to them.

Although the "request for funds" usually appears later in a letter proposal, you may include it in this section. A grantor may become very interested in your project only to discover later in the proposal that the amount you ultimately request is unrealistic. If you decide to put your grant request in this section, introduce its anticipated size by comparing your grant amount to the foundation's average grant size for your subject area. For example: "Our research has shown that your average grant size for (subject area) is $25,600. With this in mind, we encourage you to consider this $25,000 request to equip the students at XYZ School with the math and science skills they need to compete in tomorrow's marketplace."

3. The Need for Your Project

Do not describe your project in this section. Overzealous grantseekers have a tendency to immediately embark on a description of what they want to do. You should describe your project and solution *after* the funding source understands the need for *any* project or solution.

Review your research on the funding source. Remember, you are trying to demonstrate the gap between what is and what ought to be. The more you know about the fund's values and perspective, the better you can select the appropriate documentation of need. The needs section must:

- Be motivating and compelling enough to sustain the funder's interest.
- Demonstrate that you have a command of the literature and the state of the art concerning the problem.
- Appeal to the perspective and interests of the private grantor.

Review the grants pattern of the funder. Knowing the types of projects they have funded in the past and where the projects were implemented will provide valuable insight and allow you to select and tailor the data you present in the needs section. While federal and state grantors and reviewers expect statistics, research references, and quotations, foundation readers may be more motivated by an example, a story, or a case study. For instance, the needs section of a letter proposal to a foundation may include something like the following:

A recent study conducted by the Educational Testing Service revealed that American students scored lowest among 13-year-olds from five nations on an international mathematics test, and substantially lower than students from three out of four other countries in science. In our school, the average mathematics and science proficiency for students 13 and 17 years old is currently at its lowest level in 12 years.

Always start with the larger national or regional picture, and then focus on the need in your local area. Many easily retrievable education statistics can provide you with both national and state comparisons of many accepted standards of measure.

Many foundations want to be assured that their funding will make a difference in the client population they seek to impact. A case study that highlights the problem as it affects one student in that population may lodge in the funding source's mind and result in grant dollars. For example:

Alicia's story is typical of so many of our nation's female students whose math and science scores plummet when they reach high school. In the sixth grade Alicia scored in the top x percentage of her class in math and the top x percentage in science. All through middle school she continued to excel, but by high school she scored in the x percentile in both subjects, well below many of the young men she scored higher than for eight years. What can our school do to provide Alicia with the programs she needs to succeed?"

What do you do when your school's academic credentials are already very good? How can you still depict a need for Internet access or for upgrading your system? Create the motivation to give by showing how urgent it is that your students' aptitude remains high and that the only way you can do so is by providing every opportunity and advantage to your teachers and students. Emphasize that you must move *now* to remain ahead and that every day you wait is a day your students are missing out on a valuable learning experience. Even though you are accomplishing your school's objectives, stress that you could do better if you had enhanced educational aids.

Remember, the purpose of your letter proposal's needs section is to help the reader motivate himself or herself to keep on reading by documenting the gap between what is and what could be. Your challenge is to make the reader see the gap and feel compelled to do something about it, like fund your solution. This section, however, is not the place to discuss the solution. If your solution to the problem is Internet access, you must remind yourself that the Internet is a means to an end. Much as it may personally excite you, it can turn grantors off unless they know why and how you can use it to change the situation you have outlined and documented in your needs section.

4. Solution   What can be done to solve this problem? Writing this section of the proposal in the limited space available is often difficult. The previous paragraphs of the letter proposal focus on the grantor, and usually knowledge of the funding source is limited. But it is time to describe your project at this point in the proposal, or, in other words, to summarize your solution. The challenge is deciding what to include and what to

exclude. You must not describe your solution (Internet access) in such great detail that you confuse the prospective funding source and prevent them from understanding what your solution will allow you to do. Remember, you can always supply the funder with more information on request. The object of this section is to provide the prospective grantor with a *basic* understanding of the solution you have chosen to meet the needs you have outlined. To do so, ask yourself what you would want to see in the solution if you were the grantor.

Now is the time to tell the potential funding source about the Internet—not the hardware involved, but how you will use Internet access to close the gap you documented in the needs section. For example, you may tell him or her that you will use the Internet to improve your classroom leaders' lesson plans or provide your students with worldwide access to research. Keep in mind that you must give the reader specific examples. For instance, provide a list of the science and math activities you will develop through the Internet or describe how your students' ability to talk with students in other countries via email will increase their knowledge and interests. You might even propose to link your female science and math students with female "math pals" or "science pals" in countries ahead of ours in standardized scores and in retaining women in math and science.

When dealing with the whole student body, you may suggest that all students from gifted to at-risk will benefit from Internet access by researching the Arctic or searching the Louvre or the Library of Congress to prepare a report, etc.

Do not present an elaborate and overly technical description of the solution, and do not forget to include your plans for improving the phone and electric lines to your classrooms. The more sure you are that the grantor is on the same technological level as you, the more specifics you can provide. If you are not sure of his or her technological expertise, just present an overview of your approach. Most funding sources will trust that you know why you've chosen a particular approach and model of equipment and that you can substantiate your decisions. If your solution will be implemented in stages or phases, you need to provide a brief outline that suggests a time frame for accomplishing each phase, and remind the grantor that more information is available upon request. In general, keep the solution portion of your letter proposal short.

You can attach your Project Planner to your proposal or include it in your proposal. However, be sure to check with the funding source before adding it to your proposal as an attachment. If the funding source does not allow attachments, consider making your Project Planner, discussed in Chapter 3, page two of a three-page letter proposal. The Project Planner is a useful inclusion because it clearly shows the relationship between activities or methods and the accomplishment of your proposal's objectives.

Whether or not you use a Project Planner with your letter proposal, your solution must be interesting, plausible, affordable, and well organized. The objectives should be summarized in such a manner that the funder can almost "see" the gap shrink between what is and what ought to be for your students.

Be aware that some funding sources may not like your Internet solution. Even when you do your homework, you may encounter a prospective funding source that has "hidden" values, feelings, and/or prejudices related to computer or Internet phobia.

*The grantee who offers the most compelling benefits for the population valued most by the funder will ultimately receive the money.*

5. Request for Funds  How much will it cost? Foundations have limited resources. In fact, they receive many more proposals than they can ever fund. Private funders grant only an estimated 10 percent of the requests they receive. Ultimately they must judge which projects produce the best benefits for the greatest number of their target population. The applicant who can offer the most compelling benefits for the population that is valued most by the funder will ultimately receive the money.

Do not reveal the total cost of your project and then ask for a contribution at any level possible. State the exact amount you are requesting from the funding source. You will find that you will benefit from your research on the funding source at this point. Request an amount that was discussed during preproposal contact or an amount that appears reasonable based on information gathered from reviewing the funding source's tax return and the size of grants they have awarded for other projects related to education and technology.

Dividing the cost of your project by the number of students it will serve over the next several years (or at least for the life of the equipment) may be advantageous. This gives you the cost per student served. Remember, your project has a "roll-out" or future benefit because each student served will achieve more skills, better job opportunities, etc. When dealing with facilities and equipment, identify how many students will utilize the resource over its lifetime. For example, write, "We estimate that $x$ number of students and teachers will utilize the Internet for $y$ hours in the next 10 years. These are not hours spent 'surfing the net.' Rather, this is time spent enriching the learning experience." In an example like this, the cost per person served could be as little as pennies per hour, depending on the figures!

*Multiple Funders.* Obviously your letter proposal must state the amount you are requesting from the grantor. In the case of Internet access, the cost may require that you seek funding from more than one source. You should inform the funder that you are seeking additional funds from other foundations and/or corporations. But avoid saying, for example, that you hope to get funded by a number of community sponsors. State the exact number of other funders you are approaching. Also cite grantors that have already agreed to partially fund your Internet access project. Present the total amount already received and the outstanding amount.

It is crucial that the grantors know that you are tailoring your proposal to each prospective funding source and that you have done your grants homework for jointly funded projects. Some grantors may be justifiably concerned that their part of your project will get lost in the shuffle or that they will not receive appropriate credit. To alleviate these concerns, use a colored highlighter to visually separate each grantor's part of the total project on your Project Planner and refer each grantor to the Project Planner so that they can see how integral their portion is to the whole plan.

*Matching Costs and In-Kind Contributions.* Some grantors require that a portion of the project costs be borne by a grantee. While many federal grantors require matching contributions, several foundations (and corporations) also require grantees to pay for part of their projects. Even if a matching or in-kind contribution is not required, you may still want to include one to demonstrate your school's commitment to the project. Private grantors expect that organizations funded by them will be committed to supporting their projects after grant funds are expended. By demonstrating your school's commitment in advance through a matching or in-kind contribution, you confirm that you have not applied for the grantor's money without carefully analyzing your own commitment.

*What to Do if the Grantor Requests a Budget.* Only a few foundations will require that you submit a budget with your letter proposal. Of the 1,000 who may, only a few hundred will request that a specific budget format be used.

If you have developed a Project Planner, preparing the budget will be a simple task. For a letter proposal budget, provide a summary of the major line items on your Project Planner. However, be sure to let the grantor know that more detailed budget information is available upon request.

If no budget format is specified, present the budget in a paragraph or block form. Use a minimum of space and short columns instead of long ones. For example: "We are requesting a grant of $20,000 from the Appleton Foundation to provide the in-service Internet training needed to take full advantage of this online resource. To demonstrate our school's support of this important project we will provide $8,000 in matching support. A more detailed budget is available upon request." Another sample budget is provided in the following table.

|  | Request ($) | Match ($) | Total ($) |
|---|---|---|---|
| Salaries and wages | 10,000 |  | 10,000 |
| Stipends/teachers in-service |  | 7,000 | 7,000 |
| Consultants/evaluation | 3,000 |  | 3,000 |
| Equipment/lab | 7,000 |  | 7,000 |
| Printing/materials |  | 1,000 | 1,000 |
| *Total* | 20,000 | 8,000 | 28,000 |

6. Uniqueness   Why should your school get the grant instead of some other grantee? Since funding sources will ask themselves this question anyway, you should bring it up yourself: Why *should* your school get this grant? Couldn't another school initiate the methods and conduct the project just as well? The answer to the last question is no, because you have the best plan to use the Internet resource. In addition:

- You developed the idea for the project! It is your baby.
- You have documented your school's/classroom's need. The opportunity to act is at your school.
- You developed the idea with the help of experts in curriculum development, evaluation, etc. You arranged for their input, gathered them together, and worked with them. In other words, you have already invested many, many hours developing a project that will be a successful model.

Brainstorm to reveal the positive forces at work that can help convince the grantor that your school is indeed the best school to fund. For instance, in addition to superior facilities, you also employ unique individuals whose commitment and expertise make your school the funding source's most logical choice. If you are the designated project director, put in a plug for yourself. For example, "Ms. Jane Doe [*your name*] is slated to direct the project. Ms. Doe has been recognized as an outstanding educator by the State Department of Education and has more than 12 years of experience in classroom teaching. In addition, she has already provided some of our teachers with in-service education on how Internet access can enrich curriculum." Don't be embarrassed to say something good about yourself—you are not going to sign the letter. Yes, that's right. Although you may write many letter proposals, you will seldom sign them because your letter proposal should generally be signed by the highest ranking individual in your school system. So be sure to include something complimentary about yourself and your experience with the Internet. Then, when your top ranking administrator signs it, it will become the truth!

**7. Closing Paragraph**

How do you conclude your letter proposal? Use the closing paragraph to reaffirm your school's commitment to your Internet access project and to invite the funder to work with you on achieving the project's anticipated results. You should also reaffirm your willingness to provide the funding source with any additional materials that may help them make their decision. You could invite the grantor to visit your school or classroom to observe the needs firsthand.

Always include the name and phone number of your contact person in the closing paragraph. In many cases the individual whose signature appears on the proposal knows very little about the details of the project. You might say something like, "Please contact Jane Doe, the project director, at 555-879-7333 for proposal details."

**8. Signatures** Ask yourself whose signature will have the greatest impact on the funding decision. In your case, it is most likely the signature of your superintendent or building principal, although some schools prefer to have proposals signed by the assistant superintendent for instruction, the business officer, or the curriculum specialist. Some proposals are submitted with two signatures—the president of the school board's and a top ranking school administrator's. It may be appropriate to have several signatures on proposals that require special cooperation, collaboration, or coordination. For example, a consortium proposal may have the signatures of all the cooperating parties.

*Attachments* Most foundations do not allow or encourage attachments. While attachments may help answer questions that arise when a proposal is being read, the problems they create for understaffed foundations often prohibit their inclusion.

What about pictures, videotapes, audiotapes, and slides? In the age of electronics, it certainly seems that these components would be allowed. However, be sure to find out what is allowed before submitting your proposal. While electronic tools may be highly effective in preproposal contact, they may be useless during the actual proposal review. For example, the reviewer may not have access to a VCR while reviewing the proposal.

**What's in Store for the Future?** Foundations in some states are joining together to support a standard format for grant applications. However, it is unlikely that this effort will come to fruition in the near future. If you follow the information and application guidelines in the various resource books, make preproposal contact when possible, and expand your network of informal linkages, you can be fairly certain that your proposal's format will be acceptable to your prospective funding source and that it will be read.

This chapter deals with contacting foundations and writing proposals geared toward these organizations. In the next chapter, you will learn how to contact corporations and cultivate their monetary support of your Internet access project. The following sample letter proposal to a foundation (Figure 5.9) is included for your review.

..............................................................................................................................................................

**Figure 5.9**

Sample Letter Proposal to a Foundation

March 24, 1996

Ms. Laura B. Align, Trustee
Smith Foundation
123 Money Place
Jonesboro, AL 35204

Dear Ms. Align:

Emily Rogan suggested that I contact the Smith Foundation with an exciting project that deals with an area in which our school and your board share an interest. My research indicates that in a recent two-year period, the Smith Foundation made $X$ number of grants totaling $X$ number of dollars for projects focusing on increasing the math and science skills of children in grades K–12. Your granting pattern has prompted us to submit to you this proposal focusing on improving our students' skills in these areas by increasing their access to technology.

[*You could mention previous support to your school district or the number of children who have been touched by any past support. For example, "Your grant to renovate a classroom into the Smith Science Lab has directly touched the lives of over 5,000 students in four years. Scores on standardized tests have improved 40 percent."*

*If the Smith Foundation has not funded elementary or secondary education directly, show how their support for your school-based project relates to their interest in programs related*

*to the welfare of children, competing in society, preparing for
employment, and so on.]*

A recent study conducted by the Educational Testing Service
showed that American students scored lowest among 13-year-
olds from five nations on an international mathematics test and
substantially lower than students from three out of four other
countries in science. In our school, the average mathematics
and science proficiency for students 13 and 17 years old is
currently at its lowest level in 12 years.

Jennifer's story is typical of so many of our nation's students
whose math and science scores plummet when they reach high
school. In the sixth grade Jennifer scored in the top $X$ percent of
her class in math and the top $X$ percent in science. All through
middle school she continued to do well, but by high school she
scored in the $X$ percentile in both subjects. Why? Because
Jennifer no longer saw the relevancy of these subjects, and her
interest in them waned.

The solution to improving our students' math and science
skills is to link them and their teachers to the world through the
Internet so that they can share in experiences and projects that
will show them the relevancy of these subjects and motivate
them to learn.

*[Add specific examples or general, representative examples.
For instance, "By connecting our 9th grade science class to the
Internet they will be able to experience. . ."]*

However, in order to take advantage of the Internet, the most
dramatic learning tool since the pen, we must get our
classrooms rewired for both the power and the necessary
telephone service. Once the wiring is complete, we propose to
equip X number of classrooms per year with the necessary
hardware and software and provide in-service education for our
faculty and staff so that they may incorporate this resource into
their teaching.

I have included a one-page Project Planner spreadsheet
which summarizes our project. Additional spreadsheets that

document each step in greater detail are available on request. We would be pleased to present this plan to you in person at your foundation office or at our school, where you can view the use of our existing technology resources.

We are currently taking advantage of every grant opportunity possible, including state, federal, corporate, and local sources, and have raised over *X* dollars. The Jonesboro High School is fortunate to have Ms. Elizabeth Brown as our project director. Ms. Brown was named the "1995 Outstanding Teacher of the Year" by the Alabama State Education Department *[add your credibility statement here]*. She will be assisted by our Internet Technology Committee which is supported by 52 volunteers representing *X* number of local organizations and civic groups. These volunteers have already given over *X* number of hours to develop this project.

With our knowledge of your Foundation's commitment to cost efficient and effective education, we request a grant of *X* number of dollars.

*[State a specific amount which is in line with what you discovered through preproposal contact and research on the Foundation's average grant size for similar projects].*

Over the next five years, your grant will help us prepare *X* number of students for a productive future.

Jonesboro High School's tax exempt status is *123456789,* and our tax exempt number is *123-456-789*. Elizabeth Brown is available at 555-875-8451 to answer your questions and to provide additional information that will help you arrive at your funding decision.

Sincerely,

*[Official's name]*
*[Title]*
Attachment

# 6 Developing Corporate Support for Internet Access

I N ORDER to successfully acquire funds for your project from the corporate marketplace, you must first determine what motivates a corporation to contribute. In this chapter, you will learn:

- Why corporations would be interested in funding an Internet-access project.
- The four basic types of corporate support.
- How to contact corporate grantors.
- How to write a letter proposal to a corporation.

Reviewing the values of corporate funders tells us that they are motivated to give by a concern for their workers and the children of their workers, product development, and product positioning. Higher education has traditionally received the largest share of corporate support, but contributions to both elementary and secondary schools are increasing. Corporations contribute money to education because of their need for an educated work force and because good local schools are an attractive benefit for workers who have children.

**Corporate Support** It should now be evident that corporations might be interested in supporting your Internet access project for various reasons. But one thing is for sure—they do not support these types of projects simply out of the goodness of their heart. Remember, corporations want and expect an investment on their return!

The strategy you will employ for locating, developing, and sustaining corporate support for your Internet access project is different from the foundation-grants strategy that is outlined in Chapter 5. Corporate support requires much more "hands on" local involvement from your group. The most likely corporations to contribute to your project will be those in your school district because their employees' children attend these schools. The more you involve corporate officials in your project, the greater your chances of success.

Try to recruit individuals from your community's chamber of commerce to join your Internet Technology Support Group. Chambers of commerce tend to be very concerned about school resources.

Check with the chamber of commerce in your city to see if it has an education committee and/or a separate 501(c)(3) education foundation. They may be willing to submit your proposals to funding sources on their stationery and act as the fiscal agent for your project if they have a separate education foundation. This would allow your school to take advantage of the foundation's nonprofit tax status. This is particularly important if your school does not have its own foundation. In addition, the union of schools and businesses through a chamber's education foundation could provide your support group with the credibility and linkages necessary to make preproposal contact with corporate funding sources.

*Four Basic Types*
*of Corporate Support*

1. Grants awarded through corporate foundations.
2. Grants awarded through various corporate contributions programs.
3. Noncash support—such as loaned executives, adopt-a-school programs, and gifts of supplies, equipment, and company products.
4. Support provided through employee volunteer programs and union sponsorships—including cash contributions and challenge grants.

Unfortunately, there is a lack of accurate, verifiable data on corporate giving exists because only one of the four major types of corporate funding can be accurately researched and documented—the funding provided through corporate foundations.

1. Corporate Foundations

Corporate foundations must follow the same IRS rules that govern other private foundations. They must make their IRS 990 tax forms available for public scrutiny, and they must donate a minimum of five percent of their assets each year.

A corporation primarily forms a foundation in order to build a cash reserve to provide grant funding in years when corporate profits are low or nonexistent. For example, a decline in their corporate profits recently led the Boeing Company to move millions out of its foundation's asset base and donate it to nonprofit organizations through its corporate giving program.

Public disclosure by corporate foundations can assist you in assessing a corporation's interest in your school's Internet project. As with other types of foundations, you can examine a corporate foundation's tax return to determine their previous funding activities for education and technology. See Chapter 5 for a review of researching tax returns.

In most cases, corporate foundation boards consist of current corporate board members. The foundation's giving usually reflects the values of the corporation, and education is the primary recipient of corporate foundation support.

2. Corporate Contributions Programs

With more than four million corporations in the United States and only 1,700 with a foundation, your project will most likely need to elicit corporate support directly from corporate contributions programs.

Your local chamber of commerce will provide a list ranking corporations in your area by number of employees and payroll and may include product information. This list is an excellent grants research tool, but resist the urge to simply send the same hastily prepared "shotgun" proposal to every corporation on the list. Instead, review the list of corporations and devise a corporate strategy.

Linkages to important corporate decision makers and employee involvement are the key to corporate funding. Therefore, review your corporate list with school personnel and parent organizations for corporate volunteers and potential linkages, and find out if your school's records provide information on place of work for parents who have children in your school. Utilize any linkage to corporate officials that you can uncover (see the linkages section of Chapter 2). You would also benefit by involving corporate representatives on your Internet Technology Support Group. Many corporations require that their employees become volunteers or members of the nonprofit organization's support group before they award grant support to the organization. Since many corporate employees use computers in their work, and are familiar with technology, it will be relatively easy to excite and involve them in Internet access to improve the learning environment in your school.

Also, do not overlook corporate retirees as a resource. They have time to devote to your cause, as well as linkages to their former companies, and are often in favor of raising funds for school projects rather than increasing school taxes.

Do not discount smaller companies and independently owned businesses in your area. While individual companies or businesses may not be able to fund your grant idea on their own, several could band together to fund a portion of your project. Just because a company or business does not employ hundreds of individuals does not mean that it is not concerned about quality education.

In addition to corporations in your geographic area, consider nonlocal companies that may value your school's Internet access project because of its impact on their profits or marketplace. The *Standard Industrial Classification Code Book*, available at your public library, is an excellent tool to help you learn about companies and the products they manufacture. When you discover companies that manufacture products you think will be affected by your project, you can contact them about your proposal. Such products may include computer equipment; cable and phone utilities; software; and educational materials that you can test, improve, and validate.

Suppose you've already invited the local power company, phone company, cable company, and computer service and equipment suppliers to be part of your Internet Technology Support Group and they have helped you develop your plan which includes the utilization of their services and purchase of their products. Now ask them for their financial support. Also ask them to share their linkages to corporations not in your local area that could benefit from your Internet access program. They may be interested if their products will become visible to a growing marketplace. The following companies offer such discounts:

- Microsoft Corporation offers discounts on Internet-related software to elementary and secondary schools. In fact they provide several programs for free. Reach them at 800-426-9400 or http:\\www.microsoft.com/k-12.
- Apple Computer also offers free and discounted Internet-related software to schools. Through the Apple Education Initiative, schools may purchase computers at education-only discounts. Reach them at http:\\www.apple.com.
- Many other companies offer large discounts—as much as 50 percent—to schools. San Jose–based Cisco Systems

produces products and provides services and training for elementary and secondary schools to use Internet technology, and has created their Virtual Schoolhouse Grant Program. You can contacted them at: 408-526-4226; edu-grant@cisco.com; and http://www.cisco.com and http://sunsite.unc.edu/cisco.

- Also in San Jose, Asanté Networking produces Internet networking products, and provides money to schools through its Great Asanté Education Grants program. They can be reached at 821 Fox Lane, San Jose, CA 95131; phone: (408) 435-8388.
- JDL Technology provides K–12 Internet connection services and equipment and technology grants. They can be reached at: 5555 W. 78th Street, Suite E, Edina, MN; and on the Web at http://www.jdltech.com.

**3. Noncash Corporate Support** This includes gifts of technology experts, loaned executives, construction crews, maintenance, supplies, building materials, equipment, etc. Support of this nature is often overlooked, but noncash gifts can save you from having to raise all of the money. Review your Project Planner and determine which corporate sponsors have the skills or expertise to assist in making your Internet plan operational.

**4. Employee Support for Your Project** Many companies have employee groups that volunteer for community causes. These groups challenge their companies to support their efforts with loaned equipment and materials. Review your Project Planner for areas where such groups could be involved.

Unions are another valuable resource. They often provide support by making challenge grants to the companies with which they work. The companies often respond by making dollar-for-dollar matching grants.

**Corporate Research Tools** Many resource materials are available to help in your search for corporate support. Your public library or local college library should have several helpful references that can be used free. In addition, if you are near a Foundation Center National Collection or a Regional Cooperating Collection, you have access to many resources, including two of the Foundation Center's primary corporate research tools—*The National Directory of Corporate Giving* and *Corporate Foundation Profiles*.

- *The National Directory of Corporate Giving.* This directory provides information on more than 1,950 corporate foundations and an additional 650-plus direct giving programs. It also has six indexes to help you target the best funding prospects for your project.
- *Corporate Foundation Profiles.* This publication contains detailed analysis of more than 237 of the largest corporate foundations in the United States. It also breaks down corporate grantmakers' philanthropic activities by geographic area and types of support awarded. In addition, the publication includes an appendix that lists financial data on an additional 1,000 smaller corporate grantmakers.

Since most corporations' money comes from their profits, you will want to know which of your corporate prospects are profitable. Dunn and Bradstreet's *Million Dollar Directory* will help you discern the financial condition of 160,000 of America's largest businesses. A corporation that pays its creditors late and owes money should not be considered a prime target for your grant request.

**Steps for Contacting Corporate Grantors**  In this section, we discuss the various options open to you for contacting various corporate grantors.

*Linkages*  You may discover that one of your support group members or one of your members' friends or family is a linkage (mutual contact) to a corporation. Use this person to your advantage. Whenever possible, ask the person for the corporation's funding guidelines and for help arranging an appointment to talk with someone from the corporation's contributions staff.

*Letter* If your research reveals a corporate contact for grants information, you may decide to write to that person for information and application guidelines early in the grants process. The sample letter in Figure 6.1 can be sent to those corporations that have a grants staff and a preferred proposal format or application form.

---

**Figure 6.1**
Sample Letter to a
Corporation Requesting
Information and Guidelines

Date

Name
Title
Address

Dear *[contact person]*:

My research on your company's grant support indicates that we share an interest in promoting positive educational experiences and a concern for increasing our students' ability to compete in a global marketplace.

*[At this stage, mention your link, if one exists.]* John Smith, your sales representative, suggested I write to request your company's proposal guidelines and requirements for funding a project I believe you will find very interesting.

In an effort to promote the most efficient investment of both our organizations' time, I would appreciate receiving any information relative to your company's funding priorities.

Sincerely,

*[Official's Name/Title]*
Phone Number

*Telephone*   Before you telephone the corporate grantor, decide why you think the company would value your project. If you do not know who the corporate contact is, ask whoever answers the phone for the person most able to answer your questions about the corporation's grants process.

As with foundation and government granting sources, state the reason for the call. For instance, say: "I am calling to discuss the opportunity of working together on a grant that has mutual benefits to both the XYZ School and the ABC Corporation." Request five minutes of the person's time to answer your questions, and suggest that you can fax or mail background information. By sending background information, you will elicit comments to help you tailor your proposal to the corporation's needs. Be sure to explain that you are not presenting your proposal at this point.

Summarize the research that has led you to contact this particular company. Let the corporate contact know that you are approaching only a select group of corporations.

*Visit*   Corporations may actually spend more time reviewing grants than foundations do, possibly because they have more resources (employees, offices) on which to draw, even though employees who act as corporate grants contacts may have several other job responsibilities. These resources mean you can often meet with the corporate grantor in person.

You or your linkage may even want to invite the corporate person to visit your school to see the technology you currently have in place and to present the opportunities that Internet access or enhancement would provide your students and teachers.

Who Should Represent   While you may think that you, as the progenitor of the
Your School?   Internet Technology Support Group, are the best representative to meet with a corporate contact, you may want to consider someone else from your group. This is particularly true if you are a paid employee of the school, such as a teacher or administrator. In this case, letting one of the sup-

port group volunteers represent the group may be the wiser choice because a volunteer donates his or her time and may even be losing income in order to represent your school. Corporations will be impressed by the quality, commitment, and number of volunteers that your school can mobilize. But do not overwhelm the corporate funder with a massive team. Two well chosen and carefully instructed representatives will be most effective.

**What Should the Representative(s) Wear?** Remember that first impressions do count. Try to dress in a manner that is compatible with the people with whom you will be meeting, and strive to project a serious business image.

**What Should the Representative(s) Bring?** Bring materials with information outlining the need for the project. As when visiting other funding sources, you are advised to include one of the following:

• A short videotape that shows a classroom without Internet access and one with Internet access (even one in another school or school district). Include facts and, if possible, a testimony or case study for human interest.
• A slide-and-audiotape presentation on the problem or need.
• Pictures, charts, statistics, your project planner, your plan, etc.

Since corporations have their own style and vocabulary, it might be a good idea to ask a member of your support group from the corporate sector to make a short, corporate-style presentation to the funding source. This presentation might included colored charts and transparencies.

**Tracking Corporate Contacts** As with foundations, you should create a file for each of your corporate prospects. The corporate files should be kept together in alphabetical order. This will help you organize your grants effort.

Complete the corporate research worksheet in Figure 6.2 (on the following page) for your most likely funding prospects. The worksheet will help you keep an up-to-date record of the information you have gathered.

Update the worksheet as additional information and materials are obtained. The worksheet will also be a record of all contact made with the corporation.

Just as gathering personal data on foundation officers, board members, and trustees is important, gathering personal data on corporate executives and contributions officers is also important. You can uncover some information on corporate executives by examining various corporate resource materials available at your public library, including Standard and Poors' *Register of Corporations, Directors and Executives.*

The more information you collect, the better your chances of developing an approach that will appeal to the funding source. Your chances of identifying more linkages to the corporation will also increase. However, please note that you should not discount a particular corporation as a funding prospect simply because you are unable to attain personal data on the corporation's funding officials.

The worksheet in Figure 6.3 (page 100) should be used to record the information collected. The worksheet should be stored in the appropriate corporation's file.

**The Grantor Strategy Worksheet**

Complete the worksheet in Figure 6.4 (page 101) for each source for which you plan to submit a proposal. This worksheet will help tailor both your approach to each funding source and your school's proposal to each fund's viewpoint.

Every attempt should be made to analyze the funding source's granting history. Even if preproposal contact is not possible, you must at least make sure that the amount you are requesting fits the funding source's granting pattern.

Think about potential proposal collaborators and other groups that might submit proposals that better fit the funder's requirements.

**Figure 6.2**
Corporation Research
Worksheet

Create a file for each corporation you are researching and place the information you gather on the corporation in the file. Use this worksheet to:

- Keep a record of the information you have gathered
- Maintain a log of all telephone and face-to-face contact with the corporation
- Log all correspondence to and from the corporation

Corporation: _____ Deadline Date(s): _____

Corporation's Address: _____

_____

_____

Name of Contact Person: _____

Title of Contact Person: _____

Telephone Number: _____

Fax Number: _____

Email address: _____

Address of Corporate Contact: _____

_____

_____

**Figure 6.2**
(continued)
Place a check mark next to the information you have gathered and placed in the file for the corporation.

_____ Description of Corporate Giving Program from *The National Directory of Corporate Giving, Corporate Foundation Profiles,* or other source
Note Source: _____

_____ Required proposal format, grant application, and guidelines

_____ Corporate foundation's 990 IRS tax return

_____ List of corporate officers and sales representatives
Note Source: _____

_____ Corporate product information (the Standard Industrial Classification Code)

_____ Profits and dividends information—financial status of corporation from Dun and Bradstreet's *Million Dollar Directory, a* credit rating service, or other source
Note Source: _____

_____ Corporate funding staff history

_____ Information obtained from chamber of commerce (number of employees, payroll, etc.)

_____ Written summary of each contact made

_____ Grantor strategy worksheet

**Figure 6.3**
Corporation Funding Staff
History Worksheet

List any data you've uncovered that might help you. Determine ways to deal with the contact's preferences and biases. Locate other possible linkages between this individual and you, your school, a volunteer on your support group, etc.

1. Name of Funding Executive: _____

2. Title: _____

3. Residence Address:

   _____

   Phone: _____

4. Business Address: _____

   _____

   Phone: _____ Fax: _____

   Email: _____

5. Contacts: _____

6. Birthdate: _____ Birthplace: _____

7. Marital Status: ____Children: _____

8. College/University: _____ Degree(s): _____

9. Military Service: _____

10. Clubs/Affiliations: _____

11. Interests/Hobbies: _____

12. Board Memberships: _____

13. Philanthropic Activities: _____

14. Awards/Honors: _____

15. Other: _____

Notes: _____

_____

**Figure 6.4**

Grantor Strategy Worksheet

Potential Grantor: _____ Priority #: _____ Deadline: ___

**A. Strategy Derived from Granting Pattern**

1. $____ Largest grant to organization most similar to ours
2. $____ Smallest grant to organization most similar to ours
3. $____ Average grant to organization most similar to ours
4. $____ Average grant in our area of interest
5. $____ Our estimated grant request
6. Financial trend in our area of interest over past 3 years
   Up ____ Down ____ Stable _____
7. If your proposal is a multiyear proposal, how popular have these been with the funding source in the past 3 years?
   _____ many multiyear proposals funded
   _____ some multiyear proposals funded
   _____ few multiyear proposals funded
   _____ no multiyear funding
   _____ not applicable
8. Financial data on funding source: obligation levels for last 3 years for grants
   19 ___ $ _____   19____ $ _____   19____ $ _____

**B. Based on preproposal contact, which solution strategies are the most appropriate for this funding source?**

_____

_____

**C. Proposal Review System**

1. Who evaluates submitted proposals? _____

_____

2. What is the background and training of the evaluators?

_____

3. What point system will be followed? _____

_____

4. How much time will be spent reviewing each proposal?

_____

**D. Use this space to note anything "special" that will affect proposal outcome.**

_____

_____

If at all possible, find out who will read and evaluate your school's proposal. For example, will your proposal be read by staff members, board members, program personnel, or outside experts/reviewers? Besides helping you write the proposal, this information will be vital to performing a mock review of your proposal.

The prospective funding source should be ranked by prospect potential. At this point, you should not spend much time writing your proposal. Instead, you should invest your time "analyzing" your best prospects for funding.

Although some pieces of vital information will probably be missing, devise the best strategy you can, based on what you know.

**Constructing Your Corporate Proposal**

Most corporations will ask you to send them a concept paper or letter proposal. Even those with guidelines (and a few have strict formats) will usually request a short proposal tailored to their company, its perspective on your need, and how your project relates to their interests.

The basic concepts of the corporate letter proposal are very similar to those for a foundation. The differences are in using corporate vocabulary and including the corporate perspective. When writing a corporate proposal, remember that corporations think of grants as investments. They will want to know what the return will be for making Internet access available in your classroom or school. While they may have a strong knowledge of technology and its positive aspects, they will be wary of technology for technology's sake. In other words, don't be surprised if you do not elicit a positive reaction by simply stating that Internet access is great and listing all of your installation and equipment needs. Many corporations have been burned by jumping into technological advances too soon. Therefore, your proposal must include examples of how Internet access in your classroom will result in a better "product" (your students).

Mention any past corporate involvement and sponsorship in the beginning of your proposal. This is important since corporations are sensitive to being asked for money by organizations who have not done their homework. You may, however, have difficulty including this information when your proposal is aimed at a corporate giving program. It is relatively easy to obtain this information through a review of a corporate *foundation's* tax return, but the only way you can get it for nonfoundation corporate giving is through preproposal contact, linkages, and reference books. In any event, the beginning of your proposal should focus on why you have approached the company, who are their company volunteers in your project, and who referred you to them.

While corporations give where they live, they will expect a professional approach, and the project planner will appeal to them since they are familiar with and use spreadsheet formats. Include a project planner with your corporate letter proposal whenever allowed. (See Chapter 3).

The following sample letter proposal to a corporation (Figure 6.5) is included for your review.

**Critiquing Your Corporate Proposal** — Ask a group of volunteers to read your proposal and perform a mock review to help strengthen your chance of grant success. (This should be done for letter proposals to foundations, as well as to corporations.) Include a few corporate executives in the group and ask them to provide critical comments and changes they would make to elicit the best response from your corporate prospect. (See Chapter 7 for a detailed description of the mock review process.)

**Submission of Your Corporate Proposal** — After following the corporation's instructions on proposal submission, consider sending a copy of the proposal or a summary of it to your contact in the corporation. This "for your information" summary will tactfully remind your corporate friend to "push" your proposal with decision makers.

So far, this book has explained how to tap into foundation and corporation grant money. The next step is assessing federal and state opportunities for Internet access. This will be addressed in great detail in the following chapter.

**Figure 6.5**
Sample Letter Proposal
to a Corporation

March 24, 1996

Clyde L. Baker
Contributions Officer
Widget Corporation
4321 Commercial Park
Rocher, NY 14570

Dear Mr. Baker:

John Allen, your marketing manager, advised me to contact you for consideration of a grant from the Widget Corporation. John, who has volunteered more than 100 hours to our Internet Technology Support Group, has told us of your company's interest in and efforts to promote educational excellence in our community's schools.

*[You could mention previous support to your school district or the number of children who have been touched by any past support. If the corporation has not funded elementary or secondary education directly, show how their support for your school-based project relates to their interest in programs related to competing in society, preparing for employment, etc.]*

John has been instrumental in helping our group understand the changes technological advances have brought to the Widget Corporation and how these changes have affected the types of employees and skills your corporation requires.

Through our conversations with John and other corporate executives, we have realized that we must improve our children's math and science skills for them to successfully compete in tomorrow's world. The need to improve our children's math and science skills becomes very apparent when we compare our students to those in other countries. For example, the top 5 percent of the students in the United States is equal to the top 50 percent in Japan, and only eight percent of Japanese 11th graders receive math scores lower than their American counterparts.

The need to provide our students with the skills necessary to survive in the competitive future is compelling. By the year

**Figure 6.5**
(continued)

2000, the U.S. economy will create 21 million new jobs, and most will require postsecondary education. The following is a quote from an article appearing in INC. magazine in 1993.

> The modern corporation of today wants employees who can and will think about innovation, quality service, and employ techniques such as statistical process control (SPC) . . . machine tenders, trained in SPC check their own defect rates.

Yet, when we surveyed the math program in our high school we found no reference to statistical process control. And when asked to research the importance of math in the workplace, our math and business students uncovered this startling quote from the CEO of the Will-Burt, Inc. in Orrville, Ohio.

> Workers' flawed calculations resulted in 2,000 hours of rework a month which equaled a 35 percent rejection rate. Once a school was set up to teach our workers math, rework was reduced to 400 hours per month for an 8 percent rejection rate. The company's latest reports indicate that by spending 1 percent of our annual sales on remedial training the rejection rate has dropped to 2 percent.

While it would be fashionable in some school districts to spend time looking for someone to blame for this distressing situation, our school is looking for relevant ways to improve the learning environment to reverse this trend.

History has taught us that we can conquer our country's educational problems. One hundred years ago one half of the students in our public schools did not speak English. Educators had to figure out a way to teach math and science in multicultural schools. To meet this challenge, they taught their students English first, and then math and science.

Look at the changes that increased technology has brought to our country in the last ten years. Now contrast these changes

**Figure 6.5**
Sample Letter Proposal
to a Corporation (continued)

with the changes in our schools. While we may have computer labs and teach basic keyboarding and word processing, we have not been able to keep up with the technological advancements that would allow us to take advantage of Internet access and the world of educational enhancement that this access brings.

*[Add examples of classroom projects that you could accomplish if you had access, or examples from other schools with access.]*

The solution to improving our students' math and science skills is to link them and their teachers to the world through the Internet so that they can share in experiences and projects that will teach them the relevancy of these subjects and motivate them to learn.

*[Add specific examples or general, representative examples. For instance, "By connecting our 9th grade science class to the Internet they will be able to experience. . ."]*

However, in order to take advantage of the Internet, the most dramatic learning tool since the pen, we must rewire our classrooms for both the power and the necessary telephone service. Once the wiring is complete, we propose to equip *X* number of classrooms per year with the necessary hardware and software and provide in-service education for our faculty and staff so that they may incorporate this resource into their teaching.

I have included a one page Project Planner spreadsheet which summarizes our project. Additional spreadsheets that document each step in greater detail are available on request. We would be pleased to present this plan to you in person at your office or at our school, where you can view the use of our existing technology resources.

We are currently taking advantage of every grant opportunity possible—state, federal, foundation, and local—and have raised over X dollars. Rocher High School is fortunate to have Mr. Arnold Brown as our project director. Mr. Brown was named the "1995 Outstanding Teacher of the Year" by the New York State Education Department and is eminently qualified. He will be assisted by our Internet Technology Committee, which is

**Figure 6.5**
(continued)

supported by 52 volunteers representing *X* number of local organizations and civic groups.

These volunteers have already given more than *X* number of hours to develop this project. But they have done all they can do at this point. The time is now right for you to join us in preparing our students, tomorrow's employees, with the skills they will need to ensure a productive and prosperous future. With our knowledge of your corporation's commitment to cost-efficient and effective education,we request a grant of *X* number of dollars.

*[State a specific amount which is in line with the information you gathered through preproposal contact and research].*

This project is truly an investment in our community. Arnold Brown is ready to provide any additional information you may need to make your funding decision. Please call him at *555-756-4589.* Our school's tax exempt status is *123-456-789* and our tax exempt number is *123-456-789.*

Sincerely,


*[Official's name]*
*[Title]*
Attachment

# 7 Assessing Federal and State Opportunities for Internet Access

ACQUIRING government grants need not be a panic-driven process. With just a little planning and some proactive grantseeking, you can develop successful government proposals for your Internet access plan. In this chapter, you will learn:

- How the Federal Grants Clock operates.
- How to use the *Catalogue of Federal Domestic Assistance* to find approximately $75 billion in grants.
- How to contact government grantors.
- How to develop government grant proposals.

**Researching Government Grant Opportunities for Internet Access**

Federal and state grants come from tax dollars and are, therefore, subject to the Freedom of Information Act. This means that you have a right to free or inexpensive access to all information on federal grant opportunities.

Government grant opportunities for education are available to your school either directly from federal programs or indirectly from federal programs administered through the states. Some states develop their own grants programs, but there is no uniform mechanism for researching state opportunities. Since few states have grants systems that are as organized as the federal government's, you may find it helpful to check directly with your own state's education department. They can place you on their mailing list for information about the grant programs that utilize federal funds, as well as the state's program regarding Internet access and enhancement.

Direct federal grant opportunities are a different story, however. Since all prospective grantees must have an equal opportunity to learn about and apply for federal funds, there is a special system for the dissemination of federal grant information.

Ask educators in middle or elementary schools what they think of when they hear the words *federal grant opportunity,* and chances are many will describe scenes of confusion and panic. In most school districts, meeting a federal grants deadline is preceded by last-minute, chaotic scrambling. Such panic is a result of *reactive* grantseeking. Approached properly, you can develop successful federal proposals and deal effectively with the pressure of deadlines. You can even submit proposals early by utilizing the available resources to meet deadlines and developing a controlled approach to grantseeking.

Accurately determining the total number of grants and the dollars awarded by federal agencies each year is difficult. Most of the estimates are based on appropriations budgets, not on the actual grant dollars awarded. Appropriations budgets include federal program personnel and overhead expenses and are much higher than the dollars awarded. A recent search of education-related federal grants found 287 programs with more than $79 billion in appropriations. When other similar programs were searched, however, these figures rose to 549 programs with a total of $112 billion in appropriations. It is impossible, however, to calculate just how much of this is actually awarded to the recipients after the agencies pay for all of the expenses needed to run the programs.

*The Federal Grants Clock* The federal grant process follows a yearly cycle—the federal grants clock. (See Figure 7.1.) All federal granting programs operate on a similar "clock." First, the program administrator makes the applications package available to prospective grantees. The deadline, which is made public three to six months prior to the dissemination of the package, is normally four to eight weeks after the dissemination of the package and is rigidly enforced. After the deadline, the submitted proposals are read, evaluated, and scored by a team

**Figure 7.1**
The Federal Grants Clock

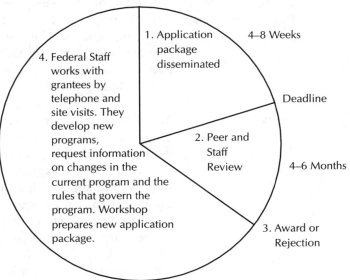

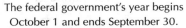

The federal government's year begins
October 1 and ends September 30.

1. Application package disseminated

4–8 Weeks

4. Federal Staff works with grantees by telephone and site visits. They develop new programs, request information on changes in the current program and the rules that govern the program. Workshop prepares new application package.

Deadline

2. Peer and Staff Review

4–6 Months

3. Award or Rejection

of reviewers, including individuals who resemble the prospective grantees (hence the term "peer review"). The peer and staff review process takes approximately four to six months. Once the funding decisions are made, award and rejection notices are transmitted to the applicants. During the remaining time, the federal officials work with grantees and begin the process of assembling another round of applications.

The key to winning federal grants is knowing what occurs during the Federal Grants Clock and how acting proactively can dramatically increase your success rate while decreasing the madness associated with a last-minute rush to meet a deadline.

Do not wait to learn about a grant opportunity. Do not postpone preparing your proposal until you receive an application package. Start now. To do so, you need to have a working knowledge of the major federal grant information publications described below.

**The Catalogue of Federal Domestic Assistance**

In the fall of each year, the federal government publishes *The Catalogue of Federal Domestic Assistance* (CFDA). This catalogue lists the 1,300 granting programs that disseminate approximately $75 billion in grants annually and provides the grantseeker with all sorts of valuable information, including deadlines.

**Why Should You Use the CFDA?**

You should know about existing federal programs for your project area even if you are planning to pursue only foundation or corporate grants. Armed with this knowledge, you will be able to explain to a prospective private grantor why you are approaching them with your Internet access project instead of a federal agency. For instance, it will be easier for you to demonstrate why private grant support is so necessary if you know for certain that no federal program funds are designated for Internet access or that federal funding for your Internet project is limited to three projects across the entire country.

*How Can You Get the CFDA?* You may purchase the CFDA from the Superintendent of Documents, U.S. Government Printing Office, Washington, for less than $50. Reach them at 202-512-1800. However, you do not have to buy your own copy; the CFDA is provided free to at least two libraries in each congressional district. (Your congressperson should know which libraries have been designated Federal Depository Libraries.) Most public libraries also have copies, as do college and university libraries and grants offices. You can also find the CFDA on the Internet: gopher://portfolio.stanford.edu:1970/1100334.

*How Do You Use the CFDA?* The most efficient way to locate the granting agencies that represent your best opportunities is to use the key words you circle on the key words worksheet for government grant-seeking (Figure 7.2, on the next page) and compare them to the indexes in the CFDA. The CFDA has five indexes. However, the subject index is the most helpful for locating grant opportunities in the Education Department and in other departments that have an interest in education.

For example, if your support group has identified math and science improvement as a target area, you can go to the CFDA and use the key subject terms "math" and "science" to search for programs interested in these areas. If you are also interested in increasing interest in math and science in high school females, you can also conduct a search with words such as "females," "girls," "minorities," etc. If you already know which agency you want to look at, you can use the agency index. In this example, we would go directly to the National Science Foundation. (NSF is a government funding agency, not a foundation.)

Each of the 1,300-plus federal programs are referenced with a number. When searching the CFDA for prospective programs for our example project, we would discover CFDA 47.076 Education and Human Resources, National Science Foundation. A sample of CFDA 47.076 is shown in Figure 7.3 (on pages 115–19) to help you understand the federal

**Figure 7.2**
Keywords Worksheet for
Government Grantseeking

The federal government uses
this subject index to
describe grant opportunities
in education. Review the list
and circle the keywords
related to your project. You
may find it helpful to briefly
note any significant ways
you could change your
solution to make it relate to
that keyword.

## Federal programs dealing with all of education

Adult education _____

Disadvantaged education _____

Early childhood education _____

Elementary education _____

Health education _____

Humanities education _____

Indian education _____

International education _____

Tools for schools _____

## Federal programs dealing with elementary education

Elementary education arts _____

Elementary education bilingual _____

Chapter 1 _____

Chapter 2 _____

Computer learning _____

Disadvantaged/deprived _____

Drug-free schools _____

Gifted and talented student _____

Handicapped _____

Homeless children _____

Immigrant children _____

Impact aid _____

Math/science _____

Migrant education _____

Elementary education minorities _____

Neglected and delinquent _____

Physical fitness _____

Private schools _____

School dropout prevention _____

Talent search _____

Upward bound _____

**Figure 7.3**
Sample of the *Catalogue of Federal Domestic Assistance*

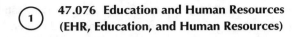

**(1) 47.076  Education and Human Resources (EHR, Education, and Human Resources)**

**(2) FEDERAL AGENCY:** National Science Foundation

**(3) AUTHORIZATION:** National Science Foundation Act of 1959, as amended, 42 U.S.C 1861 et seq.

**(4) OBJECTIVES:** To provide leadership and support to the Nation's efforts to improve the quality and effectiveness of science, mathematics and engineering education; with the ultimate goal being a scientifically literate society, a technically competent workforce and a body of well-educated scientists and engineers adequate to the Nation's needs. The program supports activities in the following areas: systemic reform; elementary, secondary and informal science education; undergraduate education; graduate education; human resource development; and research, evaluation and communication.

**(5) TYPES OF ASSISTANCE:** Project Grants.

**(6) USES AND USE RESTRICTIONS:** Grant funds may be used for paying costs necessary to conduct research, educational activities or studies, such as salaries and expenses, permanent equipment, expendable equipment and supplies, travel, publication cost, and other direct and indirect costs. Primary responsibility for general supervision of all grant activities rests with the grantee institution. Funds may not be used for purposes other than those specified in the proposal. Fellowships provide for stipends and allowances to be paid to the awardee through his/her institution. A fixed cost-of-education allowance is paid directly to the institution.

**(7) ELIGIBILITY REQUIREMENTS:**

**Applicant Eligibility:** Public and private colleges (two-year and four-year) and universities, state and local educational agencies,

**Figure 7.3**

Sample of the *Catalogue of Federal Domestic Assistance (continued)*

nonprofit and private organizations, professional societies, science academies and centers, science museums and zoological parks, research laboratories, and other institutions with an educational mission may apply.

**Beneficiary Eligibility:** Elementary, secondary and undergraduate science, mathematics and engineering teachers and faculty; secondary, undergraduate and graduate students; public and private colleges (two-year and four-year) and universities; state and local educational agencies; nonprofit and private organizations; professional societies; science academies and centers; science museums and zoological parks; research laboratories; and other institutions with an educational mission benefit.

**Credentials/Documentation:** Proposals must be signed by the principal investigator(s) and by an official authorized to commit the institution in business and financial affairs. Costs will be determined in accordance with OMB Circular No. A-21 for colleges and universities, No. A-87 for State and local governments, and No. A-122 for nonprofit organizations. Applicants for fellowship support must show evidence of ability such as academic records, letters of recommendation, graduate record examination scores, and grade point average.

**8** APPLICATION AND AWARD PROCESS

**Preapplication Coordination:** In selected areas, discussion with NSF program staff before submitting formal proposals is strongly encouraged. Other areas are eligible for coverage under E.O. 12372. "Intergovernmental Review of Federal Programs." An applicant should consult the office or official designated as the single point of contact in his or her State for more information on the process that the State requires to be followed in applying for assistance, if the State has selected the program for review.

**Application Procedure:** By submission of a formal proposal, and, in some areas, a preliminary inquiry, describing the

**Figure 7.3**
*(continued)*

planned project and the proposed amount of the grant. For guidelines, see specific program announcements and "Grants Proposal Guide," NSF 94-2.

**Award Procedure:** NSF staff members review and evaluate all proposals, with the advice of scientists, engineers, educators and other appropriate persons who are specialists in the field covered by the proposals. Panel members, who are conversant with the field covered by the application, review and evaluate all graduate fellowship applications. Awards are made by NSF on a competitive basis.

**Deadlines:** Deadlines and target dates are published in the *NSF Bulletin* and program announcements.

**Range of Approval/Disapproval Time:** From five to nine months.

**Appeals:** The principal investigator may request, in writing within 90 days of the declination or return, that the Foundation reconsider its action in declining or returning any proposal or application.

**Renewals:** Contact NSF program staff for specific renewal policies and procedures.

 **ASSISTANCE CONSIDERATIONS:**

**Formula and Matching Requirements:** This program has no statutory formula. Projects vary with regard to the required level of institutional contribution or cost-sharing. "Instrumentation and Laboratory Improvement" requires an institutional matching contribution equal to or greater than the National Science Foundation contribution.

**Length and Time Phasing of Assistance:** Up to five years. Assistance is disbursed by letter of credit or as required. For fellowships, typically nine to twelve months; up to three years of support. Assistance is disbursed to the institution for monthly stipend allotment to the fellow.

**Figure 7.3**
Sample of the
*Catalogue of Federal
Domestic Assistance
(continued)*

**(10) POST-ASSISTANCE CONSIDERATIONS:**

**Reports:** A substantive technical report is required upon completion of the project. Frequency and complexity of interim reports varies among programs depending on size, scope and program objective. Quarterly Federal cash transactions reports (SF 272) are required. For fellowships, brief annual activities reports are required.

**Audits:** Under the total audit concept, audits will be made on an organization-wide basis (rather than grant-by-grant) under GAO guidelines, "Standards for Audit of Government Organizations, Programs, Activities and Functions."

**Records:** Grantees are expected to maintain separate records for each grant to insure that funds are used for the general purpose for which the grant was made. Records are subject to inspection during the life of the grant and for three years thereafter. Not applicable to fellowships.

**(11) FINANCIAL INFORMATION:**

**Account Identification:** 49-0106-0-1-251.

**Obligations:** (Grants) FY 94 $569,033,000; FY 95 est $605,974,000; and FY 96 est $599,000,000.

**Range and Average of Financial Assistance:** $7,500 to $2,000,000; $104,500.

**(12) PROGRAM ACCOMPLISHMENTS:** In fiscal year 1994, approximately 2,573 awards were made and approximately 17,692 proposals were received. In fiscal year 1995, it is estimated that 2,642 awards will be made and 18,790 proposals will be received, and in fiscal year 1995 approximately 2,607 awards will be made and 19,675 proposals will be received.

**(13) REGULATIONS, GUIDELINES, AND LITERATURE:** 45 CFR chapter VI; 48 CFR Chapter 25; "NSF Guide to Programs, FY 1995," NSF 94-91 (no charge); "Grant Proposal Guide," NSF 94-2 (no charge).

**Figure 7.3**
*(continued)*

(14) **INFORMATION CONTACTS:**

**Regional or Local Office:** None.

**Headquarters Office:** Assistant Director, Education and Human Resources, National Science Foundation, 4201 Wilson Blvd., Room 805, Arlington, VA 22230. Telephone: 703-306-1600. Internet address: stis@usf.gov.

(15) **RELATED PROGRAMS:** 84.073, National Diffusion Network; 84.117, Educational Research and Development; 84.120, Minority Science Improvement; 84.168, Eisenhower Professional Development—Federal Activities; 84.186, Safe and Drug-Free Schools—State Grants; 84.203, Star Schools; 93,880, Minority Access to Research Careers; 93.922, NCRR Science Education Award.

(16) **EXAMPLES OF FUNDED PROJECTS:** (1) Louisiana Collaborative for Excellence in Teacher Preparation; (2) Interactive Mathematics Project—Secondary School Curriculum; (3) University of California at Irvine Alliance for Minority Participation for all areas of science; (4) Graduate Fellowship in Chemical Engineering to study reactions in super critical fluid; and (5) Evaluation of first set of statewide systemic initiative awardees.

(17) **CRITERIA FOR SELECTING PROPOSALS:** Decisions are based on the scientific and educational merit of the described project and conformance with the objectives of the program. Specific evaluation criteria vary by program activity and are addressed in the individual program announcements.

grants system. This understanding is crucial to developing a proactive grantseeking system that will enable you to start the process early and make preproposal contact with the appropriate funding source. The numbers in the left margin in Figure 7.3 are keyed to the explanation that follows.

*1. Program Title*   Education and Human Resources.

*2. Federal Agency*   This section tells you what government branch handles the program. While many grant programs will be sponsored by the Department of Education, you may also apply to the National Science Foundation, the National Endowment for the Arts, etc.

*3. Authorization*   This item tells you the source of the funding.

*4. Objectives*   This section is important because it provides the first indication of the appropriateness of your idea in relationship to the funding program.

*5. Types of Assistance*   This program funds project grants. You must know what types of assistance are provided in order to determine if the federal program is interested in funding projects or research, or if they fund on a formula basis that allocates the funds to eligible recipients through predetermined criteria.

*6. Uses and Use Restrictions*   This section helps you further determine whether the program is an appropriate source of funds for your project. In using the Internet to increase science and math skills, it would be critical to determine whether the necessary equipment would be an allowable cost.

*7. Eligibility Requirements*   • *Applicant Eligibility*—This section tells you if your school is an eligible recipient. Your school is designated as a Local Educational Agency (LEA). If your school is not eligible for funding under this program, this section tells you through which organization you can submit your proposal. In the example, your school district may fit under the category "other institutions with an educational mission."

- *Beneficiary Eligibility*—This section tells you what type of individual or organization is intended to benefit from the project.
- *Credentials/Documentation*—The Office of Management and Budget (OMB) publishes several management booklets that outline the rules for requesting, spending, and documenting expenditures under a federal grant.
- *Block Grants*—When a federal program is collapsed into a block grant that will be awarded to states, the eligible recipients will not include LEAs. Instead, state agencies or other official recipients in each state will be designated to receive the funds. Block grant funds are allocated to the states according to a formula or percentage basis. For example, if $2 billion in Internet access funds is made available by the current or future president, these monies will probably be allocated to states based upon the number of elementary and secondary students in each state. When dealing with a block grant, call your state education department. If you cannot find who holds these funds, contact the federal person listed later in the program announcement, and ask who has the money in your state. It may not be the education department, but an official appointed by the governor.

*8. Application and Award Process*

- *Preapplication Coordination*—This outlines the OMB requirements related to your state's review and knowledge of your proposal. If you have a district grants office, they will know whom to contact in your state concerning this matter. This contact is known as a "single point of contact." (For more on this, see "Intergovernmental Review of Federal Programs" on page 164.)
- *Application Procedure*—This section describes the rules for submissions, other helpful information, and agency publications.

- *Award Procedure*—This section tells you who will review and approve your proposal. Proposals submitted to this particular program will be read by program staff based on the published criteria. Experts will also read the proposals and assist the staff members. As always, the writing style and level used in your proposal should be in accordance with the background of the reviewers.
- *Deadlines*—Deadlines are established by notice published in *The Federal Register.*
- *Range of Approval/Disapproval Time*—Closing date published in the *NSF Bulletin.*
- *Appeals*—Some programs have a special appeals process.
- *Renewals*—This information is important when you are planning a project that may take several years. In this case, you must discuss this issue in preproposal contact.

9. Assistance Considerations
- *Formula and Matching Requirements*—This section outlines what portion, if any, of the project costs must be borne by your school district. It is vital that you have a plan for the match and your school's endorsement that it will commit to this share. In this example, it is difficult to ascertain what will be required. More research is needed.
- *Length and Time Phasing of Assistance*—In this case, it is up to five years.

10. Post-Assistance Requirements

Your district will be required to make reports and maintain records, and may be subject to audits. Don't let this section scare you—your school's business office will handle it.

11. Financial Information
- *Account Identification*—Account identification number.
- *Obligations*—Review this section and determine if the program is slated to increase or decrease its funding level. It is estimated that the future budget for this program will be $599 million, but this could be changed drastically by Congress or the president. In this example, program funds increased, and then slightly decreased.

- *Range and Average of Financial Assistance*—The range was $7,500 to $2 million, with the average award being $104,500.

**12. Program Accomplishments** — This section gives you important information on previously selected grantees and on the number of awards made in the past. This is your first indication of your competition— 2,607 awards made from 19,675 proposals. While this appears to indicate a 10 percent success rate, you need more information on how many Internet-related projects were supported. This section will also inform you if the program is being phased out. For example, it might read "no new awards."

**13. Regulations, Guidelines, and Literature** — This section outlines the rules and guidelines. Most of the rules mentioned pertain to your district personnel and business office. The only one that is relatively new is the drug-free-workplace-and-campus rule. You should discuss compliance with your district grants office or administration.

**14. Information Contacts**
- *Regional or Local Office*—Most regional offices were closed during the federal cutbacks of the early 1980s.
- *Headquarters Office*—This section provides the contact name, address, and phone number you will need if you select this program as a possible source of money for your project.

**15. Related Programs** — This lists the CFDA names and five-digit CFDA codes of other funding sources that have similar target populations or objectives. These are valuable leads to other programs that may be better suited to your Internet project.

**16. Examples of Funded Projects** — This section provides a sample of the solutions that the grantor valued enough to fund. In this example, the fact that secondary math and minorities are cited should make the grantseeker more interested in pursuing preproposal contact.

*17. Criteria for Selecting Proposals*

This section lists the types of criteria that the agency will follow in the evaluation procedures. Each agency has its own criteria, which may differ between programs. For example, the criteria used by NSF vary, while the Education Department usually uses EDGAR, which will be discussed in the section "Critiquing and Improving Your Federal Proposal," later in this chapter.

**Finding More Information on Federal Programs**

The CFDA is produced before many federal agencies know the exact dates on which they will require proposals to be submitted. However, your research will reveal deadline information that refers you to agency publications such as the *NSF Bulletin* or *The Federal Register*. In order to take advantage of advance notice of application and package deadlines, you can locate the referenced publications in print copy or on the Internet.

*Using* The Federal Register

*The Federal Register* is the federal government's daily newspaper. In addition to publishing the program deadline dates, *The Federal Register* provides the government with a way to acquire feedback on the rules that governed the previous year's grant-solicitation-and-award process. It is not unusual for the federal agency to publish the previous year's rules in *The Federal Register* six months before the next deadline in order to solicit public opinion on how the proposals were awarded.

A period of 30 days is usually provided to comment on the rules. The agency reviews the comments and may make changes based on them. The public is then allowed another 30 days to comment on the changes before the final rules are printed. These rules will govern the program's priorities and the scoring or review system; they also provide valuable insight into the exact requirements of the agency.

You now know that you don't have to wait until you receive a formal application package. Instead, telephone a federal program officer to ask when information on the rules and the deadline was printed in *The Federal Register*.

The information from the CFDA and *The Federal Register* enables you to make a decision on the appropriateness of the funding opportunity, and you can get started!

*The Federal Register* is available in print at your federal depository library, as well as in most public and university libraries. The Internet allows you to access *The Federal Register* quickly and easily:

- Telnet to: swais.access.gpo.gov
- Login: guest
- Point your Web browser to:
  - http://www.access.gpo.gov/sudocs/aces/aaces001.html
  - http://thorplus.lib.purdue.edu/gpo/

*Other Online Federal Resources*    Many federal agencies are creating Internet sites in order to disseminate grants-related information. Look into the following resources or use gopher or the Web to uncover other federal grants information.

GrantsWeb    This site includes information on the National Science Foundation, the Education Department, and the Education Department's Education Resource Information Center (known as ERIC). To get there, point your Web browser to: http://pc1.osr.lsu.edu/osrhtm/grants_w.htm

GrantsNet    This online grants network includes information on the Department of Health and Human Services, the Public Health Service's Center for Substance Abuse Prevention, and other federal grants programs. You can contact GrantsNet online by: email, gnet@os.dhhs.gov; gopher, os.dhhs.gov:70/11/Topics/grantsnet or peg.cwts.uci.edu; Web, http://www.os.dhhs.gov/progorg/grantsnet

The Department of Education's INet    This online library contains DOE publications, reports, press releases, legislation, a department staff directory, and links to other education-related resources. Figure 7.4 provides a menu of the grant-related information available

**Figure 7.4**
The Department of
Education's INet Web Site

through this network. To get there, point your Web browser to http://www.ed.gov/ or gopher.ed.gov.

Now you can use the information you have learned to make yourself look like a grant professional. If your Internet Technology Support Group decided to search for federal grants funding the provision of Internet access to better prepare students for the world of work, you know to first consult the CFDA.

Using your key search words, you would uncover CFDA program number 278C—the School-to-Work Opportunities Program, which is referenced in many different ways in the aforementioned databases and print resources.

You would discover that the application for this program was printed in *The Federal Register* on September 8, 1995 and that the submission deadline was November 7, 1995. The quickest way to get the application is to print it from the Internet, or you can make a copy of it at your library.

Figure 7.5 on page 128-129 illustrates what a school-to-work search of *The Federal Register* on the Internet would yield. The entire document is 24 pages long.

Selecting the first listing in Figure 7.5's search results brings you to Figure 7.6 (on pages 130–31, which shows only the first page).

Figure 7.7 (page 131) presents the Department of Education's responses to questions raised over last year's rules governing how the funds were granted. (This figure is part of the 24 pages of search results mentioned above).

**Steps for Contacting Government Grantors**

1. Contact with government agencies is encouraged by letter, phone, and when possible, in person. The first step is to send the agency a letter requesting program information and inclusion on the agency's mailing list. Use the sample letter in Figure 7.8 (page 132) when appropriate.

2. Next, telephone the federal agency that you discovered in your search. The CFDA may provide an individual's name as well as the agency's phone number. Your Internet research may have provided a personnel roster with names, phone numbers, and email addresses. Have at hand the name of the informational contact you developed from your research, but don't be surprised if the person listed in your research is not there or is not the best individual to assist you. Inform the person who answers the phone that you are calling for information concerning one of their grant programs, and tell them the CFDA reference number and the name of the granting program.

3. It usually takes one or two referrals to find the correct person and program. Introduce yourself and ask to speak with the program officer or with someone who can answer a few brief but important questions.

4. Demonstrate your knowledge, not your ignorance. Your research has provided you with a considerable amount of information; use this opportunity to validate it. Check the accuracy of the deadline dates and appropriations.

5. Tell them what you want! Ask for a few minutes of their time. These are employees of your federal (or state) government. Remember, more support staff is involved in the government grants process than in foundation or corporate, and Freedom of Information rules must be observed in tax-supported grantseeking. Staff members are

**Figure 7.5**

*Federal Register* Search
Results for: Department
of Education for the Week
Prior to 9/11/95

09/08/95 Notice of availability of funds

Office of Vocational and Adult Education; School-to-work
Opportunities; Local Partnership Grants; Application Procedures
(L-S document 535611, 60 FR 46984, 1470 lines)

SUMMARY: This notice announces the fiscal year (FY) competition for Local Partnership Grants authorized under Title III of the
School-to-Work Opportunities Act of 1994 (the Act). This notice
contains all of the necessary information and forms needed to
apply for grant funding in FY 1995. The Departments also establish final selection criteria to be used in evaluating applications
submitted under the Local Partnership Grants competition in FY
1995 and in succeeding years. The Departments also establish a
definition for the term "administrative costs," as well as a 10
percent cap on administrative costs incurred by local partnerships receiving grants under Title III of the Act.

09/06/95 Final regulations

34 CFR 74
34 CFR 75
34 CFR 76
34 CFR 81
RIN 1880-AA64

Administration of Grants to Institutions of Higher Education,
Hospitals and Nonprofit Organizations; Direct Grant Programs;
State-Administered Programs; and General Provisions Act—
Enforcement (L-S document 535336, 60 FR 46492, 527 lines)

SUMMARY: The Secretary makes technical amendments to the
Education Department General Administrative Regulations
(EDGAR) to implement amendments to the General Education
Provisions Act (GEPA) made by the Improving America's Schools

**Figure 7.5**
**(continued)**

Act (IASA). The provisions will diminish the paperwork burden for recipients, permit the Secretary to approve State plans for a period longer than three years, authorize the Secretary to take actions other than termination actions if, after a hearing, the Secretary determines that a State plan is not substantially approvable, improve the procedures and requirements governing hearings for the recovery of funds, implement other statutory requirements, and make other technical changes to EDGAR.

---

09/07/95 Notice of hearings

National Assessment Governing Board; Hearings (L-S document 535434, 60 FR 46582, 160 lines)

SUMMARY: The National Assessment Governing Board (NAGB), U.S. Department of Education, is announcing three public hearings. These hearings will be conducted as part of the Council of Chief State School Officers' contract with NAGB for the purpose of developing an assessment framework and specifications for the National Assessment of Educational Progress (NAEP) in Civics. Public and private parties and organizations with an interest in civics education and assessment are invited to present written and oral testimony to the Council. Each hearing will focus on the first draft of a framework for the national assessment of civics education for NAEP which will be given to a national sample of students in grades 4, 8, and 12. The results of the hearings are particularly important because they will provide broad public input in developing the civics education assessment framework to be used in the planned national NAEP examination. This assessment will measure American students' progress in civics education. These hearings are being conducted pursuant to Public Law 103-382 which states, "The Board shall develop assessment objectives and specifications through a national consensus approach which includes the active participation of teachers, curriculum specialists, local school administrators, parents, and concerned members of the general public."

**Figure 7.6**
CFDA Program Number
278C—the School-to-Work
Opportunities Program,
Obtained from the Internet

DEPARTMENT OF LABOR
Employment and Training Administration

DEPARTMENT OF EDUCATION
Office of Vocational and Adult Education; School-to-Work
Opportunities; Local Partnership Grants; Application Procedures

AGENCIES: Employment and Training Administration,
Department of Labor; Office of Vocational and Adult Education,
Department of Education

ACTION: Notice of availability of funds, solicitation for grant
application (SGA), an administrative cost cap, a definition of
administrative costs, and final selection criteria for School-to-
Work Opportunities Local Partnership Grants.

SUMMARY: This notice announces the fiscal year (FY) competition for Local Partnership Grants authorized under Title III of the
School-to-Work Opportunities Act of 1994 (the Act). This notice
contains all of the necessary information and forms needed to
apply for grant funding in FY 1995. The Departments also establish final selection criteria to be used in evaluating applications
submitted under the Local Partnership Grants competition in FY
1995 and in succeeding years. The Departments also establish a
definition for the term "administrative costs," as well as a 10
percent cap on administrative costs incurred by local partnerships receiving grants under Title III of the Act.

DATES: Applications for grant awards will be accepted com-
mencing September 8, 1995. The closing date for receipt of
applications is November 7, 1995, at 2 p.m. (Eastern time) at the
following address. Telefacsimile (FAX) applications will NOT be
accepted.

ADDRESSES: Applications must be mailed to: U.S. Department
of Education, Application Control Center, Attention: CFDA
#278C, Washington, D.C. 20202-4725.

FOR FURTHER INFORMATION CONTACT: Maria Kniesler,
National School-to-Work Office. Telephone: 202-401-6222.
(This is not a toll-free number.) Individuals who use a telecom-
munications device for the deaf (TDD) may call the Federal
Information Relay Service (FIRS) at 800-877-8339 between 8
A.M. and 8 P.M., Eastern time, Monday through Friday.

**Figure 7.6**
(continued)

SUPPLEMENTARY INFORMATION:

Section A. Background

The Departments of Labor and Education are reserving funds appropriated for FY 1995 under Pub. L. 103-329 (the Act) for a competition for Local Partnership Grants authorized under Title III of the Act. In accordance with the authority provided in section 5 of the Act, the Departments have determined that the administrative provisions contained in the Education Department General Administrative Regulations (EDGAR) at 34 CFR Parts 74, 75, 77, 79, 80, 82, 85 and 86, will apply to grants awarded to local partnerships under this competition.

**Figure 7.7**
Limit on Equipment
Purchases

Comment: One commentator felt that the bullet point under Criterion 4 regarding the limitation of equipment purchases would keep rural partnerships from purchasing distance learning equipment which can often play a critical role in the implementation School-to-Work Opportunities systems in rural areas.

Discussion: The Departments agree that distance learning technology can play a key role in the implementation of local School-to-Work systems in rural areas. Bullet six under Criterion 1(B) states that the Departments are looking for effective strategies for utilizing innovative technology-based instructional techniques such as distance learning. However, applicants are reminded that their overall goal should be to maximize direct services to students. Applicants proposing equipment purchases such as distance learning systems should be sure that such purchases clearly link back to the overall purpose and design of the proposed local School-to-Work Opportunities system. Applicants should also be aware that such purchases would be seen by the Departments as one-time expenditures and would not be refunded in any future years of funding.

Changes: None.

BILLING CODE 4000-01-P

**Figure 7.8**
Sample Letter to a Federal
Agency Requesting
Information and Guidelines

Date

Name
Title
Address
City, State, Zip

Dear *[Contact Person]:*

I am interested in the grant opportunities under *[CFDA #]*, *[Program Title]*. Please add my name to your mailing list to receive information on this program. I am particularly interested in receiving application forms, program guidelines, and any existing priorities statements.

Please also send any other information that could help me prepare a quality application, such as a list of last year's successful grant recipients and reviewers. I am enclosing a self-addressed envelope for your convenience in sending these lists.

I will be contacting you when it is appropriate to discuss my proposal ideas. Thank you for your assistance.

Sincerely,

*[Name]*
*[Title]*
*[Phone number]*

...................................................................................................................................

generally helpful and willing, if not eager, to provide information. Your objective is to discuss your approaches to solving the problem. Some federal programs actually request a preproposal meeting or submission of a concept paper. Believe it or not, they want you to submit the best possible proposal, even if they are unable to fund it. The better your proposal and the more requests they receive, the more their program is needed. If possible, you should visit the federal agency in Washington, D.C., but a phone conversation is your best alternative if no one from your support group can make a visit. Again, ask permission to fax or email a one-page concept paper and to call after they have had time to review it. Ask the contact person to place you on the agency's mailing list to receive guidelines, application information, and newsletters. Review the diagram in Figure 7.1, and ask where the agency is in the grants process.

- *The Federal Register*—Ask if they've published anything on their rules in *The Federal Register* or elsewhere. If they have, ask for the publication date and page number.
- *Past Grantees*—Request a list of last year's grantees. You will learn:
  - Who got how much grant money.
  - If your school or school district stands a chance of receiving funds.
  - If you should develop a consortium with other schools or districts, join with your intermediate district, or become part of a college or university's consortium.

More information on past grantees is becoming accessible over the Internet. For example, if you are interested in reviewing a list of the National Science Foundation's grant recipients, such a list is available on the Community of Science Web Server at http://cos.gdb.org/. By looking at lists of past grantees, you can see who has received grant funds from the program you are researching, the size of the average grant, and for how many years the recipients were funded. This information will help you determine your approach and the appropriate size of your request. In addition, the description of the funded projects may provide insight into how the successful grantees incorporated Internet access into their approach to solving the specific problem or area in which the federal program was interested.

- *Past Reviewers*—Ask the agency official for information on the agency's peer review system. *The Federal Register* may have information on the points that reviewers award for sections of a proposal; you need to know who reads the grant applications. Request a list of last year's reviewers; knowing the types of reviewers helps choose the style and construction of the proposal. In addition, you should ask the program officer how you can become a reviewer so you can learn more about the review process.

6. Meet in Washington, D.C., or at a federal regional office, if one exists. You could also ask the funding official to visit your school. He or she may come if you invite other schools and districts to attend an information session on grants available through that agency. You can also ask the program officer what upcoming educational conferences or professional meetings he or she is planning to attend. You may be able to meet with the official at one of the meetings.

7. You could send a volunteer from your support group to represent you at the meeting. Of course, it the best thing would be for you to accompany the volunteer. Two is the magic number when it comes to representation. But if you send more than two school representatives, the federal program officer may wonder who is back home teaching!

8. Federal program officers dress conservatively, so dress accordingly. (Programs do differ, however. For example, arts and humanities officers tend to dress more casually than those in education and science.) The older the bureaucrat, the more conservative the dress.

9. Bring materials to the meeting that will help demonstrate the need. Remember, that unless the funding source's program is specifically for Internet access, do not develop a need based upon your lack of access, cable, or hardware. The need is based on low math and science scores, the

diminishing number of females in math and science, etc. Materials may include audiovisual aides such as short (three to five minutes) filmstrips, videotapes, slides, pictures, etc. In addition, representatives may leave information on your school district, school, or classroom with the funding official, but they should never leave a proposal. Your representatives may also want to bring, or better yet, commit to memory, a list of questions to ask the program officer.

**Recording Federal Research and Preproposal Contact**

Keep copies of the information you gather on a prospective government funding source and record all contacts and correspondence on the worksheet in Figure 7.9 on the following page. Record all information you gather on agency personnel on the worksheet in Figure 7.10 (page 138).

**Selecting the Best Federal Programs for Your Project**

You'll find many programs, but don't investigate them all: use the worksheet in Figure 7.11 (page 139) to refine your list. Complete a worksheet for each funding source to which you plan to submit a proposal. This worksheet will help you develop a tailored approach to each funding source. It will also help you understand the funder's point of view.

Take full advantage of your ability to analyze the funder's granting history. Even if you haven't been able to make preproposal contact, it is imperative that the amount you request fit the source's granting pattern. Think about others with whom you could collaborate on your proposal and what group might be a better submitting organization.

Make every attempt to find out who will be reading and evaluating your proposal. For example, will your proposal be read by federal staff members or peer reviewers? This information will help you write your proposal, as well as perform a mock review. Rank the funding sources that represent your best prospects. Eventually, you will tailor your proposal to those few at the top of the list. You will probably be missing vital pieces of information, but devise the best strategy you can based on what you have, and go for it!

**Figure 7.9**
Federal Research Worksheet

CFDA No. _____

Deadline Date(s) _____

Program Title _____

Government Agency _____

Create a file for each program you are researching and place all the information you gather on this program in the file. Use this worksheet to:

- Keep a record of the information you have gathered
- Maintain a log of all telephone and face-to-face contacts made with the government agency
- Log all correspondence sent to and received from the agency

Agency Address: _____

Agency Director: _____

Telephone No.: _____

Program Director: _____

Fax No.: _____

Name/Title Contact Person: _____

Place a check mark next to the information you have gathered and placed in the file for the government agency.

_____ Program description from CFDA

_____ Sent letter requesting to be put on mailing list

_____ List of last year's grantees
        _____ Sent for      _____ Received

_____ List of last year's reviewers
        _____ Sent for      _____ Received

**Figure 7.9**
(continued)

_____ Application package, expected availability date: _____
____ Sent for      ____ Received

_____ Comments on rules/final rules from _The Federal Register_

_____ Notice of rules for evaluation from _The Federal Register_

_____ Grant scoring system (point allocation for each section)
Source: _____

_____ Sample funded proposal

_____ Federal Funding Staff History Worksheet

_____ Written Summary of each contact made

_____ Grantor Strategy Worksheet

Record of Face-to-Face and Telephone Contact:

_____

_____

_____

_____

Record of All Correspondence Sent and Received:

_____

_____

_____

_____

_____

**Figure 7.10**
Federal Funding Staff
History Worksheet

CFDA No. _____

Program Title _____

Government Agency _____

1. Name _____

2. Title _____

3. Business Address _____

4. Business Telephone _____

5. Birth date _____ Birthplace _____

6. Marital Status _____ Children _____

7. College/University _____

8. Degree(s) _____

9. Military Service _____

10. Clubs/Affiliations _____

11. Interests/Hobbies _____

12. Board Memberships _____

13. Other Philanthropic Activities _____

15. Other _____

Notes: _____

_____

**Figure 7.11**
Grantor Strategy Worksheet

Potential Grantor: _____ Priority # ___ Deadline _____

**A. Strategy Derived from Granting Pattern**

1. $ _____ Largest grant to organization most similar to ours

2. $ _____ Smallest grant to organization most similar to ours

3. $ _____ Average grant to organizations similar to ours

4. $ _____ Average grant in our area of interest

5. $ _____ Our estimated grant request

6. Financial trend in our area of interest over past 3 years
____ Up ____ Down ____ Stable

7. If yours is a multiyear proposal, how popular have these been with the funding source in the past three years?
____ Many multiyear proposals funded
____ Some multiyear proposals funded
____ Few multiyear proposals funded
____ No multiyear funding
____ Not applicable

8. Financial data on funding source: obligation levels for last 3 years for grants
19____ $ _____ 19____ $ ____ 19____ $ _____

**B. Based on preproposal contact, which solution strategies are the most appropriate for this funding source?**

_____

**C. Proposal Review System**

1. Who evaluates submitted proposals? _____

2. What is the background and training of the evaluators? _____

_____

3. What point system will be used? _____

4. How much time will be spent reviewing each proposal? _____

**D. Note anything special that will affect proposal outcome**

_____

**Developing Government Grant Proposals**

Completing a federal government application is very much like filing an income tax return. As with tax returns, the directions are usually longer than the actual forms, which aren't really that complicated. If you understand the federal grants clock in Figure 7.1 (page 111), made preproposal contact, and secured the information on the grantor strategy worksheet in Figure 7.11 (page 139), you have an advantage over an applicant who guesses what the grantor wants.

A federal grant application must be completed exactly as prescribed in the rules. In other words, if the rules require 30 double-spaced pages printed in a font of at least 12 characters per inch, that's what you must submit.

The basic format and the specific order of a federal proposal's parts are usually similar for all applications. In addition to providing an abstract, or summary, the prospective grantee is normally required to identify:

- The need.
- The plan to address the need (solution).
- The key personnel who will operate the program.
- The budget and resources required.
- How the success of the project will be evaluated.
- The adequacy of current resources.
- Assurances that federal requirements will be met.
- Attachments.

The points assigned to each area and the distribution of any additional weighing or extra points are outlined in each agency's specific proposal guidelines.

It is imperative that your proposal be easily understood by the reviewer. The reviewer must be able to read it rapidly, and the salient parts must be evident and well-documented so that a point value can be assigned to each. Remember, your proposal will be read by a reviewer who will likely evaluate each section according to a prescribed point system, read several proposals, and have very little time. In short, make your proposal user-friendly.

*Proposal Abstract or Summary*

Some proposals require an abstract, or summary. Often the abstract must fit into a designated space or specific number of lines or pages. There is some controversy about the position of the abstract in the proposal. Some experts believe it should be written last, when the grantwriter can reflect on the completed proposal; others contend that writing the abstract first helps the grantee focus on preparing the proposal. Writing a detailed outline, then the proposal, and then an abstract that reviews the proposal works well, too.

Whether you write the abstract first or last, make sure it is in the required format. The abstract should provide a short, concise description of the need, the objectives, the solution, the evaluation, and any other areas highlighted by the agency.

In an effort to efficiently use space limitations, some grantwriters push the abstract to the margins and cram in as much information as possible. The result is usually difficult to read and very confusing. When you consider that the reviewer may have already read several proposals, the "crammed" abstract may set a negative tone for the entire proposal and lead to a low score.

Review the following abstract and consider whether it sets the stage properly. Ask yourself if it:

- Shows that the grantseeker has a command of the need.
- Shows that the project has measurable objectives.
- Provides a synopsis of the methods.
- Presents the proposal's main points in an interesting manner.

Sample Abstract

This project will identify those students at risk for dropping out, will intervene and provide the motivation and tools necessary to complete their high school education, and will encourage postsecondary education and/or training. Over a three-year period, this project will extend services to 450 students, including five elementary programs that feed into three middle schools that, in turn, feed into two high school programs. Activities in this project will increase coping and daily living skills through classroom instruction, utilize community volunteers to tutor students and act as role models, increase awareness and incentive through two field trips, as well as track school attendance and classroom progress acting as a mediator between teachers, parents, and students to resolve problems as they arise.

**Analysis of the Abstract** While not necessarily the best example, this abstract does indicate that the services will be extended to 450 students, five elementary programs, and three middle schools. In addition, it provides a rough idea of the types of activities aimed at keeping students in school.

However, it does not hint at the need, nor give any measurement indicators, nor list any of the criteria for success. Also, based on the abstract, the project seems to be geared toward high schools, which makes one wonder why elementary and middle schools are even mentioned. But before we get too critical, you should know that the project summarized in this abstract was funded for approximately $97,000!

*The Needs Statement* This section could also be called "The Search of Relevant Literature," "The Extent of the Need," or simply "The Problem." One federal program refers to the needs statement as follows:

> Criterion: Extent to which the project meets specific needs recognized in the statute that authorized the program, including consideration of the needs addressed by the project; how the needs were identified; how the needs will be met; and the benefits to be gained by meeting the needs.

One successful grantee responded to this criterion by describing the extent of the need, including the following items:

1. *Target Area*—The applicant's location; data identifying a significant needs population in the student body.
2. *Need for Services*—Available school programs; the gap between "what was" and "what should be."
3. *How the Needs Would Be Met*—A general description of what was to be done.
4. *Benefits to Be Gained*—The anticipated positive outcomes of the project.

When developing the needs section, you should consider who will be reading the proposal application. The needs section should be motivating and compelling. It must demonstrate that the applicant is credible and has a command of the current literature in the field. Many excellent proposals lose crucial points when the grantee fails to gain the respect of the reviewer because he or she overlooks the needs section and places all of the emphasis on the project description and plan of operation.

The following "extent of the need" is from a grant funded by the DOE for dropout prevention.*

> The target population to be served by the project has experienced low academic achievement, high public-assistance rates, high dropout rates, linguistic and cultural differences, geographic isolation, and inaccessibility to existing career and training information. These conditions have combined to create high unemployment, underemployment, poor self-image, and a resulting low standard of living among these people. Astin's study of college attrition clearly identifies family income as a significant factor that negatively

---

\* Proposal: Four Corners School, College and University Partnership Program, Submitted to U.S. Department of Education, Division of Student Services, CFDA 84-204, by San Juan School District College of Eastern Utah—San Juan Campus, Utah Navajo Development Council, July 9, 1988.

affects student success in post secondary education and contributes to high dropout rates. Astin does note, however, that this correlation is influenced by such other "mediation" factors as ability, motivation, financial concerns, and parental education. . . .

The target population occupies a rural mountainous and desert region spanning more than 8,000 square miles, which is larger than the combined area of Delaware, Rhode Island, and Connecticut. . . .

It is pertinent to note that 79.3% of the active job applicants are ethnic minorities and that 63.5% had less than a high school diploma.*

Facts like those presented in this excerpt tell the reviewer and the federal staff that the writer has a good grasp of the situation. Including statistics in the needs section reveals a command of the situation and can make a positive impression, unlike "grant-loser statements" such as:

- "Everyone knows the need for . . . "
- "Current statistics show . . . "
- "It is a shame our students do not have . . . "
- "Several (Many, Increasing numbers of) students . . . "

When reviewers read such weak, banal statements, their frustration is reflected on the scoring sheet, and the grantseeker loses valuable points. A strong needs statement requires facts, studies, and references, and you need commitment and hard work to gather these. But remember, you will be repaid in grant success!

The extent of need in this particular proposal mentioned that the inclusion of Internet access and enrichment would combat "geographic isolation." However, the grantseeker

---

\* Alexander W. Astin, Preventing Students from Dropping Out, San Francisco: Jossey-Bass, 1977.

did not become involved in the technology, equipment, and access needs in this section because those aspects were included in the solution. This proposal developer knew how important it was to express the needs of the students, rather than the needs of the technology.

*Plan of Operation*    Your government application may refer to this section as "The Plan of Operation," "Objectives and Methods," or "The Project Methodology." This section describes an organized solution for the need and problem you have identified.

Through preproposal contact, you will determine which solutions appeal most to the prospective grantor. This information will help you decide which solution to propose. Once you have selected the best solution or approach, develop your proposal objectives. An objective is a measurable step taken to narrow or close the gap between what is and what ought to be. A well-constructed objective tells the funding source what will change as a result of the funds they provide. For example, your proposal's objective is not to allow each student Internet access for a minimum of four hours per week. You must relate how four hours of Internet access will enable the student to learn something that he or she could not have otherwise learned. Internet access is not the objective; increased learning is. The Internet is the method or means to achieve the desired end in a time- and cost-efficient manner.

Many grantseekers do not understand the difference between an objective and a method. Some actually write objectives that focus on the approaches or methods that will be utilized to bring about the change. This confuses *what* will be accomplished with *how* it will be accomplished.

To be sure you have developed a well-constructed objective, ask yourself if there is more than one way to reach your objective. If the objective you are testing suggests that there is only one possible approach, then you are dealing with a solution, not an objective. By asking yourself why you are performing a particular activity, you may back into your objective. In doing so, you will strengthen your proposal and develop a clear sense of what you will measure as you close the gap in the area of need.

An objective provides a way to measure how much change has occurred by the project's end. A method tells how this change will be accomplished. A simple rule of thumb is: *Objectives tell what you want to accomplish, and methods tell how you will accomplish it.*

Developing objectives may seem tedious, especially when you are eager to write your proposal. But keep in mind that well-written objectives that focus on the measurable change to be accomplished will make your proposal more interesting and compelling to the funder and will enable you to measure the changes the proposal suggests.

When writing a proposal, most grantseekers want to quickly explain how they will accomplish their project instead of first presenting what is to be accomplished. Grantseekers often focus on such issues as how many students will be exposed to a new piece of equipment or teaching regime rather than what the students will be able to do as a result of the experience. Well-written objectives will help combat this problem.

The grantor is the ultimate judge of a "good" objective and there are vast differences in the ways grantors prefer objectives to be written. By procuring a copy of a funded proposal and discussing your proposal idea with the funding source prior to submission, you will obtain a much more accurate idea of what they consider a "good" objective, and, therefore, have a better chance of winning support.

The following guidelines for developing objectives provide you with a secure basis for organizing your approach. In general, an objective has the following components: an action verb and a statement, a measurement indicator, a performance standard, a deadline, and a cost frame.

**1. Action Verb and Statement**

What will change as a result of the successful completion of your project? First review your needs and goals. Remember, you are not suggesting or promising that the goal will be met and the gap entirely eliminated. Rather, you are suggesting that a measurable part of the gap will be closed through the grant and the successful completion of your prescribed actions. Do not worry because you are not certain that your proposed solution, model project, or research proposal will be 100 percent successful. You are proposing a solution, and even if it is unsuccessful, the field of education will learn from the experience.

**2. Measurement Indicator**    How will you measure the area you are attempting to change? Just as there are many ways to accomplish your objectives, there are often several strategies that can measure the change in your area of need. Begin by asking what a student would do differently after you provided him or her with your solution or method of solving the problem. For example, if you decided to use the Internet to develop your students' awareness of other cultures, languages, and customs, you could expect to increase their appreciation, understanding, and tolerance for the students with whom they interface over the Internet. In fact, you could even expect that a percentage would become keypals and email each other after school.

Cognitive skills are usually the easiest to measure. Tests for this purpose already exist in many cases. For instance, there are standardized tests that can measure an increase in reading ability. If a test is not available, you can always include the task of developing one in your proposal.

**3. Performance Standard**    How much change will be necessary to consider the project successful? A grantor will consider your objectives, make note of the amount you are requesting, examine your measurement indicators, and compare the amount of your request with the expected amount of change.

For example, if you propose to use the Internet to increase the reading scores of a certain target population from the 50th to the 70th percentile as measured by the

Flockmeister Reading Scale, the percentile increase needs to be justified according to:

- The number and type of students who are in the target population.
- Internet access and equipment cost per student.
- Long-term effects of such an increase.

The grantor is likely to view the percentile increase as very meaningful if the increase can be related to an increase in the likelihood of students graduating from grade school, junior high, and eventually high school and can be achieved at a cost of $100 per student rather than $1,000.

4. Deadline How much time will be needed to accomplish the desired degree of change? This issue is usually decided for you when dealing with government grants. Most government grants are for one year due to the budget appropriation cycle. However, there is currently a movement to allow multiyear awards because of the difficulty in creating the behavioral change outlined in an objective in just 12 months. In addition, it often takes a good part of 12 months just to develop and conduct a pretest that provides the baseline data for the post-test and, in your case, to establish Internet access.

In dealing with a multiyear project, you may want to create your objectives with a one-year goal for change and increase the change shown in the measurement indicator over the subsequent years. For example, your objective could indicate a 25 percent increase in year one and a 40 percent increase by the end of year two.

5. Cost Frame How much will it cost? Include the cost of accomplishing the change in the body of your objective. This provides a stark reminder of the amount of money required to affect change. It also demonstrates that you have a total command of your proposal. You know exactly what will be accomplished, how much will be accomplished, and at what cost.

However, in most cases you cannot include cost in an objective until you have completed your budget. The Project Planner in Chapter 3 helps you develop a budget that reveals the cost of each objective. Once you have completed your Project Planner, go back to your objectives and add a cost component to each.

To determine the cost of developing change more accurately, divide the total cost of the project by the number of students to be served by the project, which gives you the cost per student served. If the cost per student served appears high, ask yourself how many students will benefit in future years once your Internet project is in place. Proposals such as yours that contain equipment may seem excessively expensive, particularly when you realize that just one classroom may be affected. But when you consider that the equipment will be utilized for many years and that it will be shared with other classrooms, the cost per student served will seem much more acceptable.

One warning: In the 1970s many demonstration models were developed that never could be replicated because the cost per person served was excessive. Funding sources are trying to prevent repeating this mistake. You can keep education grounded in economic reality by closely tracking the cost of accomplishing your objectives and creating the change you desire.

*Methods and Activities*     The project planner (see Chapter 3) helps you establish an organized approach to developing your proposed plan. Whether you utilize the project planner or not, your proposal will be evaluated on the thoroughness and clarity of the steps prescribed. Again, you can see how successful past grantees have organized this section of their proposals if you read a previously funded proposal.

You can present objectives and methods in many different ways . For instance, in Figure 7.12 (on the next page), the grantseeker presents a main objective, then a subobjective or process objective, and finally the methodologies.

**Figure 7.12**
Sample Statement of
Objective and Methods

**Objective 3: Upgrade Basic Skills**

*Process objective 3.1*
Students will be counseled and tutored during the academic year program to meet their individual academic needs and overcome areas of deficiency.

*Methodologies*
Deficiencies of participants will be documented through use of CTBS scores, transcripts, and interviews with teachers, parents, students, and counselors. Through this process, a plan will be prepared based on areas of strengths, but particularly on areas of weakness in which the student needs help. This plan will be in the form of a contract that will be signed by the student and counselor in which they agree to work together to strengthen the academic skills that need improvement.

The counselor will schedule biweekly, after-school tutoring and counseling sessions to provide academic assistance as well as emotional support.

*Personnel Responsible*
Project Counselors, tutors, and teachers from each high school.

*Resources*
Textbooks, testing and teaching materials, media centers of each high school.

---

*Quality of Key Personnel*   This section reveals your project staff's level of qualification to meet the objectives and close the gap between what is and what ought to be.

Proposal developers often face a dilemma when their key personnel have not been hired at the time of proposal submission. In this case, the proposal should clearly show that capable staff will be employed. Remember, reviewers who have read most of a proposal will want to be certain of the quality of the individuals who will implement the project. Review the sample in Figure 7.13, which is taken from a grant funded by the Department of Education.

Do you feel confident that this applicant has the expertise necessary to conduct this project? Does the grantee's statement that "no problems are anticipated in acquiring qualified personnel" make you feel comfortable? This is like betting on a horse you know nothing about, simply because someone assures you that he will be a winner. Every grantor wants to know the track records of people who will be working on the project.

In the example, the applicant could have stated that the project director would be reporting to Dr. Smith, who is currently responsible for managing X million dollars. For your information, however, the prospective grantee did at least follow the key personnel criterion with a detailed description of the major positions mentioned in the body of the proposal.

Note that many government grantors are looking for the appropriate use of personnel. If you plan to involve one

---

| | |
|---|---|
| **Figure 7.13** Sample Statement of Objective and Methods | **Key Personnel** |

*Criterion:* The quality of the key personnel the applicant plans to use in the project.

Staff will consist of a full-time project director, a full-time assistant project director, four part-time regular school year counselors, four full-time summer counselors, eight college and peer tutors, 12 part-time instructors, and a full-time secretary. In as much as project staff have not been identified at this time, resumes are not included.

The partnership would like to affirm that no problems are anticipated in acquiring qualified, experienced, highly competent personnel. At least one week will be scheduled at the beginning of the project for the orientation of staff to the goals, objectives, plan of operation, etc.

outstanding person minimally in many grants, you should be aware that some grantors ask for an outline detailing the time each staff member will commit to the project. Some federal grantors require that the project director or principal investigator commit a certain percentage of his or her time to the project. In other words, one outstanding and well-known individual should not commit 2 percent of his or her time to 50 different projects!

Be sure to include the expertise of the people in your Internet Technology Support Group in this section of your application. These individuals' advisory status and the involvement of loaned corporate executives would be very convincing to a reviewer. Your support members' degrees and Internet work experience, corporate training, and education will also help.

*Budget and Cost Effectiveness* While each federal program's proposal specifics may differ, all applications will require a budget. In most cases, the amount of the proposal (the dollar request) will be divided by the number of students who will benefit from the project so that the federal program officer can arrive at a cost per student served. A proposal reviewer's primary concern is that the budget request is reasonable, based on the steps outlined in the proposal. For example, if a project is meant to be a model for other schools, it must be affordable enough to be replicated as part of a school's technology plan that may not be benefiting from a grant.

The following sample in Figure 7.14 has been taken from a successful federally funded proposal. Note that the actual references to cost-per-student-served have been omitted to prevent the reader from calculating a formula he or she believes will result in a "preferred" cost figure. A budget narrative—an explanation of how the salaries, consultant services, equipment, and materials are related to the completion of each method or activity—may also be required.

The Department of Education's most common budget information form for nonconstruction projects is Standard

**Figure 7.14**
Sample Budget Statement

**Reasonableness of the Budget**

*Criterion:* Costs are reasonable in relation to the objective of the project.

Salaries and benefits are based on institutional schedules and policies. Supplies have been computed on the basis of local vendor prices. Travel and communication costs in such a geographically isolated location may appear to be rather extensive. These have been kept to a minimum, with rates based on institutional policies.

The overall cost per participant from federal funds amounts to $ \_\_\_\_ the first year, decreasing to $ \_\_\_\_ the second year, and $ \_\_\_\_ the third year. The budget is reasonable and cost effective, particularly considering the geographic isolation of the target area.

Form SF-424A (Figure 7.15, on the following pages). If you have completed a project planner (see Chapter 3), you have all the information needed to complete the SF-424A or any other form the federal grantor requires. The preferred budget form will be included in your federal application package.

If possible, review the budget and cash forecast format of a successfully funded proposal.

*Evaluation*  You have already outlined your basic steps for evaluation if you developed your objectives according to the methods suggested. Most projects demand some sort of preassessment survey so that baseline data can be gathered. After the completion of the intervention steps or the model project, the original baseline data can be compared with post-test evaluation data to demonstrate change in the target population or problem.

Many reviewers suggest using outside or external consultants to evaluate a project, because they tend to be unbiased. Discuss this important section of your proposal with your prospective grantors to gather as much insight as possible into their evaluation preferences.

# Figure 7.15 Standard Form 424A

OMB Approval No. 0348-0044

## BUDGET INFORMATION - Non-Construction Programs

### SECTION A - BUDGET SUMMARY

| Grant Program Function or Activity (a) | Catalog of Federal Domestic Assistance Number (b) | Estimated Unobligated Funds | | New or Revised Budget | | Total (g) |
|---|---|---|---|---|---|---|
| | | Federal (c) | Non-Federal (d) | Federal (e) | Non-Federal (f) | |
| 1. | | $ | $ | $ | $ | $ |
| 2. | | | | | | |
| 3. | | | | | | |
| 4. | | | | | | |
| 5. TOTALS | | $ | $ | $ | $ | $ |

### SECTION B - BUDGET CATEGORIES

| 6. Object Class Categories | GRANT PROGRAM, FUNCTION OR ACTIVITY | | | | Total (5) |
|---|---|---|---|---|---|
| | (1) | (2) | (3) | (4) | |
| a. Personnel | $ | $ | $ | $ | $ |
| b. Fringe Benefits | | | | | |
| c. Travel | | | | | |
| d. Equipment | | | | | |
| e. Supplies | | | | | |
| f. Contractual | | | | | |
| g. Construction | | | | | |
| h. Other | | | | | |
| i. Total Direct Charges (sum of 6a-6h) | | | | | |
| j. Indirect Charges | | | | | |
| k. TOTALS (sum of 6i-6j) | $ | $ | $ | $ | $ |
| 7. Program Income | $ | $ | $ | $ | $ |

Authorized for Local Reproduction

Standard Form 424A (4-92)
Prescribed by OMB Circular A-102

**Figure 7.15** Standard Form 424A *(continued)*

## SECTION C - NON-FEDERAL RESOURCES

| (a) Grant Program | (b) Applicant | (c) State | (d) Other Sources | (e) Totals |
|---|---|---|---|---|
| 8. | $ | $ | $ | $ |
| 9. | | | | |
| 10. | | | | |
| 11. | | | | |
| 12. TOTALS (sum of lines 8 and 11) | $ | $ | $ | $ |

## SECTION D - FORECASTED CASH NEEDS

| | Total for 1st Year | 1st Quarter | 2nd Quarter | 3rd Quarter | 4th Quarter |
|---|---|---|---|---|---|
| 13. | $ | $ | $ | $ | $ |
| 14. | | | | | |
| 15. TOTALS (sum of lines 13 and 14) | $ | $ | $ | $ | $ |

## SECTION E - BUDGET ESTIMATES OF FEDERAL FUNDS NEEDED FOR BALANCE OF THE PROJECT

| (a) Grant Program | FUTURE FUNDING PERIODS (YEARS) | | | |
|---|---|---|---|---|
| | (b) First | (c) Second | (d) Third | (e) Fourth |
| 16. | $ | $ | $ | $ |
| 17. | | | | |
| 18. | | | | |
| 19. | | | | |
| 20. TOTALS (sum of lines 16 and 19) | $ | $ | $ | $ |

## SECTION F - OTHER BUDGET INFORMATION
(Attach additional Sheets If Necessary)

| 21. Direct Charges: | 22. Indirect Charges: |
|---|---|

23. Remarks:

The evaluation section of your proposal must clearly delineate:

- What will be evaluated.
- When the pre- and post-evaluations will occur.
- How much change is predicted.
- Who will perform the evaluation.
- How much the evaluation component will cost.

*Adequacy of Resources* The information in this section should be included in every proposal whether or not the funding source requests it, because it lets the funder know why they should make a grant to your school. You need to identify what makes your school a more logical choice for funding than any other school in your area. By focusing on the problem and your proposed solution, your school will become the strongest candidate for receiving the grant.

Most federal grantors and reviewers are influenced by equipment, supplies, and facilities.

*Equipment* Demonstrate that you have enough *standard* office equipment (desks, chairs, etc.) to support the additional staff required in your proposal. You may be using equipment that you have already purchased, such as modems and VCRs. If you are not requesting funds from the grantor to purchase these items, make clear in your proposal that such equipment is being *donated* by you, the grantee, to the project. Your assurance that this equipment is available to support your project when it is funded demonstrates that you have some resources and will capitalize on them.

*Supplies/Materials* You should also note any supplies and/or materials that you will be making available.

*Facilities* Describe the facilities that will be used to support the project, especially those that are unique or different, such as existing computer labs, local area networks, or file servers. If your proposal involves another organization, demonstrate how its facilities and yours will be jointly shared to ensure the project's successful completion.

*Assurances* Your school officials will be required to provide signed assurances that the project will abide by a myriad of federal rules and regulations. Assurances deal with a wide range of issues, from drug-free workplaces to political lobbying. Your district's main office has probably signed assurances in the past and will be able to assist you in this process. The CFDA outlines the required federal assurances.

Many school districts overlook the area of human subjects review. Your school district does not need to organize an Institutional Review Board (IRB) to examine every federal proposal to assure that the human subjects involved are treated humanely. However, as a grantee you should develop a relationship with your local college or university so that you can arrange to have its IRB review and approve your federal proposals.

*Attachments* Reactive grantseeking limits the time available to write a proposal. Because of this fact, the applications of reactive grantseekers are often submitted without letters of support and agreement from cooperating organizations and community groups. This omission is a red flag to reviewers and often diminishes a grantee's credibility and costs valuable points. Be sure to take the time to gather your letters of support and agreement. Include them in your attachments.

When possible, you should also include your project planner. Other attachments may include maps, pictures, a layout of your school building, support data for the statement of need, surveys, questionnaires, and work estimates provided by local telephone, cable, and utility companies. Attachments such as these often help reviewers answer their own questions about why and how the grantee decided upon a certain cost.

Help the reviewers by referring to the attachments in the body of your proposal and including a separate table of contents for the attachment section. The easier it is to review your attachments, the greater the chance they will be reviewed. Remember, reviewers are not required to look at anything in the attachment section of your proposal; it is strictly voluntary.

**Critiquing and Improving Your Federal Proposal**

The quality of your proposal will influence how reviewers and agency staff members view you and your school for many years to come. Just as teachers do not easily forget the first impression made by a student, reviewers and federal staff members do not easily forget the first impression made by a proposal.

If you and your peers review your proposal before submitting it, you will feel more confident that you are sending the prospective grantor your best effort. And even if your proposal is not selected for funding, you can be certain it was rejected because of the competition and not because of careless mistakes.

Like many grantseekers, you may tire of the whole process, and want to submit your proposal to just get it out of your life at this point. But after coming this far, you should not jeopardize your hard work by submitting a proposal that has not passed the last test—a mock review.

Performing a mock review of your proposal will be easy if you know about the review system used by federal agencies. Through preproposal contact you should have learned how the granting agency selects reviewers, the reviewers' backgrounds, and which review system they follow. This information will ensure that your mock review is as much like the real review as possible.

The term *quality circle* best describes the process. Invite a small group of individuals who are dedicated to improving education to participate in the circle. The participants need not be experts in the grants area or in the particular subject area of your proposal. Although the members of the quality circle should mirror the types of reviewers on the real federal review committee, you should also invite several individuals who can bring a fresh outlook on the proposal to participate. For example, you could ask a business leader from your Internet Technology Support Group, a college student, a secretary, and/or an accountant to be mock reviewers. These many different perspectives will allow your quality circle to better uncover all or most of your proposal's weaknesses and strengths.

Either telephone individuals or ask them in person to participate. Brief them on the general approach you want them to take. It is important to state that you want to submit the best possible proposal and that a thorough review by a quality circle will help you achieve that goal. You should also let the group know that you, your close associates, and your Internet Technology Support Group members are so closely involved in the proposal that you need a fresh perspective. Explain that you will be sending each of them a package that includes a description of the types of reviewers and the point or scoring system that will be used. Assure them that they do not have to be experts in the subject area, but that they must make every attempt to read the proposal from the real reviewers' perspective. Use the sample letter in Figure 7.16 (on the following page) to invite individuals to participate in your quality circle.

Each federal agency that makes grants follows a different proposal review system. The fact that proposal review systems vary in selection criteria and scoring emphasizes the need for preproposal contact with the funder and early data gathering about the review process.

As previously noted, the Department of Education uses a review system known as EDGAR (Education Department General Administrative Regulations). Not all programs in the Department of Education follow EDGAR; some programs have their own published regulations with a specific set of criteria. If an education program does not have a set of published guidelines, however, you can usually assume

**Figure 7.16**

Sample Letter Inviting an Individual to Participate in a Federal Grant Proposal Quality Circle

Date

Name
Address
City, State, Zip

Dear *[Participant's name]*:

As per our conversation, I am writing to ask for your input in helping our school district submit the very best grant proposal possible. We are asking that you review the enclosed proposal from the point of view of a federal reviewer. The attached materials will help you role-play the actual manner in which this proposal will be evaluated.

Please read the information on the reviewers' backgrounds and the scoring system, and limit the time you spend reading the proposal to the time constraints that the real reviewers will observe. A Quality Circle Scoring Worksheet has been provided to assist you in recording your scores and comments.

A meeting of all the mock reviewers comprising our quality circle has been scheduled for *[date]*. Please bring your Quality Circle Scoring Worksheet with you to the meeting. The meeting will last less than one hour. Its purpose is to analyze the scores and brainstorm suggestions to improve the proposal.

Sincerely,


*[Your name]*
*[Your phone number]*

they follow EDGAR. EDGAR's main areas of evaluation include the following:

1. How the proposed project meets the purposes of the authorizing statute.
2. The extent of the need for the project.
3. How the plan of operation meets the need.
4. The availability of qualified key personnel to implement the plan.
5. Whether the budget is cost effective and realistic with respect to the plan of operation.
6. How the plan's progress in meeting the objectives will be evaluated.
7. Whether the applicant possesses sufficient resources to house the project and support the plan.

To help your volunteers review and evaluate proposals to the Department of Education, you may wish to provide them with the worksheets in Figures 7.17 (on page 162) and 7.18 (on page 163).

Try to obtain the following information from the granting agency:

• Where and how the review occurs.
• The average time reviewers spend reading each proposal.
• The number of proposals each reviewer is responsible for evaluating.

At the very least, you must give your quality circle members the point system and time constraints by which they should abide. Volunteer reviewers often try to do such a good job that in their zeal, they spend much more time reviewing your proposal than the real reviewers.

Ask the volunteers to read your proposal and to designate areas they think the reviewer will like and those they think will be viewed negatively with an asterisk. Obviously, the negative areas should be improved prior to submission.

**Figure 7.17**
Scoring Distribution
Worksheet

The numerical scores you assign to an application's response to the selection criteria must be consistent with the comments you write. Comments and scores should reflect the same overall assessment. You should never attempt to mitigate a negative comment with a positive score, or vice versa.

Comments indicate whether the application's response to the selection criteria is poor, adequate, or good; scores indicate how poor, adequate, or good. If 10 points are possible, 0–2 points is poor, 5–7 points is adequate, and 8–9 points is superior. Four points will indicate a response that is merely weak, whereas 8 points will indicate a response that is above average. Whatever amount of total points is possible, use the midpoint of the scale as adequate and choose your scores accordingly. Do not hesitate to use the full range of points.

It is perfectly acceptable to assign a score of 10 or 1, for example. Your guiding rule should be consistency in rating. Always go back and check your scores to make sure that you have written them correctly and used the appropriate point scale. You should also double-check the scores on the summary page of the Technical Review Form to make sure that they match the scores listed under each selection criterion and that the final total has been computed without error.

You may want to use the following table as a guide when assigning points.

| Total | Poor | Weak | Adequate | Superior | Outstanding |
|-------|------|------|----------|----------|-------------|
| 25 | 0–8 | 9–12 | 13–19 | 20–23 | 24–25 |
| 20 | 0–6 | 7–9 | 10–15 | 16–18 | 19–20 |
| 15 | 0–4 | 5–7 | 8–11 | 12–13 | 14–15 |
| 10 | 0–2 | 3–4 | 5–7 | 8–9 | 10 |
| 5 | 0–1 | 2 | 3 | 4 | 5 |

**Figure 7.18** Selection Review Criteria

**Meeting the Purposes of the Authorizing Statute      5 pts**

1. What are the purposes of the authorizing statute?
2. What are the objectives of the project?
3. How will these objectives further the purposes of the authorizing statute?

**Needs      25 pts**

1. What needs are outlined by the authorizing statute?
2. What needs does the applicant identify?
3. How does the applicant identify those needs, i.e., what specific documentation or evidence does the application offer in support?
4. Are the project's needs consistent with the purposes of the authorizing statute?
5. Does the applicant identify too many or too few needs for the proposed time frame and resources?
6. Are the outlined needs well-defined or generic?

**Plan of Operation      20 pts**

1. Do the project's objectives serve the purposes of the authorizing statute?
2. How well is the project designed?
3. Are the objectives consistent with the needs?
4. Are the objectives measurable?
5. How will the applicant use its resources and personnel to achieve each objective?

6. Is there an effective management plan to ensure proper and efficient administration?
7. Do the project's milestones represent a logical progression of times and tasks?
8. Does the applicant propose a realistic time frame for accomplishing the objectives?
9. Will the proposed activities successfully accomplish the project's objectives?
10. Are the planned educational approaches based on sound research?
11. Does the project have clearly developed provisions to allow equal access to eligible participants of traditionally underrepresented groups (ethnic or racial minorities, women, handicapped or elderly persons)?

**Personnel      15 pts**

1. Do the job descriptions adequately reflect the skills needed to make the project work?
2. Are the duties of personnel clearly defined?
3. What relevant qualifications do the personnel possess, especially the Project Director? (Focus on their experience and training in fields related to the project, although other information may be considered.)
4. Will the personnel need to be trained for the project?
5. How much time will the personnel actually devote to the project?

6. To what extent does the applicant encourage employment applications from traditionally underrepresented groups (ethnic or racial minorities, women, handicapped or elderly persons)?

**Budgets      10 pts**

1. Is the budget adequate to support the activities?
2. Are overall costs reasonable in relation to the objectives?
3. How much of the project's total cost is devoted to administrative costs?
4. Are budget items sufficiently justified?
5. Is the budget padded?

**Evaluation Plan      15 pts**

1. Are the proposed evaluation methods appropriate to the project?
2. Will they be objective?
3. Will they measure the effectiveness in meeting objectives?
4. Will they produce valid and reliable data on the objectives?
5. Do they measure the project's effect on its audience?

**Resources      10 pts**

1. Are the proposed facilities adequate?
2. Is the proposed equipment adequate?
3. Does the applicant have access to special sources of experience of expertise?

Send or give your volunteers the worksheet in Figure 7.19 and any other information you can gather that will assist them in their role playing. For example, information on last year's grantees may be useful, especially if the grantee mix is likely to remain the same.

You can perform the review by mail or ask the volunteers to assemble for a short meeting to review the scores and discuss the proposal's positive and negative points. The members of the circle may not want to hurt your feelings by criticizing the proposal in your presence, so ask a friend to facilitate the meeting for you.

Be sure to remind your volunteer reviewers to mention your proposal's positive areas in their evaluations. In most cases, individuals tend to focus on the negatives, although you also need to know what parts of your proposal were considered "good" by the volunteer reviewers.

Review the scores received by each section. Based on the volunteers' scores and comments, identify the areas of your proposal that need to be improved and those that should remain the same.

*Submission*

Standard Form SF 424 (Figure 7.20, on page 166) must be attached to the front of your federal grant application or proposal. Bind your proposal or staple it only when specified by the agency. Some federal funders prefer grantseekers to submit their proposals with pressure tension clips so that forms can be added or removed as needed. Others require three-ring binders, and some prescribe exactly where staples should be. Whatever the rules, follow them exactly. Include the agency's checklist of assurances and follow all of the font, spacing, printing, and page-number restrictions.

*Intergovernmental Review of Federal Programs*

Intergovernmental review provides a mechanism to coordinate funds and projects and reduce the chances that the federal government supports a program that the state does not include in its plan. Not all programs require an intergovernmental review, and not all states have the same reporting

**Figure 7.19**
Quality Circle Scoring
Worksheet

The following information is being provided to assist you in reviewing the attached federal grant application/proposal.

**Setting:** the proposals are read at
_____ The reviewer's location
_____ The federal agency's location
_____ Other site selected by the federal agency
**Time:**
_____ Number of proposals the reviewer evaluates
_____ Time reviewer spends on each proposal

| Areas/Points | Points per Area | Comments /Suggestions |
|---|---|---|

*Total Points:*

What is the background and training of the evaluators?

_____

What point system will be followed?

_____

Use this space to note anything special that may affect the

outcome of the proposal _____

_____

**Figure 7.20** Standard Form 424

| APPLICATION FOR FEDERAL ASSISTANCE | 2. DATE SUBMITTED | Applicant Identifier | OMB Approval No. 0348-0043 |
|---|---|---|---|

| 1. TYPE OF SUBMISSION: | 3. DATE RECEIVED BY STATE | State Application Identifier |
|---|---|---|

**1. TYPE OF SUBMISSION:**

Application      Preapplication

☐ Construction      ☐ Construction

☐ Non-Construction      ☐ Non-Construction

| 4. DATE RECEIVED BY FEDERAL AGENCY | Federal Identifier |
|---|---|

**5. APPLICANT INFORMATION**

Legal Name:         Organizational Unit:

Address (give city, county, state and zip code):     Name and telephone number of the person to be contacted on matters involving this application (give area code):

**6. EMPLOYER IDENTIFICATION NUMBER (EIN):**

☐☐ - ☐☐☐☐☐☐☐

**7. TYPE OF APPLICANT:** (enter appropriate letter in box) ☐

A. State      H. Independent School Dist.
B. County      I. State Controlled Institution of Higher Learning
C. Municipal      J. Private University
D. Township      K. Indian Tribe
E. Interstate      L. Individual
F. Intermunicipal      M. Profit Organization
G. Special District      N. Other (specify) _____

**8. TYPE OF APPLICATION:**

☐ New      ☐ Continuation      ☐ Revision

If Revision, enter appropriate letter(s) in box(es): ☐ ☐

A. Increase Award      B. Decrease Award      C. Increase duration
D. Decrease Duration      Other (specify):
_____

**9. NAME OF FEDERAL AGENCY:**

**10. CATALOG OF FEDERAL DOMESTIC ASSISTANCE NUMBER:** ☐☐ - ☐☐☐

TITLE:

**11. DESCRIPTIVE TITLE OF APPLICANT'S PROJECT:**

There Are Several Form Fields In This Area.
Start Typing And All Default Text Will Disappear.

**12. AREAS AFFECTED BY PROJECT** (Cities, Counties, States, etc.):

| 13. PROPOSED PROJECT: | 14. CONGRESSIONAL DISTRICTS OF: |
|---|---|
| Start Date:   Ending Date: | a. Applicant      b. Project |

**15. ESTIMATED FUNDING:**

| a. Federal | $ |
|---|---|
| b. Applicant | $ |
| c. State | $ |
| d. Local | $ |
| e. Other | $ |
| f. Program Income | $ |
| g. TOTAL | $ |

**16. IS APPLICATION SUBJECT TO REVIEW BY STATE EXECUTIVE ORDER 12372 PROCESS?**

a. YES, THIS PREAPPLICATION/APPLICATION WAS MADE AVAILABLE TO THE STATE EXECUTIVE ORDER 12372 PROCESSS FOR REVIEW ON:

DATE _____

b. NO. ☐ PROGRAM IS NOT COVERED BY E.O. 12372
        ☐ OR PROGRAM HAS NOT BEEN SELECTED BY STATE FOR REVIEW

**17. IS THE APPLICANT DELINQUENT ON ANY FEDERAL DEBT?**

☐ Yes    If "Yes," attach an explanation.    ☐ No

**18.** TO THE BEST OF MY KNOWLEDGE AND BELIEF, ALL DATA IN THIS APPLICATION/PREAPPLICATION ARE TRUE AND CORRECT, THE DOCUMENT HAS BEEN DULY AUTHORIZED BY THE GOVERNING BODY OF THE APPLICANT AND THE APPLICANT WILL COMPLY WITH THE ATTACHED ASSURANCES IF THE ASSISTANCE IS AWARDED.

| a. Typed Name of Authorized Representative: | b. Title: | c. Telephone Number: |
|---|---|---|

requirements. However, if an intergovernmental review is required and your district has a grants office or a formal grants procedure, they will most likely handle the review.

If you must handle the review, contact your state's single point of contact to ensure that you comply with your state's requirements for coordinating your grant with other programs in your state. A list of contacts is provided on the following pages

You now know how to solicit money for your Internet access project from foundations, corporations, and government sources. Chapter 8 discusses some concepts behind raising funds through means other than grantseeking.

# State Single Point of Contact Offices

## Alabama
No single point of contact office

## Alaska
No single point of contact office

## Arizona
Janice Dunn
Arizona State Clearinghouse
Office of Economic Planning and Development
3800 North Central Avenue, Suite 140
Phoenix, AZ 85012

## Arkansas
Tracy L. Copeland
State Clearinghouse
Office of Inter-Governmental Services
Department of Finance and Administration
1515 West 7th Street, Room 412
Little Rock, AR 72203

## California
Grants Coordinator
Office of Planning and Research
1400 Tenth Street, Room 121
Sacramento, CA 95814

## Colorado
State Clearinghouse
Division of Local Government
1313 Sherman Street, Room 521
Denver, CO 80203

## Connecticut
No single point of contact office

## Delaware
Francine Booth
Executive Department
Thomas Collins Building
Dover, DE 19903

## District of Columbia
Rodney T. Hallman
Office of Grants Management & Development
717 14th Street, NW, Suite 500
Washington, DC 20005

## Florida
Suzanne Traub-Metlay
Intergovernmental Affairs Policy Unit
Executive Office of the Governor, Room 1603
Tallahassee, FL 32399-0001

**Georgia**
Charles H. Badger,
    Administrator
Georgia State Clearinghouse
254 Washington Street, SW
Room 401J
Atlanta, GA 30334

**Guam**
Giovanni T. Sgambelluri,
    Director
Bureau of Budget and Management Research
Office of the Governor
P.O. Box 2950
Agana, GU 96910

**Hawaii**
No single point of contact office

**Idaho**
No single point of contact office

**Illinois**
Steve Klokkenga
Office of the Governor
107 Stratton Building
Springfield, IL 62706

**Indiana**
Frances E. Williams
State Budget Agency
212 State House
Indianapolis, In 46204-2796

**Iowa**
Steven R. McCann
Division for Community Progress
Iowa State Department of Economic
    Development
200 East Grand Avenue
Des Moines, IA 50309

**Kansas**
No single point of contact office

**Kentucky**
Ronald W. Cook
Office of the Governor
Department of Local Government
1024 Capital Center Drive
Frankfort, KY 40601-8204

**Louisiana**
No single point of contact office

**Maine**
Joyce Benson
State Planning Office
State House Station
Number 38
Augusta, ME 04333

**Maryland**
Roland E. English, III
State Clearinghouse for Intergovernmental
    Assistance
Maryland Office of Planning
301 West Preston Street—Room 1104
Baltimore, MD 21201-2365

**Massachusetts**
Karen Arone
State Clearinghouse
Executive Office of Communities and
    Development
100 Cambridge Street
Room 1803
Boston, MA 02202

**Michigan**
Richard S. Pastula,
    Director
Office of Federal Grants
Michigan Department of Commerce
P.O. Box 30225
Lansing, MI 48909

**Minnesota**
No single point of contact office

**Mississippi**
Cathy Mallette,
    Clearinghouse Officer
Office of Federal Grant Management and
    Reporting
301 West Pearl Street
Jackson, MS 39203

**Missouri**
Lois Pohl
Federal Assistance Clearinghouse
Office of Administration
P. O. Box 809
Truman Building, Room 760
Jefferson City, MO 65102

**Montana**
No single point of contact office

**Nebraska**
No single point of contact office

**Nevada**
Department of Administration
State Clearinghouse
Capitol Complex
Carson City, NV 89710

**New Hampshire**
Jeffrey H. Taylor,
    Director
New Hampshire Office of State Planning
Attn: Intergovernmental Review
2 ½ Beacon Street
Concord, NH 03301

**New Jersey**
Andrew J. Jaskolta
State Review Process
Division of Community Resources
New Jersey Department
    of Community Affairs
CN 814, Room 609
Trenton, NJ 08625-0814

**New Mexico**
George Elliott,
    Deputy Director
State Budget Division
Bataan Memorial Building, Room 190
Santa Fe, NM 87503

**New York**
New York State Clearinghouse
Division of the Budget
State Capitol
Albany, NY 12224

**North Carolina**
Chrys Baggett,
    Director
North Carolina State Clearinghouse
Office of the Secretary of Administration
116 West Jones Street
Raleigh, NC 27603-8003

**North Dakota**
Office of Intergovernmental Assistance
600 East Boulevard Avenue
Bismarck, ND 58505-0170

**North Mariana Islands**
Planning and Budget Office
Office of the Governor
Saipan, CM
North Mariana Islands 96950

**Ohio**
Larry Weaver
State Clearinghouse
Office of Budget and Management
30 East Broad Street, 34th Floor
Columbus, OH 43266-0411

**Oklahoma**
No single point of contact office

**Oregon**
No single point of contact office

**Pennsylvania**
No single point of contact office

**Puerto Rico**
Norman Burgos, Chairman
Jose E. Caro, Director
Puerto Rico Planning Board
Minillas Government Center
P.O. Box 41119
San Juan, PR 00940-9985

**Rhode Island**
Daniel W. Varin, Associate Director
Department of Administration
Division of Planning
One Capitol Hill, 4th floor
Providence, RI 02908-5870

**South Carolina**
Omeagia Burgess
Grant Services
Office of the Governor
1205 Pendleton Street, Room 477
Columbia, SC 29201

**South Dakota**
No single point of contact office

**Tennessee**
Charles Brown
State Planning Office
John Sevier Building, Suite 309
500 Charlotte Avenue
Nashville, TN 37243-0001

**Texas**
Tom Adams, Director
Intergovernmental Coordination
P.O. Box 13005
Austin, TX 78711

**Utah**
Carolyn Wright
Utah State Clearinghouse

Office of Planning and Budget
State Capitol Building, Room 116
Salt Lake City, UT 84114

**Vermont**
Nancy McAvoy
State Single Point of Contact
Pavilion Office Building
109 State Street
Montpelier, VT 05609

**Virginia**
No single point of contact office

**Virgin Islands**
Jose George
Office of Management and Budget
#41 Norregade Emancipation Garden Station
Second Floor
St. Thomas, VI 00802

**Washington**
No single point of contact office

**West Virginia**
Fred Cutlip, Director
Community Development Division
West Virginia Development Office
State Capitol Complex
Building 6, Room 553
Charleston, WV 25305

**Wisconsin**
Martha Kerner, Section Chief
State/Federal Relations
Wisconsin Department of Administration
P.O. Box 7868
Madison, WI 53707

**Wyoming**
Sheryl Jeffries
Herscher Building
East Wing, 4th floor
Cheyenne, WY 82002

# 8 The ABCs of Fund-Raising for Internet and Technology

ALTHOUGH you can garner a hefty sum of money for your Internet-technology project by grantseeking, it will seldom capture all the capital that is necessary to implement and maintain your ambitious project. The rest of the money will come from other fund-raising techniques. In this chapter, you will learn:

- Where the money from private donations goes.
- How to relay your Internet Technology Support Group's mission to potential donors.
- The importance of building a strong donor pyramid.
- The advantages to be gained by utilizing a tax-exempt status.

In this book so far you have learned how to gain access to a portion of the federal government's $75 billion in grants for Internet access and enhancement. In addition, you now know how to work with your support group to develop your plan for securing a portion of the $16 billion in foundation and corporate grants.

You know from reading Chapter 4 that $114 billion in gifts from individuals to nonprofit organizations is left to explore. These monies are accessed by fund-raising techniques other than grantseeking. Even if grants provide all the necessary up-front funds to facilitate your Internet access project, you will still need to incorporate other fund-raising strategies for ongoing support for the repair, replacement, and upgrading of equipment. Only through the implementation of a variety of fund-raising strategies can you insure the future of your Internet project.

**Where Does the Money Go?**

Figure 8.1 shows that approximately 45 percent of private philanthropic support goes to religious organizations. The remaining $50 billion is shared by other nonprofit organizations in a variety of areas including education, and this amount increases each year. For this reason, your school has untapped potential in this marketplace.

You can access individual contributions for your Internet project by understanding:

- Who gives the money.
- Who gets the money.
- What type of system you need to establish to capture your share.

❖

*What are you to do when your support group members tell you: "We'll do anything to help, but please don't ask us to ask our friends for money?"*

❖

If you have applied the techniques suggested in the grantseeking chapters of this book, you are already on your way to developing your fund-raising system. You know from reading Chapter 4 that individuals are most responsible for private sector support of nonprofit organizations through individual gift giving. You also know that you must ask people for money in order to receive it. Unfortunately, however, many people feel uncomfortable asking for money.

What are you to do when your support group members tell you: "We'll do anything to help, but please don't ask us

**Figure 8.1**
Uses of Charitable
Contributions (in $billions).
*Source:* Giving USA 1995,
*American Association for
Fund-Raising Counsel Trust
for Philanthropy*

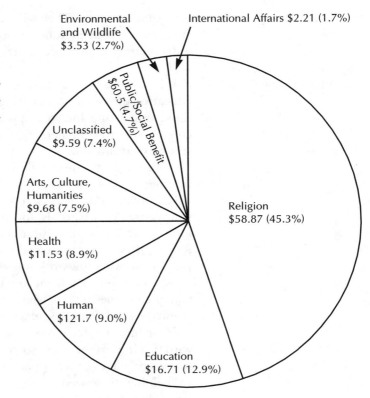

Environmental
and Wildlife
$3.53 (2.7%)

International Affairs $2.21 (1.7%)

Public/Social Benefit
$60.5 (4.7%)

Unclassified
$9.59 (7.4%)

Arts, Culture,
Humanities
$9.68 (7.5%)

Health
$11.53 (8.9%)

Human
$121.7 (9.0%)

Religion
$58.87 (45.3%)

Education
$16.71 (12.9%)

to ask our friends for money"? First, you can help your Internet Technology Support Group become comfortable with the idea of raising money by increasing their knowledge of fund-raising. Give the group the basic facts just as you did when you helped them develop their grants strategy. After all, they are well aware of your project's monetary need and have already "bought into" the plan. They now need to understand the group's specific mission. Don't assume they know this just because they volunteered to join your support group. They will need to have a specific under-standing of your mission in order to succinctly convince individuals to contribute money to the cause.

**Your Mission Statement**   You have already documented the gap in the learning and education of your students. By developing your plan and all those interesting Internet applications for your students, curriculum, and teachers, you have all the ingredients for stating your mission.

Your mission should include a short description of your Internet Technology Support Group's purpose as well as what potential donors need to know to be willing to support your cause. Your cause is not to wire a school building for Internet access or to raise money to purchase equipment. Rather, it deals with the end results or the ideal situation you are working toward (improving students' grades, etc.).

What do you want from your efforts? Is it an Internet system or equipment? If so, what would this provide your community, school, students, teachers, and staff?

Your Internet Technology Support Group must grapple with this important issue, so don't just give them a mission statement and ask them to accept it. When asked why they are helping, they need to feel comfortable with and under-stand their own reasons. Let your support group members try to develop their own mission statement.

If your support group's mission is to provide your stu-dents with a window to the world and the great educational opportunity provided by Internet access and technology, your case could state something similar to the following:

The purpose of the Internet Technology Support Group is to provide a forum in which to discuss the opportunities that Internet access can provide, such as enhancing school curriculum, student learning, and student interest in learning. This group is dedicated to developing the community's knowledge of the educa-tional opportunities the Internet can provide to the teacher, the student, the parent, and the community. The group's purpose is to raise the funds needed to make this resource available to our school. This includes raising funds to remodel, rewire, and equip our schools and to educate our teachers, staff, administrators, and parents on the proper educational use of this dynamic resource.

You may decide to select a logo or a symbol to bring recognition to your support group. Try to select a logo that is related to the mission and your case. For example, a mouse would make more sense than a polar bear because the "mouse" is a widely recognized computer peripheral. Two computers joined by wires would work well also.

**Building a Base for Your Funding**

One model for teaching the basics of fund development utilizes a pyramid such as that in Figure 8.2. The pyramid is used in fund development because it anchors fund-raising on a sound base.

The pyramid consists of three donor levels: levels A, B, and C. Donors become attracted to an organization (in this case, your Internet Technology Support Group) because they have been educated about it and somehow involved in its cause. As donors become better associated with the organization's mission they move up the pyramid. The goal at

**Figure 8.2**
The Donor Pyramid

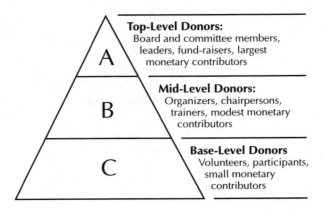

each donor pyramid level is to involve a subset of donors at the next level. The objective is to provide donor movement up the pyramid levels, from C to B to A. Each level relies on donors to qualify themselves by achieving higher levels of financial support or personal involvement through increased volunteering. The triangular shape of the donor pyramid represents the donors' ability to move up to the next level. Most organizations begin with an appeal to level C. These initial fund-raising activities are followed by activities designed to move the donors to level B and eventually to level A. Each sequential level solicits donors who are more involved and receptive to the organization's fund-raising objectives, organizational activities, and purposes. This all results in larger donations with less fund-raising effort. For example, at the A level, board members encourage each other to make large gifts. The real beauty of this is that today's board members were yesterday's level C donors!

*Level C*  Level C, known as the donor base, is characterized by a larger number of donors than levels B and A. Level C comprises individuals who have responded to the organization's invitation to participate in a fund-raising event, or have volunteered for or taken an active part in the organization within the last year.

Level C provides the base for both current and future fund-raising activities by directing its activities toward:

- Increasing the organization's position (recognition) in the marketplace.
- Promoting the general public's awareness of the problem, need, or condition of the organization's beneficiaries.
- Developing an increasing willingness in donors to contribute funds to the organization's goals and objectives.
- Increasing the number of individuals who volunteer to assist in the organization's program and fund-raising activities.

Level C is responsible for the continued strength of the donor pyramid. Just as in construction, if one builds on an inadequately prepared and maintained base, the foundation will not support the weight of the structure and the whole thing will collapse. After the funding "base" is laid, the goal is to continually maintain it by reaching out and involving new donors and volunteers to take the place of those lost for whatever reasons. Fortunately, donor and volunteer "maintenance" at level C is relatively low. Level C fund-raising activities do not require a lot of time or money. Many fund-raising activities that are considered "special events" are found in this section of the pyramid.

Remember that beneath (and indeed all around) level C lies an even deeper "base" of potential donors who have not yet risen to level C. The organization has not yet managed to position itself, its goal, its objectives, its programs, or its beneficiaries with these potential donors in a manner that has compelled them to participate. Your organization's potential depends on the percent of this group whose values will compel them to become involved in your mission to make the Internet and its benefits available to your students. They will participate when they realize that they can retain their own personal values along with yours. To elicit donor support, you must try to insure that the potential donor does not experience conflict in his or her value system when responding to your mission statement.

In order to entice a donor into your donor base, you must, of course, first identify and contact the donor. Organizations often have many donors who contribute small, anonymous amounts through low-level involvement, wherein a name and address are difficult to elicit. For example, 5,000 individuals may participate in a "Flower Day" and donate $1 for a bloom. Although they are contributors, without their names, addresses, or phone numbers you cannot personally invite them to participate in future fund-raising activities that would encourage them to ascend your organization's donor pyramid. Therefore, when planning your fund-raising strategy, be sure to develop activities that allow you to get your donors' names and addresses. For example, offer your donors the opportunity to purchase five flowers to become a member of the Bunch Club, or encourage them to increase their gift level by allowing them to enter a Bunch Club prize drawing for a round trip ticket for two if they purchase 10 flowers.

The area of the pyramid in Figure 8.3 that is designated as "volunteers" represents a percentage of the level-C donors who freely agree to perform minimal tasks related to the organization's service, educational, or fund-raising activities without monetary compensation. Examples of these tasks include selling raffle tickets or flowers, flipping pancakes at a special fund-raising breakfast, tending bar at a dinner/dance, and distributing public relations materials. By taking on these tasks, donors are demonstrating their loyalty and commitment to the cause. By performing these types of tasks, they qualify to become members of a very special group—donor volunteers.

Naturally, not all donors become volunteers. But whether a donor or a donor volunteer, the individuals in level C form the basis for the early growth and later expansion of your

**Figure 8.3**
Volunteers and the Donor
Pyramid

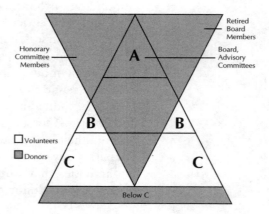

organization. Because of this, your fund-raising plan must always include public relations activities that increase public knowledge of your organization and add to the new donors and volunteers. This is especially important since new people are always needed to replace those lost through attrition. Even organizations with an established plan to maintain their current membership level or size will be affected by the loss of interest of some donors or members, and eventually by the aging and/or death of members. This time period is referred to as the "donor life." Without a conscientious review of its donor constituency and a consistent effort to recruit new donors and volunteers at its base level (level C), the organization will eventually fall prey to an inadequate donor base. If an organization does not continually plan level-C activities and no one is being recruited to replace the level B and A volunteers and board members, the organization may become terminally ill.

*Level B*  To move from level C to level B, donors must respond to invitations to become more involved, both financially and personally. The amount of money that qualifies a donor must be determined by the organization and should be based on the financial makeup of the organization's constituency. For one organization, the qualifying donation from level C to level B may be $1,000 in one year; for another it may be $100. In the Internet-technology interest area, $100 should qualify the donor to move from level C to the beginning of level B.

Volunteers qualify themselves by becoming organizers, captains, chairpersons, trainers, etc. Volunteers at level B are more involved and better able than those at level C to convince their friends and associates to join the cause. While the level-B donor may coordinate a special events fund-raising activity and donate to a variety of level-C activities, he or she is ready for more sophisticated requests based on a greater monetary commitment. For example, a $200 per couple dinner/dance.

*Level A*   The top level of the pyramid represents the cream of the crop. This level includes a small number of donors who made it this far through significant identification with and financial commitment to the group. Most level-A donors are high level volunteers who form the nucleus of the advisory committees and volunteer groups. They are the organization's leaders and have helped shape the organization through their knowledge, leadership, and involvement. They are the strategic planners who will transfer their legacy of purpose and service to the next generation. These individuals position the organization in the marketplace. They lend credibility to the organization because they have donated their time, money, and names.

Level A provides the most low-cost, high-return fund-raising. The fund-raising activities of personal solicitation, unsolicited gifts, bequests, and tax deferred gifts occur at this level. Unfortunately, the size of the level-A gifts and the ease in obtaining them can tempt an organization to ignore the donor base and the constant need to build a new constituency. Do not assume that you will be able to disband your Internet Technology Support Group once you have achieved your objective. Money is a constant necessity.

One of the more perplexing problems associated with the top level of the pyramid is deciding how to acknowledge this group's generosity while gradually moving them out of level A to allow for new growth from level B. In an effort to avoid dealing with this issue, many organizations choose to keep level-A members "forever." However, this can easily result in stagnation. Developing advisory groups comprised of past board members, and/or establishing a policy of a mandated rest before readmission to the board makes more sense.

In the succeeding chapters, you will analyze your current fund-raising strategies and evaluate your donor development structure for its strengths and weaknesses. Before you choose the fund-raising strategies that are best for your group, consider the legal implications of using a nonprofit umbrella under which to raise funds.

**Understanding and Utilizing Tax-Exempt Status** If your school system has created an educational foundation, you need to consider placing your Internet Technology Support Group under the foundation's umbrella. By doing so, you can take advantage of the foundation's status as a federally approved tax-exempt charitable organization.

Schools and school districts are usually nonprofit and exempt from paying sales and certain other taxes. However, this status is very different from being recognized by the Internal Revenue Service as a not-for-profit charitable organization. The vast majority of school foundations are designated as either 509(a)(1) or 509(a)(3) organizations under the tax code. Charitable organizations—including school foundations—can provide donors with receipts that may be counted when they take the contribution as a deduction on their income tax return.

If your school does not have a foundation, then you have other options. It is not mandatory to start a foundation to be able to legally and effectively raise money for your Internet project. There are several community-based organizations that can help by allowing your group to use their tax status. Many of these non–school-related charitable organizations will be designated as 501(c)(3)s by the Internal Revenue Service.

Check with the following groups to see if any of them would be willing to share their tax-exempt status with you:

- Your community foundation.
- Your Chamber of Commerce's foundation.
- Youth clubs such as 4-H, YMCA, YWCA.
- The Junior League.
- The United Way.

Collaboration with one of these groups will also enhance and legitimize your group's image in the community.

It is not mandatory that your Internet Technology Support Group provide donors with a tax deduction. You can still sponsor fund-raising activities if your school does not have a foundation and you cannot elicit any other organization to share their tax-exempt status with you. However, you must make clear on all of your public relations information, tickets, etc. that even though the donation is to support Internet access for your school, it is not tax deductible.

Now that you understand the basics of grassroots fund-raising and the donor pyramid, it is time to discuss just why people donate money and time to certain organizations. The next chapter will provide you with important information you need to know before approaching donors for money for your Internet Technology Support Group.

# 9 Why People Give, Using Consultants, and the Ethics of Fund-Raising

As a fund-raiser, you must identify your potential donors and develop plans for approaching them. You must also understand donors' motivations. In this chapter, you will learn:

- Why people give money to certain organizations.
- How to solicit donations and how much money to request.
- The use of fund-raising professionals.
- The ethics of fund-raising.

The famous French author Alexis de Toqueville wrote:

> These Americans are peculiar people. If, in a local community a citizen becomes aware of a human need which is not being met, he thereupon discusses the situation with his neighbor. Suddenly a committee comes into existence. The committee thereupon

begins to operate on behalf of the need and a new community function is established. It is like watching a miracle, because these citizens perform this act without a single reference to any bureaucracy or any official agency.

Sounds like your Internet Technology Support Group, doesn't it? You and your volunteers noticed a need and want to give your students the best opportunity for learning. So you invited others to join in meeting your goals and objectives. You don't need to form a formal organization because people don't give money to organizations; they give money to people.

Individuals contribute $130 billion annually to causes that are larger, more far reaching, and more meaningful than anything they could do alone. Together your group and your donors will invest in the future of your young people. Your donors will buy your dream (enhanced levels of student achievement and interest) by paying for your methods (Internet access). But first you must identify your potential donor groups, their values, and with which part of your mission they will identify.

As stated throughout this book, you must know how your project reflects the donor's personal values in order to encourage him or her to become involved in your organization. Determine how your activities will reinforce the donor's values and enhance the exchange of money. You must remind yourself and your volunteers that people are entitled to their own values. Fund-raising is therefore not aimed at teaching individuals to value your cause, but to awaken values they already have that are the closest to those you represent. The freedom to value is an important concept that will help the fund-raiser understand donor motivation.

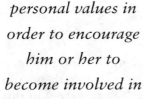

*You must know how your project reflects the donor's personal values in order to encourage him or her to become involved in your organization.*

**Why People Give** "The Charitable Behavior of Americans," a study conducted by Yankelovich, Shelly and White, Inc., examines individual giving in the United States.* Commissioned by the Rockefeller Brothers Fund, this study provides valuable insight into the factors that influence an individual to make a donation. The following summarizes selected findings contained in the report.

1. Although some donors felt that they were asked for donations too often and by too many groups, the study revealed that 38 percent of the donors thought they should be giving more. When asked why they did not contribute more, 23 percent said they "did not get around to it" and 14 percent said they were not asked. Based on these findings you clearly must build a follow-up plan into your fund-raising efforts which will allow you to reach those who need a little push to persuade them to give. In addition, you must ask more individuals to make sure you reach those who say they are never solicited. (The study documents that the individual donor marketplace is not oversubscribed and that there is room for growth.)

2. Individuals make contributions based on their values. The amount of discretionary income left to potential donors after their own needs are met is an important factor in the giving decision. There are wide variations in what individuals perceive their needs to be, but you can safely assume that your organization and constituents will be considered after an individual's own needs. While many religious groups espouse giving from need rather than from excess, most individuals apparently do not heed this.

3. About 77 percent of individuals with incomes in excess of $50,000 feel that they have sufficient discretionary income to make contributions. While individuals with incomes less than $10,000 donated 2.8 percent of their

---

* "The charitable Behavior of Americans: A National Survey." Yankelovich, Shelly and White, Inc., 1986.

income, only a small percentage used discretionary funds; they gave from funds they needed. However, remember that 2.8 percent of $10,000 translates into as much dollar value as 1.5 percent of $60,000. Therefore, if your school is in an economically depressed community, your local donors may not be able to sustain the upper level of your donor pyramid, and you will be forced to locate individuals outside of your community who have the necessary discretionary income to help support your project.

4. Around 25 percent of individuals under 35 years of age with moderate discretionary incomes were donors, compared to 40 percent of those over 35 years of age. Apparently, the younger donor with the means to give was either not responding or not approached. The study does not give concrete reasons why the under-35 group was behind the over-35 group. It just documented that a difference existed. Of course, we all know people who are in stark contrast to these findings, but citing them will not help our programs. Instead, you should review your fundraising activities for ways to target the portion of the under-35 age group that possesses discretionary funds. This strategy is especially good since the under-35 group represents your future donors and it is likely that they may have more knowledge of how the Internet can be used in education than the over-35 group.

5. The survey documents that the 35- to 64-year-olds with incomes in excess of $50,000 should be the prime targets of contribution programs.

6. This study found that three out of five high level donors (those making gifts of 3 percent or more of their annual income) were also active as volunteers.

7. Approximately 78 percent of those interviewed for the study agreed that individuals should volunteer for

nonprofit organizations. But the interesting fact is that only 47 percent said they actually did. As you review your fund-raising activities for volunteer involvement, remember that many more people feel they should volunteer than actually do.

8. The old adage that "people give to other people" is well documented by this study. Individuals utilizing face-to-face solicitation found it to be the most effective form of fund-raising. Among larger donors, it was even more effective if the solicitor and donor knew each other before the solicitation.

9. The study documents the "geographic perspective" of giving—62 percent of the individuals interviewed believed in helping people they knew or who were members of their community before helping those elsewhere. While these same individuals may make a short term commitment or donation to something like disaster relief in another area, their geographic philanthropic "homing device" is always operating.

10. Study results confirm that volunteers donate to the groups in which they volunteer. Hence, attracting many volunteers is important for more than one reason. Clearly defined, short-term, minimal time investments, with a definite beginning and ending date will appeal to the beginning volunteer. Volunteer training materials and the description of tasks to be performed must be well organized in order to attract the volunteer who is only marginally interested.

11. The system used to collect donations or pledges can influence people to give. Your pledge system and the organization of your approach will have a tremendous effect on your donors' decision to give. After sharing this data about individual giving with your Internet Technology Support

Group, you are ready to identify your potential donors and develop your plan for approaching these donors. Brainstorm the types of individuals who would be most likely to respond favorably to your Internet access project and why they would value it. Use the worksheet in Figure 9.1 and add more potential donors to the list.

**Figure 9.1** Types of Individuals to Approach for Financial Support of Your Internet Technology Project

| Rank | Type | Shared Values/Concerns |
|---|---|---|
| | Parents | • improving achievement of children |
| | | • improving children's motivation and interest in learning |
| | | • _____ |
| | | • _____ |
| | | • _____ |
| | Teachers | • improved resources teaching |
| | | • enhanced curriculum |
| | | • interaction with other teachers |
| | | • _____ |
| | | • _____ |
| | Retired Teachers | • _____ |
| | | • _____ |
| | Grandparents | • _____ |
| | | • _____ |
| | Local Employers | • improved workforce |
| | | • _____ |
| | | • _____ |
| | | • _____ |
| | _____ | • _____ |
| | _____ | • _____ |
| | _____ | • _____ |
| | _____ | • _____ |

Make copies of your completed list and let each member of your support group rank the suggested donor groups by their strength of conviction and identification with the Internet project and its benefits. Collect the sheets and place the four groups with the highest ratings in the center quadrant of Figure 9.2. Work out from the center of the figure by placing the next four highest groups in the next ring and the next eight groups in the outside ring. This visual provides a quick reference for building your fund-raising focus. It will also help you develop your strategy for approaching your "best" potential donors.

**How Much and How Often Should You Ask ?**

Many people involved in fund-raising are so influenced by their own values, commitment, financial resources, and personal reasons for donating that they transfer their own feelings about giving to the prospective donor. By doing so, the well intended fund-raiser limits the freedom of the prospective donor to make a commitment at his or her own level.

**Figure 9.2** Targeting Your Donor Groups

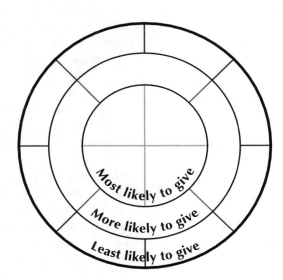

The following Donor Emancipation Proclamation will help you educate the members of your support group about the problems created by impinging upon the freedom of a donor.

**Donor Emancipation Proclamation**

Prospective donors are free to decide how much they value our organization, goals, objectives, and programs. I will not determine their level of commitment by forcing my values on them. Donors are free to decide:

- How much they contribute.
- How often they contribute.
- Their level of involvement/volunteering.

**Soliciting Donations**

The volunteer solicitor who wrongfully assumes that the donor holds the same values as he or she does can also wrongfully view the request as a gift to the solicitor. The solicitor must remember that the donation is to the organization and its mission. The volunteer solicitor is making a contact to:

- Involve donors in a cause they feel strongly about.
- Educate donors concerning the project and its benefits.
- Allow donors to meet their personal need through their contribution.

The donor develops a fear of donor rejection when the solicitor confuses the issue of why he or she is asking the donor to become involved. Solicitors are asking donors so that donors can meet their own needs, values, and motivations. The situation is analogous to asking a friend if he wants to hike the Appalachian Trail. He may say, "No thank you," but add that he would like to meet you along the way and cook out by a campfire. He is not insulted that you asked him to hike the whole way, and is comfortable with the fact that he could respond at a level of commitment appropriate for himself. Likewise, if an individual agrees to donate to your support group's mission, you must allow him or her to give at a comfortable level, not necessarily the level with which you feel comfortable.

The Donor Emancipation Proclamation provides the basis for considering some of the ethical issues involved in donor solicitation, including repeated requests to a donor. Remember, the donor is free to say yes and equally free to decline a request, so don't be afraid to ask more than once. Don't be illogical and say to a prospective donor, "Now give as much as you would ever give to our Internet technology project because I am uncomfortable inviting you to support our project more than once a year. I won't come back until next year, so consider how much you value the enhancement of our students' education and give all of your donation right now!" This sounds foolish, but that is essentially the impression you give when you approach the donor once annually.

Tests on soliciting membership of organizations through direct-mail fund-raising reveal that the optimum number of requests yearly is between four and seven. Your support group must understand that they limit the donor's freedom by asking only once. This finding does not necessarily mean you should appeal to your members seven times per year. Rather, you should develop a variety of creative approaches or "special" appeals to upgrade your donors on a repeat basis. For example, you could form a "Friends of the Internet Society" appeal for a new software program. The members of such a group would want to donate regularly; they would want to be a consistent part of your organization; and they would want to be allowed to express their freedom of choice concerning contribution frequency. If you receive a few irate letters or complaints from some of your donors because of your repeated requests, just develop a mailing list code that will enable you to distinguish those who should be solicited only once or twice a year.

**Using a Professional Fund-Raising Consultant**

You must educate your Internet Technology Support Group members so that they can make sound fund-raising decisions. Neither you nor your team members need to be development experts to raise money. Likewise, you do not necessarily have to hire a fund-raising consultant to assist you. Consider the following advantages and disadvantages of hiring a professional consultant before making this important (and potentially costly) decision. In the end, you may find that one or two well-designed fund-raising strategies undertaken by your volunteers will net more money for your cause and foster a better community image than using a portion of your proceeds to pay a profit-making fund-raising firm.

*Advantages*
- Professional fund-raising consultants know about your local funding marketplace.
- They can save time developing your fund-raising plan.
- They have already learned from their past mistakes and can reduce problems.
- Support group members tend to listen to professional fund-raisers since their services cost money.
- They can help you develop a fund-raising plan that incorporates many fund-raising strategies to help you build a strong donor pyramid.
- They are knowledgeable of specific techniques that may not be cost efficient for you to undertake on your own, such as telemarketing and direct mail.

*Disadvantages*
- Your support group may say: "Let the professional raise the money. That's why we're paying him or her." But they need to understand that the consultant's job is to guide and coordinate your efforts, not actually solicit money.

- Donors will be wary about the percentage of their gift that will be used to pay the fund-raising professional, and your cost per dollar raised will be closely watched.
- Your support group's fund-raising expertise, competency, and confidence is not enhanced when you hire out your fund-raising needs.
- Your group may become dependent on the professional and find that it cannot act independently of a fund-raising consultant.

**The Ethics of Fund-Raising**    Your Internet Technology Support Group should be comfortable with the basic ethics involved in raising money. Here are some pertinent questions to review:

- Will the funds be used for the needs/project described?
- Have you selected the most cost efficient method to acquire these funds?
- Did you portray your constituency (students, teachers) fairly? Did you capitalize on their condition to elicit donor sympathy or base your appeal on enhancing their capacity?
- Have you followed all state laws on disclosure, and have you filed all appropriate forms related to the costs of fund-raising?
- If you utilize fund-raising consultants, do they abide by a code of ethics?
- Has your organization taken necessary safeguards to ensure that donor restrictions and wishes are respected?
- Have you followed financial standards outlined by certified public accountants?

The National Society of Fund-Raising Executives (NSFRE) and the Center of Philanthropy are two organizations dedicated to promoting ethical and value-based philanthropic fund-raising.

The National Society of Fund-Raising Executives (NSFRE) was founded in 1960. Its focus is on fund-raising training, certification, and ethics for nonprofit organizations, smaller consulting companies, and individual fund-raisers. NSFRE has grown tremendously within the last 26 years, with chapters in cities across the United States. You can obtain the name and phone number of the chapter president nearest you by calling NSFRE's Arlington, Virginia office at 800-666-FUND. In addition to discussing your organization's fund-raising needs, NSFRE can provide information on the ethical standards and practice codes to which they subscribe. The Chicago NSFRE chapter has developed an excellent resource titled "Honorable Matter: A Guide to Ethics and Law in Fund-Raising."* For ordering information call 708-655-0134.

Because of its concern with preserving the spirit of philanthropy, the Lilly Endowment, Inc., awarded a grant in 1987 to develop the Center of Philanthropy at Indiana University, Purdue University. The Center promotes a variety of services to the field of philanthropy, including training programs through the Fund-Raising School. The Center of Philanthropy can be reached at 800-962-6692.

Ethics in fund-raising are of critical importance, and the responsibility for ethical conduct extends beyond the professional fund-raising consultant; it is shared by all members of your Internet Technology Support Group.

*Payment of Consultants* Many ethics-related questions asked by members of support groups and fund-raising committees deal with the payment of fund-raising consultants. One of the foremost associations of fund-raising corporations, the American Association of Fund-Raising Counsel (AAFRC), addresses this issue in its fair practice code. The code serves as a model for those of other fund-raising associations and

---

* NSFRE, Chicago Chapter. "Honorable Matter: A Guide to Ethics and Law in fund-raising," 414 Plaza Drive, Suite 209, Westmont, IL 60559.

includes the following provisions on payment of services. Member firms believe it is in the best interest of the clients that:

- Fees be mutually agreed upon in advance and be based on the level and extent of services provided, except that initial meetings with prospective clients are not usually construed as services for which payment is expected . . .
- Contracts providing for a contingent fee, commission, or percentage of funds raised should be avoided . . .
- The services of professional solicitors who receive a contingent fee, commission, or percentage of funds raised should be avoided . . .
- Any potential conflict of interest should be disclosed to clients and prospective clients.*

Commission-based fund-raising is, in effect, a polite term for "skimming off the top." It diverts funds intended for the charity, and it misleads donors. Due to the pressures faced by your Internet Technology Support Group to raise funds right now, you could fall prey to the consultant who promises to "do it all" for you for a percentage of the funds raised. But remember, a fixed fee paid from an organization's budget is far more likely to generate donor confidence and contribute to the development of a sound donor base.

Professional fund-raising consultants are paid for their experience and the time they allocate to a project. In fact, they are paid for their work even when, with their assistance, the desired amount of money is not raised. This is because the ability to interest a donor is not necessarily

---

* American Association of Fund-Raising Counsel, Inc., Fair Practice Code, pp. 22–23. AAFRC, 25 West 43rd Street, Suite 1519, New York, NY 10036.

related to the skill of the consultant, but rather to the organization, its position in the funding marketplace, and the salability of its project.

Difficulties can arise when the consultant is made to feel that he or she is being paid to bring in as much money as possible, as quickly as possible. This pressure could force the consultant to ask donors who have not been sufficiently cultivated for support or to ask those who are not yet ready to give at a higher level. And, since the consultant may be gone tomorrow, he or she may practice techniques that are damaging to the future of your organization.

However, in defense of fund-raising consultants, most are ethical, will be around tomorrow, and prefer to develop long term relationships. But beware—the temptation for both nonprofits and consultants to act in an unethical manner is a real and ever-present problem. Money can corrupt even faster than it can create.

The next chapter gives you a basic knowledge of the different fund-raising techniques. It also teaches you how to organize a fund-raising event and describes the different types of events you may want to undertake.

# 10 Selecting the Most Efficient Fund-Raising Strategies

THIS chapter describes in detail a variety of fund-raising strategies you can employ. Whether your fund-raising effort is on the classroom, building, or district level, you will learn to use a fund-raising matrix to help you determine which strategies are the best for you. In this chapter, you will discover:

- How to analyze your fund-raising costs.
- How to develop a fund-raising organizer.
- The pros and cons of the most common and popular fund-raising strategies.

Many people who contribute to fund-raising efforts wonder how much of their donation is actually allotted to the cause and how much is spent on fund-raising efforts. The expense of fund-raising is definitely an important issue. The following fund-raising organizer (Figure 10.1) will help you develop and track the actual costs of your present and future fund-raising activities. This spreadsheet will allow you to

**Figure 10.1**
Fund-Raising Organizer

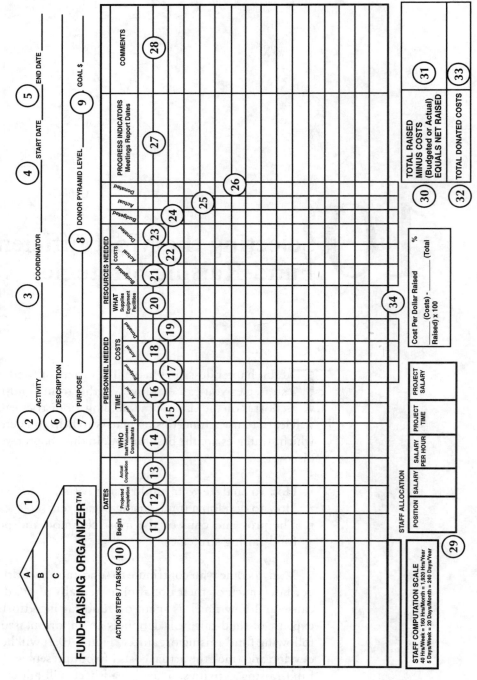

**Figure 10.1**
Fund-Raising Organizer (continued)

ACTIVITY (35) _____

| MEETINGS (36) | | | TELEPHONE LOG (37) | | | COMMITTEE MEMBERS (38) | | KEY INDIVIDUALS (39) | | MISC. EXPENSES (40) | | |
|---|---|---|---|---|---|---|---|---|---|---|---|---|
| DATE | INDIVIDUALS PRESENT | RESULTS | DATE | WHO | RESULTS | NAME | PHONE NUMBER | NAME | PHONE NUMBER | DATE | AMOUNT | EXPLANATION |
| | | | | | | | | | | | | |
| | | | | | | | | | | | | |
| | | | | | | | | | | | | |
| | | | | | | | | | | | | |
| | | | | | | | | | | | | |
| | | | | | | | | | | | | |
| | | | | | | | | | | | | |
| | | | | | | | | | | | | |
| | | | | | | | | | | | | |
| | | | | | | | | | | | | |
| | | | | | | | | | | | | |
| | | | | | | | | | | | | |
| | | | | | | | | | | | | |

TOTAL

budget each activity, and to compare your budget to actual costs. It will also enable your volunteers to visualize where they fit into your fund-raising equation by seeing how their efforts reduce costs, increase efficiency, and lead to the involvement of more volunteers and donors.

When developing a cost analysis system, remember that fund-raising activities should not be judged solely on their revenue production. For example, when trying to construct a healthy Donor Pyramid, you may have to engage in fund-raising activities that require many volunteers, or provide your cause with much-needed public relations. However, you should still be able to determine how much of your valuable resources was expended to achieve these other ends, even when you select fund-raising activities to meet these and/or other criteria. Whether you are asked about your fund-raising costs by a government agency or about the allocation of a gift by a donor, your completed fund-raising organizer will help you accurately answer these questions and present your funding plan in a credible manner.

**Developing a Fund-Raising Organizer**

The following steps outline the process for completing a fund-raising organizer. The sections below are numbered to correspond with the labels on Figure 10.1.

*1. Logo*

The fund-raising logo at the top of the organizer is to remind the user that all fund-raising activities should be related to the donor pyramid and that each activity should be placed in the appropriate level (A, B, or C).

*2. Activity*

This space is used to record the name of the activity (e.g., pancake breakfast).

*3. Coordinator*

Who will be the lead person, or individual in charge of the activity? Co-coordinators may be listed here, but their individual tasks should be designated on the fund-raising organizer. Or, you can develop additional fund-raising organizers based upon specific responsibilities.

*4. Start Date*    This date reflects the first day of the earliest task for the activity. You need to do many of the tasks more than a year in advance. For example, if you're planning a gala dinner/dance, you must procure hotel accommodations, reserve function rooms, schedule orchestras, etc. Recording the start date will keep you from delaying decisions and missing the "right" dates or places—variables that could affect the gross amount raised.

*5. End Date*    This is the effective date for compiling all income and paying all expenses. At times, the start date for the next year's activity will overlap the end date for the current year's activity. In these instances, you need to keep the activities separate so that you can calculate your cost per dollar raised for each activity each year.

*6. Description*    Not everyone will be familiar with the activity named on line 2 of the organizer. This line provides space to explain the activity in a little more detail. For example: "Pancake breakfast that the Kiwanis Club does each February at a local hotel."

*7. Purpose*    This space is for a statement concerning how the activity will benefit the organization. For example, the Pancake Breakfast may be held to raise money, develop public awareness of your organization, provide endorsement by a major service club in order to recruit more volunteers, and/or qualify donors or volunteers.

*8. Donor Pyramid Level*    List the level (A, B, or C) or list more than one level if the activity has components involving two or three levels. Each person involved in the activity should know and understand the target group and purpose of the activity in developing the donor base. For example, the pancake breakfast may have donors who contribute all the food (level B) and others who purchase tickets (level C).

9. *Goal*    This is the anticipated gross that will be raised by the activity. (The net money realized/expected from this activity will be expressed later.) This total could represent several subactivities such as ticket sales, a raffle, or silent auction proceeds.

10. *Action Steps/Tasks*    List the tasks that must be performed to complete the fundraising activity. You may enter a task in a general way—such as "advertise the pancake breakfast"—or you could be more specific and write something like "advertise the pancake breakfast: (a) develop posters, (b) print 5,000 posters, (c) make a presentation at five Kiwanis Clubs, and (d) organize a volunteer group to distribute 1,000 posters at each Kiwanis Club."

11. *Begin Date*    As opposed to the start date for the entire project, the begin date is the task initiation date for each step in your fundraising plan.

12. *Projected Completion*    This column represents the ideal time frame for completion of the task. While you are practicing sound planning techniques, in reality you must also be flexible. Many activities could be undertaken simultaneously, while others must be accomplished in a definite order. For example, layout, design, and printing of posters must occur in sequence. Committees can be set up at the same time or in sequence as needed. Another way of representing the relationships among activities is through the use of a diagram.

13. *Actual Completion*    Immediately after completion of the task, record the date. Use this date next year to develop a more accurate plan.

14. *Who*    List individuals from your support group who will be responsible for each task. If this is a district-level effort, list support staff, volunteers, and consultants. Estimating how many people will be involved in leadership roles is difficult,

but by keeping an accurate log you will be in a better position to anticipate the required personnel the next time you carry out the fund-raiser.

**15. *Time: Estimated*** Place an estimate of the time required of each individual listed in column 14 ("Who"). Using a fund-raising organizer will insure that everyone has a job description and that the time estimates allocated to the tasks are logical. The individual who is estimated to work 50 percent of his or her time must be able to see that the tasks add up to a 50 percent commitment over the time frame of the activity. The 50 percent or half-time should be based on the staff computation scale (number 29) located at the lower left hand corner of the fund-raising organizer. One of the most common mistakes in time allocation occurs when an individual works nearly full-time for three months, and then at a 25 percent rate for several months. By averaging time allocation during the year, the individual may appear to be at 50 percent. However, careful analysis may reveal that the individual is overextended for months at a time.

Failure to plan and analyze the time allocation for each group member can cause confusion, fatigue, and fund-raising burnout. The inclusion of the fund-raising organizer in your fund-raising plan is welcomed by everyone, and fulfills their need to know what is expected of them. The fund-raising organizer may appear awesome at first. But you will use it repeatedly once you become familiar with its benefits.

The staff computation scale (number 29) will help you allocate any personnel you decide to use. But notice that vacation leave, medical, and personal days have not been accounted for. You must deduct these from the scale according to your organization's personnel policies.

**16. *Time: Actual*** Place the actual time dedicated to the fund-raising activity in this box. The logging of actual completion dates and time expended will help you obtain future staff or volunteers. If your school bases its service awards to volunteers on number of hours volunteered, the fund-raising organizer will provide this data.

The allocation of personnel to tasks provides the data necessary for sound decision making related to additional staffing needs if you are undertaking a large district-level fund-raising effort. An analysis of the information provided on the fund-raising organizer will allow you to determine when additional staff are cost-efficient (i.e., generate more money than they cost).

Many board, advisory committee, and support group members are from the for-profit world and are well aware of the necessity of cost efficiency. Hence, use of the fund-raising organizer to analyze the cost efficient utilization of personnel will be eagerly accepted.

*17. Personnel Needed:*
*Costs Budgeted*

Insert the budgeted costs of the individuals who will be paid for their time for performing the tasks. This column is based on the estimated time for each individual, and the cost per unit of time that you choose to utilize (cost per hour, day, week, etc.). Refer to the staff computation scale (number 29) and to the Staff Allocation Box on the fund-raising organizer for salary rates. Do not assume that the school staff will be willing to take reservations or sell tickets. Forecast these activities in their time allocations, and ask the school officials to donate their involvement.

*18. Personnel Needed:*
*Costs Actual*

Multiply the actual time (column 16) by the cost per unit of work, and enter the figure in this column. You may want to highlight those tasks performed that are under budget by using a different color of ink or a highlighter pen. By drawing attention to tasks completed under budget, you reward the individual in charge for performing at a superior level. You can also highlight all the "actual" figures in a different color of ink to make them stand out from the rest of the form. This is particularly helpful whenever the organizer is used as the basic planning document for the next year's fund-raiser.

*19. Personnel Needed:* Note all donated personnel in this column from school staff,
*Costs Donated* volunteers, and consultants. This column is useful in calculating total in-kind or donated costs. These donations are an
indication of community support for the activity and for
your project.

*20. Resources Needed* Itemize the necessary resources for the successful completion of each task. These include all supplies, printing,
postage, travel, donor recognition awards, and the like.
Failure to pay close attention to this area can transform a
cost-efficient fund-raiser into a fund-raiser with an unac-
ceptable cost per dollar raised.

Share your fund-raising organizer with your support
group members, advocates, and friends and ask them if they
know of a way you can borrow, share, or lease equipment
and supplies. Look through your phone directory to locate
potential sources of corporate donations or loans for these
necessities. Corporations may, for example, be willing to
donate used equipment that has been reconditioned or to
tell you who has purchased new equipment from them,
which could assist you in locating potential donors. You
can also look through the *Standard Industrial Classification
Code Book* (see Chapter 6) for manufacturers that may
make donations that could significantly lower your fund-
raising costs.

*21. Resources Needed:* This column provides the opportunity to estimate the costs
*Costs Budgeted* of the nonpersonnel resources needed. Estimates and quotes
for the tasks omitted may not always be exact, but a phone
call to a printer or bulk mailer for an estimate of costs for
handling a direct mail piece will give you enough information to estimate your net proceeds before committing your
group to a particular strategy.

*22. Resources Needed:* Place all costs and billing charges in this column as they
*Costs Actual* occur. Your fund-raising organizer enables you to determine
where you are under and over budget.

23. *Resources Needed:* This is the column that will help turn a "ho-hum" fund-
*Costs Donated* raiser into a highly efficient and profitable event. Each
donor who underwrites a portion of your fund-raising costs
provides you with a lower and more attractive cost per dollar raised. When you can logically demonstrate how the
donation affects the "bottom line," the donor will feel
appreciated and motivated to say, "Yes, I'll volunteer my
products/services."

24. *Subtotal Costs:* Place the total of columns 17 and 21 in column 24. You may
*Budgeted* choose to use a dotted line across the fund-raising organizer to separate each task.

25. *Subtotal Costs: Actual* Place the total of columns 18 and 22 in column 25. This is
the subtotal that will be an integral part of the planning for
next year.

26. *Subtotal Costs:* Place the total of columns 19 and 23 in column 26. Take a
*Donated* look at this donated subtotal before repeating the fund-
raiser. This will enable you to anticipate the impact additional donated services would have on the success of the
activity.

27. *Progress Indicators:* Record the target dates for the completion of those activities
*Meeting and Report Dates* that comprise the action step or task.

28. *Comments* Place important notes and comments concerning any cost
savings for the activity or ideas on how to improve the activity in this column.

29. *Staff Allocation* Record the staff position, the fringe benefits, and the wages
for that position, and the percentage of time and total salary
for that position that will be charged to the fund-raising
activity.

30. *Total Raised* Place the total amount of income generated from the activity in this box.

*31. Minus Costs*  Budgeted costs from column 24 are totaled and entered on line 31. Enter the actual costs (column 25) rather than the Budgeted costs when they are available.

*32. Equal Net Raised*  Subtract line 31 from line 30 to obtain the net amount of funds raised.

*33. Total Donated Costs*  Place the total from each task subtotaled on column 26 in this space. You should know the value of the donated costs, but be careful not to add this item into the costs (line 31), since the result will be a significantly lower net-raised amount (line 32) and could adversely affect your cost of fund-raising.

*34. Cost Per Dollar Raised*  Enter line 31 (costs) and divide by line 30 (total raised), and then multiply by 100 to get the cost per dollar raised or percent. For example:

$$\text{actual costs} \div \text{total raised} \times 100 = \text{cost of fund-raising}$$
$$100 \div (400 \times 100) = 25\% \text{ cost of fund-raising}$$

The resulting figure allows you to compare all your fund-raising activities for their effectiveness. You must remember that the cost per dollar raised should not be the only way to evaluate a funding activity. Some excellent fund-raising activities cost more money than they generate in revenue for three years, but become quite efficient over a four-year period.

Many states require that you report the cost per dollar raised by your organization or the amount of the budget that is expended on fund-raising. Several professional fund-raising groups question the fairness of these regulations because they favor organizations that utilize fund-raising activities with a low rate of return and a high initial cost that have a great payoff over several years. These professional groups believe that such rules make strategic planning more difficult for all nonprofits, especially those like your

Internet Technology Support Group that are newly formed. The reverse side of your fund-raising organizer provides a log for recording the information usually just jotted on loose paper or stick-on notes.

*35. Activity*    Place the activity title or name from number 2 on this line.

*36. Meetings*    List meetings related to the fund-raiser. Log individuals who attend, and record the results or additional tasks generated from the meetings.

*37. Telephone Log*    List frequently called and other important phone numbers, and/or important telephone calls made and received. Include dates, names, and results.

*38. Committee Members*    List committee members, staff, volunteer names, and phone numbers.

*39. Key Individuals*    List the individuals who are not staff or volunteers but are critical to the fund-raising activity's successful completion. Also list corresponding phone numbers.

*40. Miscellaneous Expenses*    The budget on the opposite side of the organizer provides a record of unallocated miscellaneous expenditures. As the fund-raiser is launched, you will invariably encounter personal expenses that were not anticipated, or perhaps were too difficult to place on the organizer. For example, keep a log of parking fees, mileage costs, and last-minute supply expenses that never seem to get recorded. Place them here as they occur and you will know exactly how much additional support your group should request payment for or receive credit for donating.

**Strategies for Raising Funds**    The following fund-raising matrix (Figure 10.2) is provided to help you evaluate different types of fund-raising activities including: special events, thons, personal solicitation, annual campaigns, membership drives, direct mail, telemarketing,

Figure 10.2 Fund-Raising Matrix

| A<br>Type of Fund-Raising Activity | B<br>Donor Level | C<br>Personnel Costs | D<br>Volunteer Involvment | E<br>Public-Relations Value | F<br>Response Rate | G<br>Donor Qualification Factor | H<br>Activity Life | I<br>Up-Front Costs | J<br>Return on Investment |
|---|---|---|---|---|---|---|---|---|---|
| Special events | B/C | Med/High | High | High | Med | Med | Med | Med/Low | Med |
| Thons | B/C | Low | High | High | Med | Med | High | Low | High |
| Personal solicitation | A/B | Low | High | Low | High | High | High | Low | High |
| Membership drives/Annual Campaigns | A/B/C | Med | Med | Low/med | High | High | High | Med/High | High |
| Direct mail | B/C | Med | Low | Low | Low | High | High | Med/High | High |
| Telemarketing | B/C | High | Med | Low | Med | Med/High | Low | Med/High | High |
| Memorial giving | A/B | Low | Low | Low | High | High | High | Low | High |
| Capital campaigns | A/B | High | High | High | High | High | Low/Med | High | High |
| Bequests/planned giving | A/B | Low/Med | Med | Low | Med/High | High | High | Low/med | High |
| Credit cards | A/B | Low | Low | Low | Med | Med/High | Med | Low | High |
| District bond issues | A/B/C | Low | Med/High | High | High | Low | Low | High | Variable |

memorial giving, capital campaigns, bequests and planned giving, credit cards, and district bond issues. Factors that will help you compare the major types of fund-raising activities are listed across the top. These include: donor level, personnel costs, volunteer involvement, public relations value, response rate, donor qualification factor, activity life, up-front costs, and return on investment. Each variable for each fund-raising activity has been given a rating of either low, medium, or high. By understanding the different aspects of each of the fund-raising activities, you will be able to determine which strategies are the most feasible for you to implement based on your group's specific constraints, strengths, and needs. You will then be able to develop a strategic mix of activities based on their optimum cost-benefit return, public relations value, activity life, etc.

For example, when your support group is just formed, you probably will have few resources to expend on up-front costs and paid staff (personnel). Therefore, as you review the fund-raising matrix, you must focus on those fund-raising activities that can be accomplished with the limited resources you have available and the constraints within which your group must operate. Your main fund-raising objective will be to alert the public of your mission in the most cost-efficient manner possible. You will need to generate the maximum return (more donors and more money) for whatever investment you make.

If your group has been functioning for a while and already raising funds, you will be able to focus on more sophisticated activities that qualify donors, move them up the donor pyramid, and increase the size of their gifts.

Review the fund-raising matrix and develop a draft of a two- or three-year plan that will include initiating and changing the activities you select to meet your funding goals. After selecting the activities in a general sense (special event, "thon"), refine your ideas (gala, math-a-thon), and estimate the net funds needed to meet your project goal of adding to and improving your school's Internet technology.

*1. Special Events*
Most groups begin their fund-raising efforts by sponsoring a special event.

Column A: Type of Fund-Raising Activity
This column lists the major categories of fund-raising. The term "special events" as it relates to fund-raising is commonly used to describe only certain types of events that raise funds. In actuality, any attempt to raise money could be considered a special event, especially if your organization has not previously attempted it. "Special event" is commonly used as a catch-all term that: (1) applies to an event with a definite time frame and a special appeal, and (2) covers any event that is not included in any of the other fund-raising categories. It includes such activities as raffles, bingo, carnivals, balls, celebrity banquets, auctions, flower days, dances, concerts, candle sales, book sales, craft sales, card sales, duck races—you name it!

Column B: Donor Level
Special events fund-raising is usually designed to appeal to the C and B levels. The $100-per-ticket gala dinner/dance could be considered a qualifier for the B level; while a $5 pancake breakfast or barbeque would be a level-C event. By increasing the cost of a special event the target level of the donor can move from level C or B– to level B+. In addition, some special events can have several levels of donor commitment and, therefore, include donors from all levels of the donor pyramid.

Column C: Personnel Costs
This column is designed to help you evaluate the allocation of paid personnel to the different types of fund-raising strategies. Some fund-raising techniques require paid staff or consultants. While volunteers may be suitable substitutes for paid personnel when implementing certain fund-raising activities, using nonprofessionals in other fund-raising activities may be difficult, or may significantly alter the success of the activity. Naturally, your ability to use paid personnel will depend upon your financial resources, as well as the availability of paid staff. While a district-level effort may

have access to staff, a building-level Internet Technology Support Group may have to rely more heavily on volunteers and will have to consider this factor when selecting which fund-raising strategies to use.

Special events fund-raising normally requires a medium to high commitment of paid personnel. While the gala may appear to "go off without a hitch," that impression arises because a paid person worked with the decoration committee's volunteer chairperson or the public relations committee to insure that the fund-raiser was not a disaster.

**Column D:**
**Volunteer Involvement**

The need for volunteers is another important consideration when evaluating the various types of fund-raising activities. Some fund-raising activities are extremely cost-efficient due to the high use of volunteers. Using volunteers rather than paid personnel can have a dramatic effect on the net revenues raised by an activity. Remember, volunteers are in limited supply and must be used wisely. You may feel tempted to encourage volunteers to commit to a fund-raising activity by assuring them that many other volunteers will help out. A real mess will develop if the other volunteers do not materialize, or if those who do have weak skills.

*One key to the success of a special event is volunteers with a high level of commitment and the willingness to follow up on all details.*

Most special events fund-raising requires a high level of volunteer involvement. Hence, one of the keys to the success of a special event is to recruit volunteers with a high level of commitment and the willingness to follow up on all details.

**Column E:**
**Public-Relations Value**

Almost every fund-raising activity is said to have a public relations value. Fund-raising activities that promote the organization's name and mission, or position the organization as a credible group with a positive image, warrant a high public relations score. Many fund-raising activities promote an organization's name, but not its purpose and mission. Name recognition is indeed important, but it is not as useful as the recognition and promotion of both the name and the cause.

Special events usually have a high level of public relations value. Even those individuals who do not purchase a ticket to the dinner/dance or the pancake breakfast see and hear the advertisements endorsing the organization's cause.

**Column F: Response Rate**  This column is used to record the expected rate of response from the total number of potential donors contacted. The expected rate of response varies with each type of fund-raising activity. For example, a direct mail response rate of 2 per 1,000 contacts would be considered excellent, while a one to five donor response would be considered very poor for face-to-face fund-raising.

Special events fund-raising usually generates a medium rate of response. While a high rate of response is always wonderful, three out of four people you ask will not buy a ticket to your pancake breakfast.

**Column G: Donor Qualification Factor**  This variable rates each type of fund-raising activity by the degree of loyalty a donor must have to want to repeat the activity. This is an important factor since it is what leads individuals to qualify themselves. Conversely, excessive focus on this area may influence fund-raising decisions that are targeted away from donors who respond with lower levels of involvement and smaller gifts. Special events fund-raising has a medium donor qualification factor. A special event fund-raiser can either be targeted toward the loyal "old guard" that attends every event or be designed to appeal to a new and larger donor population. To determine how loyal your donors are to your special event, ask yourself how many donors would "miss" the event if you did not repeat it next year. How many would call your school to ask for the date of your Internet Technology Computer-Rama because they wanted to be sure not to miss it?

**Column H: Activity Life**  This column deals with either the length of time during which, or the number of times that, a fund-raising activity can be successfully repeated. Some special events have a very long activity life. Donors may look forward to the event and attend it for years. An annual "bash" at a private secondary school could have an activity life of well over 20 years, with some of the original donors attending every year, and new members attending for an average of five years. Raffles and pancake breakfasts may not have the same life span. Therefore, the "activity life" rating for special events is medium.

Most special event fund-raisers reach a peak after three or four years. Then they plateau and begin to show a decline in both the number of attendees and net revenue. Fundraisers must always be ready to add a new component to a special event or to demonstrate flexibility in replacing events that are losing their ability to draw donors and participants.

**Column I: Up-Front Costs** This variable is important because it allows you to evaluate the true costs of each type of fund-raising. With limited capital available, you need to plan events according to your cash flow, and you must choose a mix of fund-raising activities that best provides the income needed for your Internet/technology project. Wide diversity exists here. For example, suppose your group decides to sponsor a raffle to generate funds to develop an Internet-based exchange program with students in Mexico. The prize, a trip to Mexico, has been jointly donated by a travel agency and an airline. In this instance, the up-front costs are minimal and basically consist of printing the raffle tickets for students to sell. The risk associated with not selling the projected number of tickets is small because the prize is donated and the sales vehicle consists of volunteers. The price of the raffle tickets would be based on how high the up-front costs are and who the purchasers will be. If the purchasers will primarily be students and parents, the tickets might be priced at $2.00 with a special sales offer of three for $5.00. This pricing is acceptable because the up front costs are low.

When the up-front costs increase significantly, the scenario changes dramatically. Consider the situation of a group that wants to raffle a car. Suppose the car was arranged to be supplied at cost from a concerned car dealer who wants his daughter's school to increase its Internet/technology resources. The problem is that the up-front cost of the car must be paid no matter how many tickets are sold. If only a few tickets are sold and little money is generated, the car must still be raffled off. This result means the group experiences a major net loss!

So while you may be able to sell tickets to a dance before you pay the deposit for the band, the up-front costs and the risk of having to carry out the event at a loss are real. When dealing with high priced admission or raffle tickets, you should test your donor base first to see if you have "enough" individuals with the interest and resources to participate.

In most circumstances, special events fund-raisers have low to medium up-front risk costs. The more that is donated for the special event, the lower your up-front costs and the lower your risk. If the car group had arranged for a local antique car collector to donate a vintage car, the benefactor would have received a tax deduction, and most of the group's up-front costs and risks would be eliminated.

*When dealing with high priced admission or raffle tickets, you should test your donor base first to see if you have "enough" individuals with the interest and resources to participate.*

**Column J: Return on Investment**

This factor requires careful examination. You should be concerned with both the cost per dollar raised and the return on the time it takes to invest in the activity. The time factor is a critically important aspect when evaluating the return on your fund-raising dollar. Some fund-raising strategies, such as planned giving and bequests, have an excellent return when evaluated over the long term. However, it is imprudent planning to have your school listed as a beneficiary in an estate 20 years after you have discarded your dream of Internet access and enhancement due to a lack of funds.

The reverse is equally true and very common. Some groups never consider bequests or other long-term strategies. Although special events have a medium return on investment, one must realize that these events take time each year to sponsor. However, you only have to develop a bequest and/or planned giving program once, and once you have done so, you can use your time to plan and implement other fund-raising activities.

Developing a mix of fund-raising activities is the real key to fund-raising success; and your ability to do so will depend on the factors listed on the fund-raising matrix and other variables such as your geographic area and the number and wealth of the donors in your area.

Special events have been used by schools to raise funds for school projects for years. However, you will find it difficult to realize enough net funds from bake sales and other product sales to improve access to the Internet and affect your technology needs. Therefore, you must brainstorm special events that focus on your group's mission and have the potential to raise a significant amount of funds in a cost-efficient way.

One special event you may wish to try is a Mystery Ball. Volunteers could sell the tickets to the ball for $25 each, and the mystery would be to discover where the ball was to be held. In actuality no ball would take place, so all the ticket proceeds would go to your project, and your only real up-front costs would be the printing of the tickets!

The best special event fund-raiser has yet to be devised. You don't necessarily have to copy what some other organization has done. Once you know your donors, your prospective donors and your community's special interests, it will be easy to devise your own. But whatever you sponsor, have the special event focus on your mission whenever possible.

Reinforce your mission from the title of the event to the activities that occur. For example, if you choose to have a raffle, offer a prize that is related to the Internet and technology. If you are raising funds for Internet access, don't raffle off a dinner for four at an exclusive local restaurant. Instead, raffle a modem, a one year's subscription to America Online, a new laptop, or a laser printer.

❖

*The best special event fund-raiser has yet to be devised.*

❖

*2. Thons*  A "thon" is a form of special event fund-raising that employs a large group of volunteers who enlist sponsors to pay them a predetermined amount of money for the completion of a selected activity.

Column A: Type of Fund-Raising Activity  Common thon activities include:

- Answering math questions correctly (math-a-thon).
- Riding a bike a number of miles (bike-a-thon).
- Completing a number of ski runs (ski-a-thon).
- Walking a number of miles (walk-a-thon).
- Dancing for a certain number of hours (dance-a-thon).
- Bowling a certain number of pins (bowl-a-thon).

If you can measure it and sponsor it, you can "a-thon" it. For example, you could even sponsor a "roll-a-thon," in which children roll their pennies, nickels, and dimes, and sponsors pay a fee for each roll assembled.

Thons are based on a pyramid principal. A captain is selected to enlist five volunteers, who then get 25 sponsors to pay for each mile walked, math problem answered correctly, or book read. The base of the pyramid can be extended dramatically if a service club, church group, or other group that can utilize its members is involved. A bowling league could get teachers to enlist in a bowl-a-thon, for example, and pay a certain amount per pin.

Your ability to sell your mission and convince multiple donors (sponsors) to pay for the activity performed by each volunteer will determine the success of your fundraiser. In addition, you will need to recruit coordinators who will herd the volunteers, who in turn solicit the sponsors and collect the funds. Competition between offices or teams, and prizes for groups can be very effective in thon endeavors.

Column B: Donor Level  Thons are basically level-C activities except for the qualifying volunteers (level B) and some corporate donors who contribute food, prizes, etc. (level B). Thons are C-level fund-raisers that involve many people and are a lot of fun.

Column C: Personnel Costs

Thons have low personnel costs. They are designed to be volunteer intensive and should involve a minimum of paid staff or consultants.

Column D: Volunteer Involvement

Thons score high when it comes to the use of volunteers. They utilize a large number of volunteers for a variety of activities—including everything from public relations, to committee membership, to sponsor recruitment, to thon participation.

Column E: Public-Relations Value

Thons score very high in this category. They are highly visible events in which the news media can get involved and will usually cover. In fact, involving television and radio personalities in the thon and getting a local broadcasting company to sponsor it will considerably boost the event. In terms of media involvement, radiothons and telethons are at the high end of the continuum and differ from a walk- or bike-a-thon in that the repetition is not miles ridden or walked, but the marathon of hours they stay on the air to raise the funds.

In order to entice individuals to telephone with pledges, you must create a pledge system that is automated and allows you to mail pledge cards and return envelopes immediately. This can be accomplished by computer or through the use of carbonless pledge forms.

Each day that elapses before pledge cards and envelopes are sent out will result in an estimated loss of 10 percent of the total amount pledged during the thon. The public has a very, very short memory.

The sample fund-raising organizer in Figure 10.3 outlines the results from the second year of a radio-thon that had a built-in pledge reminder system. A pledge reminder system did not exist in the first year of the radio-thon. Through the use of a late last-minute mailing of pledge

# Figure 10.3  Sample Fund-Raising Organizer

**FUND RAISING ORGANIZER™**
David G. Bauer Associates, Inc.

ACTIVITY: Radio-thon  COORDINATOR: M. Schmidt  START DATE: 3/1  END DATE: 10/1

DESCRIPTION: WBEE On-Site Radio-thon

PURPOSE: Public Relations / Raise money  DONOR PYRAMID LEVEL: C  GOAL: $ 20,000

| ACTION STEPS / TASKS | Begin | Projected Completion/Completion | Actual Completion/Completion | WHO Staff, Volunteers, Consultants | SALARY PER HOUR | SALARY | PERSONNEL NEEDED — TIME | PROJECT TIME | PROJECT SALARY | COSTS Budgeted | COSTS Actual | RESOURCES NEEDED — WHAT Supplies, Equipment, Facilities | COSTS Budgeted | COSTS Actual | SUBTOTAL COSTS Budgeted | SUBTOTAL COSTS Actual | PROGRESS INDICATORS Meetings, Report Dates | COMMENTS |
|---|---|---|---|---|---|---|---|---|---|---|---|---|---|---|---|---|---|---|
| A. Set up committee. | 3/1 | 4/1 | | Vol. Coord. WBEE Staff | | | 2 days | | | $? | | | | | | | | |
| A-1 Review last year's event for | | | | | | | | | | | | | | | | | | |
| suggestions / changes | | | | | | | | | | | | | | | | | | |
| A-2 Report dates selected by | | | | Exec. Asst | 125 | | 1 day | | | | | | | | | | | |
| WBEE | | | | | | | | | | | | | | | | | | |
| B. Print list of last years | 5/1 | 4/1 | | Vol. Coord. Consultant | | | 3 days | | | $? | | list of donors 200 | | | | | Can we mail to last year's who |
| pledges. (2,000+) | | | | | | | | | | $? | | | | | | | didn't phone in |
| B-1 Select largest givers (500+) | | | | INFRO | | | | | | $? | | Sort list 100 | | | | | this year? |
| to receive a special | | | | WBEE | | | | | | | | labels/Mail 200 | | | | | |
| thank-you or put in special | | | | | | | | | | | | Bold Stuff | | | | | |
| contest for repeat gift | | | | | | | | | | | | Postage 110 | | | | | |
| B-2 Set up upgrade contest | | | | Vol. Coord. | | | | | | | | | | | | | |
| or mailing | | | | | | | | | | | | | | | | | |
| B-3 Set up matching or special | | | | | | | | | | | | | | | | | |
| promo | | | | | | | | | | | | | | | | | |
| C. Set up location. | 5/1 | 6/30 | | Vol. Coord. WBEE | | | | | | | | | | | | | |
| C-1 Power requirements | | | | | | | | | | | | | | | | | |
| C-2 Refreshments | | | | Exec. Asst | | | .5 day | 62.50 | | $? | | | | | | | |
| D. Print pledge forms / envelopes | 5/15 | 6/30 | | Vol. Coord. | | | | | | | | 3000 NCR 4 part form 250 | | | | | |
| D-1 Use cardboxless forms and | | | | | | | | | | | | 3000 envelopes 15 | | | | | |
| instant mailer envelopes | | | | | | | | | | | | 2000 stamps 500 | | | | | |
| E. Get sponsor to put up $500 to | 4/1 | 4/1 | | Vol. Team | | | 1 day | | | | | | | | | | |
| for t-shirts and promos | | | | | | | | | | | | | | | | | |
| E-1 Volunteer team to get sponsor | | | | | | | | | | | | | | | | | |
| F. Put on -thon (date to be determined) | | | | Exec. Asst. Vol. Coord. Committee | 125 | | 1 day | 125 | | | | 10 phone lines 250 Refreshm. | $? | | | | Will need $25,000 in pledges to |
| Estimated August / September | | | | | | | | | | | | | | | | | get $ 20,000 in |
| F-1 Set up promos for volunteers – | | | | | | | | | | | | | | | | | Phone lines |
| Volunteers for 16 hours of | | | | | | | | | | | | | | | | | donated last year |
| -thon | | | | | | | | | | | | | | | | | Call R. Bittner |
| G. Follow-up | | | | Vol. Coord. INFRO | | | 1 day | 125 | | | | | | | | | |
| G-1 Pledge Cards mailed | | | | Exec. Asst | | | 1 day | | | | | | | | | | |
| G-2 Tally funds—provide report | | | | | | | | | | | | | | | | | |
| H. Mail reminders to pledges of | | | | Exec. Asst | 125 | | 1 day | 125 | | | | | | | | | |
| $5.00 and over. | | | | | | | | | | | | | | | | | |
| TOTAL COSTS | | | | | | | 562.50 | | 562.50 | | | | 1425 | | 2197 | | Estimate |

STAFF ALLOCATION:

| POSITION | SALARY | SALARY PER HOUR | PROJECT TIME | PROJECT SALARY |
|---|---|---|---|---|
| Exec. Asst | 30,000 | 125/day | 4.5 day/s | 562.50 |

STAFF COMPUTATION SCALE:
40 Hrs/Week = 160 Hrs/Month = 1,920 Hrs/Year
5 Days/Week = 20 Days/Month = 240 Days/Year

Cost Per Dollar Raised = 11 %
$2,197 (Costs) ÷ 20,000 (Total Raised) x 100

| | |
|---|---|
| TOTAL RAISED: | 20,000 |
| MINUS COSTS: (Budgeted or Actual) | 2,197 |
| EQUALS NET RAISED: | 17,813 |
| TOTAL DONATED COSTS: | |

reminders, the loss was reduced to $12,000. In other words, of the $30,000, only $18,000 was collected. To avoid the problem of unpaid pledges in the second year, pledge cards were mailed to previous donors in advance of the thon. Pledge cards were also mailed as soon as gifts were phoned in. These two simple steps dramatically reduced the difference between the amount pledged and the amount received. When done properly, most thons collect 80–90 percent of their pledges.

Column F: Response Rate    The participation rate of those contacted to become involved in a thon is medium. This includes both the volunteer performing the activity (riding the bike, dancing) and the donor sponsoring the volunteer. Not everyone will say yes, but you should expect at least one in 50.

Column G: Donor Qualification Factor    Individuals who enter the Donor Pyramid through a thon may become attached to the activity, whether biking, inline skating, or swimming, and prefer to continue it for many years. Because many look forward to the annual thon, participate in it year after year, and get sponsors to become involved every year, the donor qualification factor for the thon is fairly good (medium).

Column H: Activity Life    Thons have a life of their own and, therefore, score high in this category. By tracking the revenue generated by a thon that is repeated yearly, you will be able to determine when the activity has peaked and when you may be losing donor interest.

Column I: Up-Front Costs    Thons do not require much capital support. Since they are volunteer-based and rely heavily on face-to-face fund-raising, they have low up-front costs. Costs include such things as printing flyers, purchasing prizes, etc.

Column J: Return on Investment    Thons provide a high rate of return for the small amount of capital and staff/volunteer time invested, and they can provide a good source of revenue for your Internet technology project. You have a resource in your students who will enjoy both participating in the thon and soliciting sponsors for their activity. Donors (sponsors) have a hard time turning down a student who is willing to do something (dance, bike, walk, do math problems) for a cause.

*3. Personal Solicitation*     Personal solicitation is the most effective way to attract donors. People give to other people, and especially to people they know.

Column A: Type of Fund-Raising Activity     Most fund-raising strategies involve a person asking another for money. The personal solicitation strategy is distinguishable from the others in that a gift is the purpose of asking— not tickets or products. You ask for money to support the mission. Since no exchange of a tangible product takes place (except possibly a token of recognition), this form of fundraising is very efficient for securing a maximum of net funds.

Column B: Donor Level     While people ask other people for money at all donor levels, personal solicitation is not the same as solicitation for a raffle ticket. Personal solicitation typically generates medium to large size gifts and is an A- or B-level activity. If you have few donors at the A/B level, you must cultivate them and allow them to grow. The most common starting point is to have your support group or founders ask each other for a donation.

Column C: Personnel Costs     Since the effectiveness of face-to-face fund-raising increases if the solicitor is a peer and friend of the prospective donor, the best programs are volunteer based. Therefore, personnel costs should be low to nonexistent for this fund-raising activity.

Personal gift solicitation is the pinnacle of donor development. Donors who are personally solicited should have already responded to low-level-involvement fund-raising, volunteered, and qualified themselves by moving from the C level to the B or A level. Even if they are dedicated members of your support group, these high level donors need to be asked to contribute more, to increase their commitment, and to solicit their fellow members.

**Column D:**
**Volunteer Involvement**

Volunteer involvement in personal solicitation is critical to its success. However, personal solicitation does not require a tremendous effort by a lot of volunteers. What it does require is board and support group members willing to dedicate a minimal amount of time to generate a large amount of money. To be successful at personal solicitation, volunteers must have a clear sense of their group's mission, familiarity with the Donor Emancipation Proclamation, and a commitment to giving themselves.

**Column E:**
**Public-Relations Value**

The public relations value of personal solicitation is relatively low. Except for the token certificates, pens, mugs, and plaques there is little recognition of the personal solicitation of donations. The public relations realized from a special awards dinner is about as much as you can expect. Real public relations is seen in the fact that a current donor cared enough to ask a friend for money for the cause.

**Column F: Response Rate**

The level of response to personal solicitation is normally high (20–70 percent). The 70 percent rate is for solicitation by a peer for a project of which the donor has prior knowledge. The 20 percent rate is for a capital campaign.

❖

*Personal solicitation*
*is the most effective*
*way to attract donors.*

❖

You can take several steps to insure that you will have a high rate of response to personal solicitation when the time comes. First and foremost, you must initiate several C-level events to develop your donor base and discern the responsiveness of your potential donors. Never, for example, should you jump into a large capital campaign dependent on personal solicitation before you have qualified donors. This effort would meet with a high rate of rejection and a rate of response well below 20 percent; and whenever your personal solicitation response rate falls below 20 percent, you can expect to have a difficult time helping your volunteer solicitors deal with the rejection they are receiving.

**Column G: Donor Qualification Factor**  Personal solicitation is the most satisfying form of fund-raising for the donor and has a high donor qualification factor. The giving transaction is complete when the donor hands the check to the solicitor, who of course says, "Thank you." The sense of completion and satisfaction is addictive, and when the giving transaction is undertaken properly, it is an experience that the donor will want to reinforce and perform again. In fact, the donor will expect to be asked again.

**Column H: Activity Life**  Since the life-blood of nonprofit organizations comes from this fund-raising activity, the organization ceases when personal solicitation does. This form of fund-raising has a high activity life.

**Column I: Up-Front Costs**  The up-front costs for personal solicitation are low. The cost for printing the necessary materials is minimal, and the only other costs are for the training of the volunteer solicitors.

**Column J: Return on Investment**  Personal solicitation has the highest return on investment of all fund-raising activities. However, organizations usually do not start with this form of fund-raising as their first activity. Personal solicitation is so productive because both the solicitor and the donor have not only been involved in the organization, but also have qualified themselves by donating time, and feel it would cause a values conflict *not* to support the organization. In addition, a peer (or another person known to them) is making the request and, provided they have the money to reply positively, they will.

Compare that scenario to one in which a solicitor approaches a stranger who has never supported his or her organization. As you can well imagine, the outcome would be quite different.

*4. Membership Drives Annual and Campaigns*

A membership drive is a fund-raising approach that is employed by many school foundations and school technology support groups. After checking with any other existing technology-fund development groups at your school, your Internet Technology Support Group may decide to explore this option.

Column A: Type of Fund-Raising Activity

The concept is based upon designating a defined period of time during which a public relations campaign is undertaken to promote the payment of a fee for membership in your group. Whether your scope of concern has transformed your initial Internet access and technology group into a full fledged tax exempt organization with a board, or you are operating under the tax status of an other organization, a membership drive will provide you with:

- An early test of the acceptance of the other fund-raising activities included in your plan. For instance, if individuals aren't willing to join your group for $25, you can be pretty sure they won't make a $100 gift to you later.
- The beginnings of your donor pyramid with the donors' names, addresses, phone numbers, and the level of their membership and commitment.

In order to work properly, donors must understand that joining your membership drive does not mean you are asking them for a one-time gift. Asking your donors only one time per year for a contribution would be a violation of the Donor Emancipation Proclamation. However, since many groups begin this way, membership drives are often referred to as "annual appeals," and that sounds like one request per year. In reality, the membership fee paid by the donor should be considered an entrance fee into your donor pyramid. Members should understand that your organization not only has different membership levels, but that you also have other fund-raising activities throughout the year.

The principles of sound fund-raising can be employed to make the event more exciting and effective whether it is held in conjunction with a yearly membership drive or an annual funding campaign. Using levels of annual giving are very effective in upgrading donors. Levels of giving can also increase participation in and revenue generated by direct mail and telephone campaigns.

Column B: Donor Level
Annual campaigns appeal most to donors from levels A, B, and C who are already committed and involved with the organization. Attracting new members, those who are currently outside of the donor pyramid, requires a substantial amount of additional effort.

Column C: Personnel Costs
The development of printed material and the management of member names lists can require a significant investment of time by paid staff or personnel if your support group is taking the route of hiring paid staff. Analyze the costs by examining the estimated and actual times listed on your fund-raising organizer. In general, annual campaigns and membership drives require a medium level of investment in personnel costs.

Column D: Volunteer Involvement
Annual campaigns can utilize a significant number of volunteers and therefore have a medium rating for volunteer involvement. However, many organizations use volunteers ineffectively in annual campaigns and membership drives by having them type labels, fold brochures, stuff envelopes, etc. These activities can be professionally accomplished at a reasonable rate, thereby freeing volunteers to perform other tasks that have a greater impact on the cost per dollar raised.

Column E: Public-Relations Value
The annual campaign or membership drive has limited public relations value. The mailing to past members serves as a reminder of your important work, and a renewal of their commitment. If the mailing is to prospective donors, some

benefits come from name recognition. Generally speaking, the public relations value of annual campaigns or membership drives is low to medium unless you can involve the community and get free support through radio, television, or newspaper.

Column F: Response Rate    The annual campaign differs from other fund-raising activities because members expect to be solicited, and in essence, position the event in their minds. Therefore, the expected response rate is relatively high (60–80 percent). Recapturing lapsed donors can be a problem in the annual appeal, just as it is in direct mail and other fund-raising activities such as special mailings. You can use a follow-up phone to re-enlist the tardy or lapsed donor.

Column G: Donor Qualifications Factor    The annual campaign has a high degree of donor loyalty. Donors expect, and some even wait for, the appeal.

Column H: Activity Life    Annual campaigns and membership drives have a high activity life. Some fund-raisers wish annual appeals would die, but they tend to recycle instead. For example, the March of Dimes is one organization that developed a special annual appeal. The appeal was so successful it lived beyond the health problem for which it was created—polio. And now, its annual appeal is directed toward birth defects.

Column I: Up-Front Costs    Annual campaigns and membership drives have medium-to-high-level up-front costs that are primarily incurred through printing, postage, and the handling of related membership materials.

Column J: Return on Investment    Annual campaigns and membership drives have a high return on investment. This is particularly true if they are not thought of as happening only once per year.

5. *Direct Mail*    Direct mail is an extremely effective fund-raising tool. Most experts would rank it second only to personal solicitation.

Some experts would argue that without direct mail you have fewer donors to solicit in person, and that, therefore, direct mail is the most important form of fund-raising.

**Column A: Type of Fund-Raising Activity** Direct mail fund-raising involves the solicitation of small and medium sized donations through written communication to prospective donors, current donors, or past donors. The word *direct* distinguishes this form of fund-raising from appeals that are included in newsletters or distributed at meetings. Direct mail fund-raising can be used to attract first time donors, to upgrade existing donors, or to enhance a telemarketing program wherein you phone donors as well as contact them through the mail. (The fund-raising matrix analysis of direct mail is based upon the conventional model of mailing to both new and existing donors.)

In direct mail fund-raising, pictures and words are used to convince people to write and mail a check. Motivating a donor to give is difficult no matter what, but it is a particular challenge when no one from the organization is actually present. For this reason, direct mail has a high failure rate. Whether a direct mail activity is successful or not depends on the rate of response to the number of pieces mailed.

**Column B: Donor Level** Direct mail marketing targets the C- and B-level donors who are currently giving or have given in the past but have lapsed. It can also be aimed at prospective donors who have yet to be approached (below level C).

**Column C: Personnel Costs** Whether you use a consultant or staff to create your direct mail piece, manage your donor list, and target and purchase mailing lists, the personnel costs related to direct mail are medium to high. If staff need to be trained in this area, your personnel costs may be very high. The adage "It takes money to make money" certainly applies to direct mail fund-raising.

The cost of consultants alone will appear expensive as you analyze this activity, especially when you consider that consultants can make mistakes, too! To determine whether you should "do it yourself" or not, get quotes from several consultants and get references. The quotes should be for exactly the same services to the same level of donor lists or groups and to potential donors lists. By obtaining quotes and checking references, you should be able to dramatically cut your risks.

The most crucial variable is the choice of mailing lists when using direct mail to acquire level-C donors. The more you use direct mail to solicit first time donors, the more costly the acquisition becomes. Therefore, you must have a good idea of the type of donor most likely to respond to your cause, and to the amount you are seeking. Companies specializing in direct mail have lists that are divided into categories including practically everything from income and neighborhood to the number of cavities the head of the household has! These prospect lists come in the thousands, tens of thousands, and hundreds of thousands. You can select lists and purchase them, or borrow them from other nonprofit groups. Many nonprofits purchase lists and labels, and have bulk mailers handle the process of sorting, folding, stuffing, and mailing the envelopes. The size and cost of the mailing will be a factor in your decision to try it yourself. Deciding whether to do it yourself also depends on who your target group is. If the mailing is going to target your past donors, then you are mailing to a qualified list of individuals, and you can expect your response rate to be much higher than the nondonor (prospect) group. Since your response rate will be greater, your risk will be lower, and you may decide to do it yourself.

> *Over 14 billion pieces of mail were sent out by nonprofits last year, and they will continue to mail because direct mail brings in money.*

**Column D: Volunteer Involvement**

The involvement of volunteers in direct mail is generally low. Qualified volunteers can be used to assist in your direct mail campaign, but, if possible, you may not want to use them to perform menial tasks such as folding materials, stuffing envelopes, sealing envelopes, placing labels on envelopes, or sorting letters in zip code order. These tasks can be better performed by machines and are inexpensive to have done. For example, the machine folding and inserting of letters into envelopes costs approximately $15 per thousand sheets.

**Column E: Public-Relations Value** Direct mail fund-raising uses recognition value. The donors remember seeing your name. There is some positioning value to the recognition, and any knowledge that prospective donors may obtain is beneficial. However, the level of public-relations value for direct mail is low since many prospective donors discard appeals before they even read them.

**Column F: Response Rate** A direct mail response of 1 percent of the number mailed is considered good, and a 2 percent response rate is excellent. The low response rate is compensated for by the large number of pieces mailed. You can assume that ten thousand pieces mailed may get a response of 100 donors, and that would be good. Over 14 billion pieces of mail were sent out by nonprofit groups last year, and they will continue to mail because direct mail brings in money.

The tremendous potential of direct mail to generate funds—even with a .6–1.2 percent response rate—is illustrated by David Barnes Associates, Inc., in Figure 10.4 (on pages 230–31). Barnes, like other direct mail consultants, has enhanced many donor pyramids with his fund-raising techniques. As you review the Barnes example, keep in mind that although Barnes's "average" came from years of record keeping, your organization is by no means "average." (Barnes Associates produces *National Fund-Raiser,* a monthly "how to" newsletter. To request a sample copy or to subscribe, call 800-231-4157.)

The key to direct mail success is to target new mailing lists and to remail those who do not respond. Between 15 and 20 percent of your donors will drop off your lists each year. Professional fund-raisers have demonstrated the need to mail to lapsed donors four times while you appeal to

**Figure 10.4
Acquiring New Donors
through Direct Mail
Prospecting—
Why It Makes Sense**

Direct mail prospecting for new donors is expensive. It is almost certain that you will spend more to acquire brand new donors than you will bring in. So, why should you invest in donor acquisition when your initial return is less than expenses? Here are two very good reasons:

1. No matter how sophisticated your development program, you will experience a normal attrition rate of 15–20% each year. If you do not acquire new donors, your current, active base will be reduced by more than half in five short years.

2. Each group of newly acquired donors will cost you money in their first year of giving. In the second year, that same group will return a handsome profit on the second-year investment and reduce the cumulative loss significantly. In the third year and each year thereafter, your return per dollar invested will soar. It is important to realize that your initial investment is to secure *donors* not dollars. As you cultivate, mature, renew and upgrade new donors, your investment begins to yield high dividends.

The following illustration shows you the *profitability* of direct mail prospecting: Assume that you mail 100,000 prospecting letters this year to selected people who have never contributed to your organization. Your results are likely to be 0.6–1.2% response with an average gift of $20–25. Each package will cost about 35–45¢ (including name rental and postage).

**First Year**

| Packages mailed | 100,000 | Gifts received | @0.9% |
|---|---|---|---|
| | | Response | 900 |
| Cost per package | .40 | Average gift | $23 |
| Total investment | $40,000 | Total income | $20,700 |
| | | Net loss | (19,300) |

You now have 900 brand new donors. In the second year you will mail up to four or five packages to get these 900 to renew. If a donor doesn't respond to your first mailing, mail again in 90 days. For those who still don't renew, mail a third, then a fourth time. These first-time renewals should total 60% of your original 900.

**Second Year**

| Packages mailed | | Total gifts received | |
|---|---|---|---|
| 900, 745, 610, 510 | 2,765 | 155, 135, 100, 150 | 542 |
| Cost per package | .50 | Average gift | 28 |
| Total investment: | $1,383 | Total income | $15,120 |
| | | *Net income* | *(13,737)* |
| | | *Cumulative loss* | *(5,563)* |

In the third year, your original 900 donors will be split into two groups—the 540 who gave for the second consecutive year (ongoing donors) and the 360 who gave in the first but not the second year (lapsed donors). Mail up to four or five personalized packages to renew the ongoing and reinstate the lapsed by year end.

| Third Year | Packages mailed—ongoing | | | Gifts—ongoing | |
|---|---|---|---|---|---|
| | 540, 420, 330, 255 | 1,545 | | 120, 90, 75, 147 | 432 |
| | Cost per package | .50¢ | | Average gift | $33 |
| | Investment—ongoing | $773 | | Income—ongoing | $14,256 |
| | Packages mailed—lapsed | | | Gifts—lapsed | |
| | 360, 338, 318, 299 | 1,315 | | 22, 20, 19, 11 | 72 |
| | Cost per package | .50¢ | | Average gift | $28 |
| | Investment—lapsed | $658 | | Income—lapsed | $2016 |
| | Total investment | $1,431 | | Total income | $16,272 |
| | *Net income 3d year* | | | | *$14,841* |
| | *Cumulative net income after 3 years* | | | | *$9,278* |

By the fourth year, your original 900 donors will be split into 504 ongoing and 396 lapsed donors (432 ongoing who renewed in third year plus the 72 who were reinstated = 504 as your new ongoing total for the fourth year).

| Fourth Year | Packages mailed—Ongoing | | | Gifts—ongoing | |
|---|---|---|---|---|---|
| | 504, 393, 307, 239 | 1,443 | | 111, 86, 68, 138 | 403 |
| | Cost per package | .50¢ | | Average gift | $40 |
| | Investment -Ongoing | $722 | | Income—ongoing | $16,120 |
| | Packages mailed—lapsed | | | Gifts—lapsed | |
| | 396, 372, 307, 239 | 1,447 | | 24, 22, 21, 12 | 79 |
| | Cost per package | .50¢ | | Average gift | $28 |
| | Investment—lapsed | $724 | | Income—lapsed | $2212 |
| | *Total investment* | | | | *$1,446* |
| | *Total income* | | | | *$18,332* |
| | *Net income 4th year* | | | | *$16,886* |
| | *Cumulative net income after 4 years* | | | | *$26,164* |

During this four-year period, you have invested $44,260 and have received $70,424. Even with the original loss, you have received an average 15% per year net profit on your investment. With this same group of 900 originals donors, a 10-year summary might look like this:

| | |
|---|---|
| Your investment | $53,000 |
| Total income | 306,000 |
| Net income | 253,000 |
| Average percent return | 48% per year |

*©1986 Barnes Associates, Inc.; © 1991 (revised), Barnes Associates, Inc.*

your ongoing donors to upgrade and increase their gifts. You will have to explain the concept of repeat mailings to your support group.

**Column G: Donor Qualification Factor** The individuals who respond to your direct mail appeal will have an unusually high response to further appeals. In addition to responding again, their average gift will increase over the years as they requalify themselves. For these reasons, the donor qualification factor is high for direct mail.

**Column H: Activity Life** This type of fund-raising has a high activity life. With changes in the appeal, the use of direct mail has a place in new donor acquisition, reinstating lapsed donors, and soliciting active donors.

**Column I: Up-Front Costs** Direct mail fund-raising has medium to high up-front costs. The printing, postage, and mailing lists have to be paid before the direct mail piece elicits any money.

**Column J: Return on Investment** In general, the return of investment for direct mail is high. However, how high and how soon the return will be depends on the purpose of your appeal and whom you target. If you mail to donors and lapsed donors who have been assimilated into your other fund-raising activities, your costs will be low and your return high. If you mail to nondonors, "cold" names, or lists purchased from mailing houses, your initial costs will be high, but will begin to pay off handsomely over the course of a few years.

Although we have barely scratched the surface of direct mail fund-raising, you now have a grasp of the fundamentals that need to be considered before talking to a consultant or embarking on a "do-it-yourself" program. You can try your own direct mail fund-raising and test it before you invest in mailing to thousands. You may be able to obtain lists of potential donors from your school or school support groups. Or you may decide to use a consultant for all or part of the direct mail process.

If you do decide to test your own approach, look at the mailing piece from the prospect's point of view. Since donor response is the key to success, what will your mailing look like in his or her hand? Consider these important factors.

- How do you pick up and sort your mail?
- How do you separate it into trash and nontrash?
- What do you look at and look for?
- Do you write out checks every time you open the mail? Or do you wait, and write all of your checks out at once?
- What do you retain besides the return envelope when you make out your check (letter, pledge card, etc.)? A large percentage of direct mail pieces are never opened.
- What do you open and why?
- How much are you influenced by the label, window, return address, etc.?

The trick is to make your direct mail piece not look like junk mail. For example, donors may respond better to an appeal that has an envelope with your logo on it. However, the prospective donor may throw the envelope away if he or she is not familiar with your work. In this case, the prospective donor may react better to an envelope with a window that reveals business-like and inviting contents, such as an investment opportunity too good to pass up or, better yet, a check.

Before you write your direct mail copy, examine what you receive in the mail. What entices you to donate? You can gain some helpful insights. When you read a good letter you:

- Feel as if it is written to you personally.
- Can picture the need.
- Think of the reason why you should give (narcissism, guilt, altruism, etc.).
- Have empathy and concern.
- Are motivated to give.
- Learn about the charitable organization.

Your direct mail request *must* contain a remittance envelope—usually a No. 9 (3⅞ × 8⅞″) or a No. 7 (3¾ × 6¾″). Since donors may set aside the mail until they make out their checks to pay bills, you should place a strong motivational message on the outside of the back flap.

*6. Telemarketing*

Telephone fund-raising often results in a much higher return than other forms of fund-raising. It can also be quite successful when used in conjunction with other fund-raising activities such as special events and direct mail. For example:

- Individuals can first be invited by mail to a special event and then called to confirmed their attendance.
- A request for a gift could be mailed to a lapsed donor and then followed up with a phone call.

Column A: Type of Fund-Raising Activity

Evaluate telemarketing as an adjunct to your other fund-raising activities by performing an experiment. What effect would it have to phone donors *before* you mail to them? What about *after* you mail to them? A phone call should not be viewed as an intrusion into your donor's life; it should be viewed as a connection to your organization. For those donors who like to talk, think things over, or ask questions, the phone call is often the missing link to the "feeling" they want to achieve from giving.

Do not let your personal feelings about telemarketing influence your decision whether to include it in your funding plan. You may not personally like it, but it is a highly successful strategy!

Column B: Donor Level

Telemarketing is primarily aimed at the C and B levels.

Column C: Personnel Costs

Telemarketing is best accomplished by paid consultants and/or trained staff. Studies demonstrate a 25–50 percent difference in contributions and response when comparing telemarketing performed by paid professionals and that

❖

*Don't let personal feelings about tele-marketing influence your decision to use it in your funding plan. You may not like it personally, but it's highly successful!*

❖

performed by volunteers. Telemarketing is not usually staff intensive, but it is often consultant intensive and therefore generally has high personnel costs.

But don't let this information intimidate you if you are involved with a small building-level Internet Technology Support Group. You can still embark on a telemarketing campaign by setting up a few phones manned by volunteers in an area in your school where you have multiple phone lines.

Since telemarketing that utilizes consultants or paid staff is expensive, the recommended approach is to test the benefit with a sample of your donors. Compare the difference in the amount of revenue generated by volunteers as compared to paid staff.

**Column D: Volunteer Involvement**  Volunteers can be effectively trained to staff the phones and make the calls. Many volunteers will not like the rejection they get, so a positive environment with a lot of reinforcement will be helpful. Due to the public's wariness of telephone solicitation, volunteers must be able to answer questions about the program for which they are soliciting. In your situation, your volunteer telemarketers must be able to understand the basics of the Internet and how Internet access and enhancement will benefit your students. In general, telemarketing has a medium level of volunteer involvement.

**Column E: Public-Relations Value**  Telemarketing has a low public relations value unless telemarketing is used in conjunction with another type of fund-raising like a radiothon or telethon.

**Column F: Response Rate**  When used to contact lapsed donors, this activity regularly produces a 40 percent or medium-to-high success rate.

**Column G: Donor Qualification Factor**  Telephone contact does increase donor loyalty and has a medium to high donor qualification factor. Evidence suggests that when a $50 direct mail donor upgrades to a $100 donation over the telephone, his or her telemarketing gift does not reduce later direct mail gifts, but rather increases them.

**Column H: Activity Life** Telemarketing can be eliminated, added to, or used in conjunction with other forms of fund-raising to achieve the desired results. However, people normally will not look forward to an organization's annual telemarketing activity. Therefore, telemarketing has a low activity life.

**Column I: Up-Front Costs** The up-front costs associated with telemarketing are medium to high. Up-front costs can be dramatically reduced by using volunteers and donated facilities and phones. One organization used an employee/volunteer service group from a local phone company to help them in their telemarketing effort. They asked the employees/volunteers to solicit their phone company to donate its telemarketing center and the cost of the calls. They then trained the employees/volunteers in telephone solicitation and had them make calls after work for six days. They raised $50,000!

**Column J: Return on Investment** The return on investment is generally high when using this technique.

**7. Memorial Giving** This fund-raising activity will affect donors who already feel strongly about the value of your support group. By making a memorial gift to your group, for example, they honor relatives and friends supported your Internet technology project, or technology in general, but have passed away.

A memorial giving program is usually publicized among donors (members) and your support group through a brochure or newsletter. When a donor's or support group member's friend or relative dies, a donation is sent to the support group in memory of the deceased. The donor includes with their gift the name and address of one of the deceased individual's family members. This individual is then notified that a gift in honor of their loved one was received. The name of the contributor is noted, but the amount of the gift is not. The donor is sent a thank you note and a receipt for his or her tax deductible contribution.

**Column A: Type of Fund-Raising Activity**

The memorial giving program can take many forms. One variation is to produce a packet for donors that consists of a card to be sent to the family of the deceased and an envelope for the card. The card should recognize the loss of the loved one and include a statement that introduces the mission of the group. For example, "A gift has been made to the Internet Technology Support Group in memory of a life that has been lost. This gift will be used to pave the road for young people who are just beginning their journey . . ."

Your group could sell the memorial package in advance to make it easier for the donor, who could purchase a package of five or even ten memorial gifts and use them as needed.

**Column B: Donor Level**

This is a level-B or -A activity. The memorial giver must already value the organization.

**Column C: Personnel Costs**

Memorial giving is not labor-intensive, does not normally require paid staff time, and thus has low personnel costs.

**Column D: Volunteer Involvement**

This is an excellent fund-raiser for volunteers. It is cost-efficient and allows the volunteer to help the member or donor, the organization, and the family of the deceased. The low level of volunteer involvement in this activity is due to the time efficiency of the activity.

**Column E: Public-Relations Value**

The public relations value of memorial giving is low. The family of the deceased learns of the organization, but widespread public knowledge is not likely.

**Column F: Response Rate**

The percentage responding is usually quite high—a response of 35–50 percent is not unusual. The higher up the donor pyramid, the greater the response.

| | |
|---|---|
| Column G: Donor Qualification Factor | This activity has a high degree of loyalty and repeated use. Once initiated, it will continue. |
| Column H: Activity Life | Once initiated, it takes a long time for this activity to peak. Therefore, it has a high activity life. |
| Column I: Up-Front Costs | Memorial giving has low up-front costs. If your organization has paper, envelopes, and stamps, then you are in business. One of your volunteers can design the card, and you may be able to convince a local printer to print it at little or no cost. |
| Column J: Return on Investment | While you will still have to employ other fund-raising activities, memorial giving has a high return on investment. It is only limited by the number of donors who will utilize it. |
| 8. *Capital Campaigns* | The traditional capital campaign is an organized, multiyear fund-raising program that utilizes many activities to raise a significant amount of money. Because of its complexity, this type of campaign is usually undertaken by large district-level fund-raising organizations. Originally, funds raised for capital expenditures were for buildings, renovations, and new equipment. However, the original definition has been altered, and nonprofit organizations now raise capital for a variety of purposes, including endowment programs and expansion. In fact, capital campaigns to most nonprofit staff members mean large fund-raising programs for a lot of money. Most nonprofits limit themselves to one campaign at a time, but the campaign may include many components such as capital for expansion, capital for remodeling, capital for equipment, etc. |
| Column A: Type of Fund-Raising Activity | Nothing relies more on your long-range and strategic planning than the decision to embark on a capital campaign. The need must be both clear and compelling, and the plan and goal must be feasible. Also, it is imperative that you test |

*all* assumptions concerning your capital campaign. For example, your support group needs to:

- Understand the concepts outlined in this book.
- Have a well-developed donor pyramid.
- Find a public relations program that positions your mission in the minds of the donors.

If your Internet access inventory reveals the need for renovations, rewiring, and equipment totaling $575,000, naive group members may typically say, "Okay, let's plug in five donors at $115,000 each." While this solution may be mathematically correct, the practical solution usually works according to a very different formula. Although you know that those gifts and grants may indeed be available, can you acquire them?

A professional in capital campaigns can develop a gift table or chart to illustrate the scale of giving necessary to accomplish the organization's funding goal. Figure 10.5 (on the following page) is an example of a scale of giving that is based on case studies of successful campaigns and the shared experiences of fund-raising professionals.

The likelihood of reaching the goal depends on the:

- Number of existing donors who can be placed on the gift table.
- Ability to interest a target group of prospective donors.
- Ability to attract foundation and corporate grants and gifts.
- Ability to set up a team of solicitors who will call on the donors.

A feasibility study should be performed before delving into a capital campaign. An outside consultant is the best person to analyze whether you really have the potential donors and the ability to raise the funds. Naturally, a reputable consultant will charge a fee for helping you test your assumptions.

**Figure 10.5**

Scale of Giving

| Gifts | Prospects | Gift Range ($) | ~Total ($) |
|---|---|---|---|
| 2 | | 50,000 | 100,000 |
| 4 | | 25,000 | 100,000 |
| 4 | | 15,000 | 60,000 |
| 5 | | 10,000 | 50,000 |
| | 15 Pacesetter gifts | | 310,000 |
| 10 | | 5,000 | 50,000 |
| 15 | | 3,000 | 45,000 |
| 25 | | 1,500 | 37,000 |
| 30 | | 1,000 | 30,000 |
| | 80 Leadership gifts | | 162,500 |
| 35 | | 600 | 21,000 |
| 70 | | 400 | 28,000 |
| 100 | | 200 | 20,000 |
| 200 | | 100 | 20,000 |
| | 405 Major gifts | | 89,000 |
| | 500 Pacesetter, Leadership, & Major gifts | | 561,500 |
| | Numerous small gifts | | 13,500 |
| Total | | | 575,000 |

But, the size of the fee depends on the amount of preliminary work you have completed.

In order to ascertain the level of interest, and therefore the likelihood of contributions, the consultant will need to review your mission statement, list of needs, plans, benefits, and the names of potential donors you have at each gift level. Most consultants will conduct interviews on a sample of prospects from each level. These interviews will allow them to estimate the number of prospects you will need at each level to generate the number of donors you must have.

Listen to these experts. Fund-raising consultants do not like their clients to embark upon doomed efforts. If the consultant says your campaign is not feasible, you should listen. If you decide to continue to use the services of the consultant after your feasibility study is completed, many will reduce their contract fee for their post-feasibility services by the amount they charged you to conduct the feasibility study.

But remember, the consultants do not raise money. They plan, train, develop background material, and organize, but your teams of volunteers do the actual fund-raising. Your Internet Technology Support Group's level of giving and their dedication to the success of the campaign will set the pace for your entire community.

Look at Figure 10.5 again. Do you have the people who can and will support your Internet technology project at the necessary level? The latest data suggests that you need one gift for ⅓ to ½ of the total campaign and that 15 gifts should raise 60 percent of the total.

Column B: Donor Level    The donor level for a capital campaign is A/B. There may be activities that attempt to raise money at level C, but the majority of the funds will come from A and B.

Column C: Personnel Costs    The personnel commitment to a capital campaign is high. Even when a consulting firm is employed, capital campaigns require a major commitment of paid staff time and often the addition of staff members.

Column D:
Volunteer Involvement    An extremely high level of volunteer activity is required for a capital campaign to succeed.

Column E:
Public-Relations Value    The capital campaign requires a high degree of visibility and public relations. The real value is in encouraging large gifts. There is a value to the organization and to the donor pyramid, but that will have minimal effect on current fund-raising activities, especially if the campaign is successful.

Column F: Response Rate    Since a capital campaign relies heavily on personal fund-raising, the response should be high, around 30–50 percent. One capital campaign rule is to secretly carry out some fund-raising before a public campaign is announced. After you have raised 50 percent or more of the goal, announce the campaign. If the percent of contacts who respond is unusually low, you may not reach 50 percent of the goal, and therefore choose not to announce the campaign.

**Column G: Donor Qualification Factor** The capital campaign is a true test of the donor's loyalty and strength of feeling for the organization. Since a multi-year pledge system is employed in capital campaigns, a bonding with the campaign is encouraged. The donor qualification factor is high.

**Column H: Activity Life** Twenty-five years ago, the activity life of a campaign would have been limited to every 10 or 20 years. More recently, however, some groups have had great success having successive capital campaigns. Therefore, estimating this variable is difficult. Most donors and staff, however, need a period of rest between campaigns. Therefore, the capital campaign's activity life is rated from low to medium.

**Column I: Up-Front Costs** Capital campaigns have high up-front costs.

**Column J: Return on Investment** Capital campaigns have a high return on investment. While the investment is one of the larger ones a nonprofit will make, the return is also large.

**9. Bequests/Planned Giving** You may be shocked that you should consider bequests as soon as you begin your fund-raising plan. In your quest to raise the money you need right away, do not forget this valuable tool. In addition to simple techniques like having your Internet and technology needs addressed in your volunteers' wills, you can examine more sophisticated deferred giving strategies such as life insurance policies that list your organization as the beneficiary.

**Column A: Type of Fund-Raising Activity** The marketplace for a gift that is planned during life but granted only after death is huge because eight out of ten

Americans die without a will. Planned giving allows donors to, in a very real way, continue their presence in your organization even after their exit from the world. A donor who normally gives $100 per year to your organization could endow that yearly donation by making a bequest of $2,500 (at 4 percent per annum) from his or her estate. After death, that money would provide for the benefits supported during life.

The number of your potential donors who do not have wills is almost unbelievable. For example, six out of ten college graduates in America have none. The small percentage of individuals who have died with wills has generated a total of $80 billion in bequests since 1955! And remember, the baby boomers are aging. The percentage of individuals over 65 will increase by 20 percent in the next 10 years.

Helping your donors develop wills would be a genuine favor to them. The problems associated with the probate of wills, custody of children, and the loss of money to estate taxes are reason enough for you to assist your donors in this area. Through planned giving and careful use of tax advantages, your program will allow large and small donors alike to make significant contributions to your organization while they are still alive.

**Column B: Donor Level** Bequests and planned gifts normally come from donors who know the organization, value its goals, and have qualified themselves. They are usually from levels A and B.

**Column C: Personnel Costs** The costs of finding and employing a full-time planned giving expert limits the feasibility of this activity for most non-profit groups. Placing a staff person in charge of this area and arranging a 10 percent allocation of staff time is more than enough to begin the bequest/planned giving process. Personnel costs for this activity are low to medium.

**Column D: Volunteer Involvement** Volunteers from the trust offices of local banks and law firms can begin the process of raising awareness concerning wills and planned gifts. Free financial planning seminars for your donors could provide you with prospects. Volunteer involvement in this area is medium.

Column E: Public Relations    The public relations value is low.

Column F: Response Rate    Start by targeting 100 of your donors who have the financial means and an interest in the future of your organization. You can expect a medium to high rate of response.

Column G: Donor Qualification Factor    The loyalty and continuity qualifications of this fund-raising technique are high. For instance, studies have shown that 42 percent of all bequestors usually are individuals who had not given an annual gift in the five years prior to their bequest.

Column H: Activity Life    The area of planned giving has a high activity life. Individuals who have made planned gifts while still alive should be invited to ceremonies and other special events, and encouraged to bring their friends. The acceptance of planned gifts and the increase of the population in the over-65 age group insure that this activity has a long life.

Column I: Up-Front Costs    The up-front costs can be minimal when volunteers perform this activity in an integrated manner.

Column J: Return on Investment    The return on investment is very high. While bequests must wait until the donor dies, the planned gift provides instant revenue and value.

*10. Credit Cards*    This fund-raiser has evolved from being one type of special event into its own fund-raising strategy. The concept is that a bank and a credit card company issue a credit card with your fund-raising group's name on it. You then receive a percentage of the purchases made with the card.

     While the banks are helpful in developing your market and agreeing to special first-year introductory offers (like no fee for one year), your real success will be determined by the number of your constituents who request and use the card. The Fairfax County Public School Foundation started a credit card program in 1995 and generated a sizeable income from a base of 5,000 cardholders making credit card purchases of $2,000 per year. Before you initiate this strategy, analyze the factors on the matrix.

Timing may be more important than you think. Many credit cards have already positioned themselves with users by giving credit toward gasoline purchases and automobiles, cash back, and frequent-flyer miles. These benefits may outweigh your Internet technology appeal.

Column B: Donor Level  You need donors who are committed to and knowledgeable of your mission for a credit card strategy to work . These include primarily B-level donors and possibly upper C-level donors.

Column C: Personnel Costs  You do not necessarily need hired staff for this fund-raising activity. The bank does the work for you once the cardholder is signed up and starts using the card.

Column D: Volunteer Involvement  Credit cards require low volunteer involvement. However, your core support group will help begin the program and to promote an annual event to encourage usage and re-signing when the first year of benefits expires. A telemarketing campaign can be used to effectively re-sign cardholders.

Column E: Public-Relations Value  The public relations value is low. Except in the initial or annual promotion, most of the public-relations value comes with card usage and the opportunity of the user to tell a vendor that he or she supports the Internet technology project at your school.

Column F: Response Rate  The rate of response depends on the manner in which the card is marketed. If individuals are soliciting their peers, you should experience a medium level of response. If your volunteers each ask 25 individuals to sign up and five to ten do, most of your volunteers will be willing to continue asking. But if only one in 25 responds favorably, your volunteers will feel rejected, and your program will languish. If direct mail is used to market the card, the key will be to deliver the names of A- and B-level donors. The percent of donors expected to respond will be a critical issue to the participating bank since they will be paying the marketing costs up front.

**Column G: Donor Qualification Factor**  This must be medium to high in order to keep the credit card strategy working. The donor/cardholder must derive enough satisfaction in your group's communication with them, that they are willing to use the card to contribute to the technology needs of your school.

**Column H: Activity Life**  At this point, this strategy is still new to school technology fund-raising, and the use of it by other nonprofits has had mixed results over the long term. Competition in this area, along with the availability of low interest loans gives this strategy a medium activity life.

**Column I: Up-Front Costs**  The credit card strategy incurs low up-front costs. The bank sponsor fronts the marketing costs, so the fund-raising group's financial responsibility is minimal. However, you will have difficulty attracting a bank sponsor if you cannot provide the necessary support services such as computer generated mailing lists, endorsements, and some marketing through your own vehicles.

**Column J: Return on Investment**  Since you are not required to invest anything other than support, this effort can have a high return on investment.

**11. District Bond Issues**  If you employ other fund-raising strategies first, you have a better chance of convincing district administrators, parents, teachers, and the community to vote positively on a bond issue to cover the costs of your Internet technology plan.

Evaluate the techniques you can use based on your limitations of staff and volunteers, and your current donor base. Develop your fund-raising plan for the next two or three years. Estimate the net you can realistically expect to make available for your school's Internet access and technology needs. If it appears that the funding will not be enough to produce the change your group wants to develop within the time frame you desire, you may want to consider issuance of bonds to provide the resources required in a more timely manner.

The bond issue should be considered seriously only after your support group has determined that the other strategies will require too much time, or that the revenue generated by the other strategies will not be great enough to establish your Internet technology plan. Remember, if your plan will take six years to implement, you will have to adjust the estimates of the amount you need to raise so that the funds raised cover the increases in the cost of renovations and technology due to inflation. In addition, each year it takes to implement your plan is another year that another group of students passes a grade level without the educational advantages provided by Internet access and increased technology.

By implementing the process and strategies outlined in this book, you will be able to educate your constituency so that you can develop the support necessary to undertake a successful vote on a bond issue.

**Column A: Type of Fund-Raising Activity**  There are three major types of bond fund-raising mechanisms: the standard bond issue, the mini-bond issue and certificates of participation.

*Standard Bond Issue.*  Developing a strong public relations campaign and strategic plan is the typical approach to the standard bond issue. This approach will require a well-orchestrated effort that garners support from citizens beyond those who have children in your school. In fact, developing support from business people and senior citizens will be a key to your success. If your students can convince their grandparents to support the bond issue vote, you will likely succeed. While high voter turnout by your supporters is a necessity, low voter turnout from your critics would also help!

Voters can be particularly critical of technology and Internet related bond issues. The renovations required to make a school building technology-accessible may be feasible only when the costs are spread over several years, but the technology related equipment that must be purchased may be worn out or outdated by the time the bonds are paid. You can avoid this voter criticism by providing the voters with a plan showing how you will update and replace equipment and software without requiring another bond issue.

In 1993, the West Bloomfield School District in Michigan utilized the standard bond issue to raise $26 million and proposed that $10 million of this be spent on technology related school renovations and equipment.

*Mini-Bond Issue.* The major difference between the standard bond issue and the various mini-bond strategies is who purchases the bonds and, therefore, collects the interest. Banks and large financial institutions and investors purchase standard bonds in large monetary blocks, while mini-bonds can be sold for lower amounts ($500) to local citizens. The local citizen is then entitled to receive the interest paid on the bond.

This concept provides your school and support group with the opportunity to implement a unique fund-raising strategy. For example, John and Sue Smith purchase a $500 technology bond that will be repaid over five years at $100 per year plus a fixed rate of 5 percent interest. At the end of year one, your school sends the Smiths two checks (one for $100 and one for the interest) with a letter. The letter explains how their funds have been used to increase Internet access and technology and improve teaching and learning. It then asks them to consider the following.

1. Making the interest check a tax-deductible donation to the school foundation (or other foundation that acts as the school's intermediary).
2. Donating both checks (the $100 payment and the interest) to the foundation.

This concept could be compared to taking out a loan with a repayment plan that allows the repayment to be converted into a donation. Whether the loan is for $100 or $100,000, the concept is the same.

Use your fund-raising knowledge to develop a strategy to keep the Smith's donation coming each year. In addition to including a remittance envelope with the checks and letter, you could follow with a phone call inviting the Smiths to become members of your technology investors group for donating the interest check back, or of your high-tech investors group for donating the $100 yearly payment plus the interest. Whether you decide to use mini-bonds or standard bonds, you must first check all of the legalities.

Some states allow nonprofit groups to perform functions similar to the mini-bonds through other, less-regulated mechanisms. In New York state, one nonprofit group sold sub–venture certificates to its members. These certificates were for $25 each, paid a set amount of interest, and could be purchased in installments. The group set out to raise $30,000 and actually raised $65,000 in one month! If they had requested the purchasers to donate back their interest or payment, they could have realized an even greater return.

*Certificates of Participation.* This strategy involves selling certificates of deposit (loans) through an investment firm and putting up school property as collateral. By taking advantage of the assets of the school district, existing debt and needed cash for technology can be rolled into a single refinancing plan. This is like a personal bill-consolidation loan that can reduce your monthly payments by spreading them over several years.

By consolidating and spreading out the district's debt over 30 years, the new payment may be lower than the existing payments. By adding in the cash needed for technology, the new payment can be made equal to the school's existing payments. Of course, the same question will arise relative to the usable life of the equipment that will be paid for, for over 20 years. The best approach would be to expend the majority of the bond funds on building improvements rather than software and equipment.

The other bond mechanisms (standard bonds and mini-bonds) require voter approval. Certificates of participation can be entered into by the school board without a public vote. However, there must be strong community support if the board is to effectively utilize this strategy. Piscataway Township Schools in New Jersey utilized this technique to consolidate $15 million of old debt and add $9 million dollars for technology and technology related building improvements.

Whether using standard bonds, mini-bonds, or certificates of participation, fund-raising activities such as these will only be successful after you have convinced the public that your Internet technology project is worthy of support.

**Column B: Donor Level**  The bond issue strategy could be an A-, B-, or C-level activity. In fact, a person who is not even in the donor pyramid may purchase a mini-bond simply because of the interest rate it promises to pay. Of course, the higher up the donor pyramid you go, the greater the support should be. One college raised $1 million dollars by asking 10 A- and B-level donors to loan them $100,000 each for 10 years with a repayment of $10,000 plus interest each year. Over the 10 years, the college actually had to repay only a small portion of the $1 million. Most of the money was donated back to the college.

**Column C: Personnel Costs**  The personnel costs associated with bond strategies are high. Bond issues require the involvement of existing school personnel and often the hiring of additional staff and consultants. For these reasons, bond issues are typically district-level fund-raising activities.

Column D: Volunteer Involvement
Volunteer involvement in this activity is medium to high. The dollar size of the project requires a sound base of public acceptance even when paid support staff is available to assist in the effort. From speaking at service clubs to knocking on doors, volunteer involvement is substantial.

Column E: Public-Relations Value
The public must be well educated about the value of the Internet and technology before they buy into bond issues. Therefore, this must have a high public-relations value.

Column F: Response Rate
Since this requires a majority vote and strong support, the response rate should be high (around 50 percent).

Column G: Donor Qualification Factor
This factor is low. Once utilized and supported, donors will feel that the problem has been solved and will not want to borrow more money to keep the program going.

Column H: Activity Life
This technique takes several years to complete. Although it can be reused after it is paid off, it is not usually repeated before then. Therefore, its activity life is low.

Column I: Up-Front Costs
The up-front costs are high. The costs of consultants and legal counsel and the fees paid to brokers, make this a cost intensive strategy. The large amount of cash realized in one lump sum warrants these expenses. In some cases, the costs are amortized over the years called for in the bond issue so that they are not all up-front. If you utilize volunteer lawyers and the mini-bond issue or another simple strategy, the up-front costs may be reduced to the medium level.

Column J: Return on Investment
The return on the investment is variable. While this strategy may provide you with Internet access and the other technology resources your school desires, it can also provide

you with high costs if you are paying interest, consultants, lawyers, and commissions. However, if you try to use volunteers and recover your debt payments and interest as charitable gifts, this strategy can have a high return for your investment.

**Conclusion**  At this point in the book, you have been presented with a plethora of information to help you decide your best fundraising strategies. Remember, your Internet Technology Support Group does not need to be part of a huge district-level organization in order to garner funds for a technology plan. No matter what your group's size, you can pick and choose the right strategies for your particular vision and needs.

# 11 Developing Your Funding Strategy and Putting It All Together

**Y**OU ARE NOW ready to use everything you learned from this book to develop a funding plan that will provide a better teaching and learning environment to your school through Internet access and technology. You have:

- Developed an Internet/Technology Support Group comprised of knowledgeable, committed individuals.
- Learned how the grants marketplace can get you started.
- Examined many fund-raising strategies that can complete or enhance your Internet access project and fund it into the future.

In reviewing the fund-raising strategies, you have learned to assess both the feasibility and the cost benefit of each strategy and whether you can make the strategy work for you. Now you must put it all together.

Start by placing your steps to success on a fund-raising organizer for each year of your strategic plan. What will you implement each month for the next 12 months? Who will be responsible for each step in your plan? What events will you plan to generate enough cash to develop the next event?

Involving and educating key individuals is the basis of your fund-raising plan. Begin by addressing grants. Your support group will believe this area is where the "easy money" is. Once you have their commitment, proceed to the other fund-raising strategies.

Be certain to include some highly visible activities that promote public relations and reinforce that the education environment in your community is positively changing due to the funds that have been raised from your initial efforts. With funds in your treasury, you can implement those strategies that have up-front costs, but also produce a good return on your investment. The number and types of fund-raising strategies you will be able to implement will depend on your donor base and the volunteers you have attracted to your cause.

Your Internet Technology Support Group will be ready to consider bond issues when they feel they do not have enough time or money to catch up with other schools. But first they must thoroughly analyze the feasibility of the other types of fund-raising strategies so that the community and the school board do not feel as if your support group is just looking for an easy way out. When your support group presents your school board with its findings regarding the need, the cost, and the time frame for your solution, you must take every measure to insure that they will be impressed with the work your group has done. In addition, the more support you develop through your donors, the more likely you will be to get a bond issue passed.

The path to successful fund-raising is different for each school and each school district. The personalities of the volunteers are different, and the demographics of the potential donors vary widely. Therefore, it is not worthwhile to blindly copy the techniques employed successfully in another community.

When working with a school in a low income neighborhood, an expensive raffle ticket for a car would not meet with the same success it would in a wealthy suburban school. Those schools located in communities that have fewer donors with extra money will need to rely more heavily on grants and corporate support. However, this probability should not prevent you from trying to raise money from individuals in less affluent populations. Their support will reveal their level of commitment to grantors. Grantors will be impressed by the fact that the community is willing to come to the aid of their school's technology needs even though the residents do not have much money.

Fund-raising does not require any special magic. You can now see that success depends on developing a base of donors that you know, cultivate, and invite to qualify themselves by moving up the donor pyramid.

Some of the steps outlined in this book may seem a little obvious, while others are more complicated. But remember, fund-raising should be kept simple. Simple, however, does not mean easy. There is no short-cut to success—you must plan your work and work your plan. Good Luck!

# Glossary

**Active Phase (of a Campaign)**  The period of public solicitation that usually follows successful completion of a campaign's nucleus fund and the establishment of a pattern of giving; campaign solicitation activity as opposed to campaign preparation.

**Ad Hoc Committee**  A group of people in an organization or institution who are named to accomplish a specific objective; upon completion of the task, the committee disbands.

**Administrator**  The person, appointed by a court, to settle the affairs of a decedent who died without leaving a valid will. The duties of an administrator are similar to those of an executor, but, because his or her powers and rights come from the state law, they are often more restricted than those generally given to an executor by a will.

**Advance Gifts**    Gifts given or pledged in advance of a public announcement of a campaign. Advance gifts are solicited before a campaign is announced because the success or failure of a campaign may depend upon the size of advance gifts.

**Advisory Board**    A prestigious group of individuals, usually influential and prominent, whose endorsement of the campaign objectives implies credibility.

**Advocacy Groups**    Organizations that actively support a particular ideology or cause.

**Alumni(ae) Campaign**    A fund-raising campaign of an educational institution that is focused on individuals who have attended the institution.

**Alumni(ae) Fund**    An annual, organized effort by educational institutions (publicly as well as privately supported colleges, universities, and secondary schools) to obtain gifts from their alumni(ae).

**Annual Fund (Appeal; Giving Program)**    Any organized effort by a gift-supported organization to obtain gifts on a yearly basis, usually to support general operations.

**Annual Report**    A yearly report of financial and organizational conditions prepared by the management of an organization.

**Beneficiary**    An individual or organization that receives funds from any source.

**Big Gifts**    A general term used to identify contributions that are large relative to the magnitude of the campaign.

**Board of Directors**    Individuals selected (e.g., by other directors or members) in accordance with law (usually reflected in bylaws) in order to establish policy and oversee the management of an organization or institution.

| | |
|---|---|
| **Bulk Rate Mail** | Second, third, or fourth class mail that qualifies for special postage rates, which are lower than first class postage. |
| **Campaign** | An organized effort to solicit funds for an organization or institution. |
| **Campaign Leadership** | Top volunteers who are an essential ingredient of any campaign organization and one of the three major pedestals on which fund-raising success must rest—the other pedestal being the case and sources of support. |
| **Capital Campaign** | A fund-raising campaign, usually extending over a period of years, to raise substantial funds to finance major projects and/or programs requiring extensive outlays of capital; a campaign designed to obtain donations for capital rather than annual income. |
| **Capital Expenditure** | An expenditure to acquire an asset with an expected useful life for more than one year. |
| **Case Statement** | A carefully prepared document that sets forth, in detail, the reasons an organization needs and merits financial support. In the context of the "case is bigger than the institution," it documents its services, human resources, potential for greater services, current needs, and future plans. |
| **Categorical Grant** | A grant from an agency of the United States government, usually for a program with relatively narrow guidelines, including eligibility requirements, time for completion, and beneficiaries. |
| **Challenge Gift** | A substantial gift made on condition that other gifts will be obtained on some prescribed formula, usually within a specified period, with the objective of stimulating fund-raising activity. |

**Challenge Grant**   A grant made on condition that the donee organization is able to raise additional matching funds from other sources. Such a grant is used to stimulate giving from other donors.

**Charitable Deduction**   The value of money or property transferred to a 501(c)(3) organization, deductible for income gift, and estate tax purposes. In most cases, the term "charitable deduction" refers to the portion of a gift that can be deducted from the donor's income subject to federal income tax. A donor's charitable deduction should not be confused or equated with the value of the gift, i.e., gifts for purposes of life income agreements are not federally deductible at their full value.

**Charitable Institution**   A private organization that operates on a nonprofit basis— classified 501(c)(3)—and, therefore, exempt from income tax.

**Charity**   A cause; a 501(c)(3) organization; an organization, institution, or advocacy group that seeks philanthropic support.

**Commitment**   An individual's, corporation's, or foundation's expression of significant support to an organization through service and/or financial assistance.

**Community Foundation**   Most often, a publicly supported organization that makes grants for social, educational, religious, or other charitable purposes in a specific community or region. Funds are derived from many donor sources, and retaining such funds as endowment is usually encouraged. The income, including that earned by the endowment, is then used to make a grant.

**Company-Sponsored Foundation**   A private foundation whose corpus is derived from a profit-making corporation or company and whose primary purpose is the making of grants. It may maintain close ties with the donor company, but it is an independent organization, most often with its own rules and regulations.

**Constituency**  The members of the "family" of an organization (such as the faculty, alumni, medical staff, employees, users, parents, donors, and members); financial support usually comes from these general categories: individuals, foundations, government(s), and corporations.

**Contingent Gift**  A gift that is subject to certain conditions that may occur in the future.

**Corporate Foundation**  The philanthropic organization established to coordinate, over a period of time, the philanthropic interests of the founding corporation. Corporate foundations are very explicit as to their fields of interest, often limiting grants to causes related to corporate profits and interests, such as the communities where they are headquartered or the communities where they have branches.

**Cost/Benefit**  A concept of economic and social ramifications, concerned with getting the most and the best for the least cost.

**Cost per Dollar Raised**  The amount of money from each dollar raised that can be attributed to the expenditure of resources used to attract that gift. Several state attorneys general suggest an overall average of approximately 35¢ per $1 raised.

**Cultivation**  The process of developing the interest of prospective contributors through exposure to institutional activities, people, needs, and plans, to the point where they are considered ready to give at acceptable levels.

**Current Giving**  Gifts to existing operations or projects of an organization.

**Database**  A collection of information specific to an operation or organization.

**Declining Grant**  A multiyear grant that grows smaller each year in the expectation that the donee will raise other funds to close the gap.

**Deferred Giving Program**

**Deferred or Planned Gift**  A commitment or gift established legally during the donor's lifetime, but whose principal benefits usually do not accrue to the recipient until later, often after the donor's death. The term is usually applied to any arrangement whereby money or property is irrevocably (except for will commitments) set aside for future receipt by a nonprofit organization, frequently where income is paid to the donor and/or someone else for a period of time. Annuities, trusts, gifts of insurance, and will commitments are all generally referred to as deferred gifts.

**Demonstration Grant**  An initial grant made to show how an innovative project will function as a model and can be capable of duplication with or without modifications.

**Development**  A term used to define the total process of organizational or institutional fund-raising, frequently inclusive of public relations and (in educational institutions) alumni affairs.

**Development Board**  A group of volunteers usually entrusted with overall responsibility for an organization's fund-raising program in matters of policy and top-level decision making.

**Development Committee**  A volunteer committee of the board of a nonprofit organization that is charged with the responsibility for oversight of fund-raising and other related activities.

**Direct Mail**  Solicitation of funds by mail.

**Discretionary Funds**  Gifts that can be expended by an organization's designee according to the donor's wishes.

**Donor List**  A list of contributors prepared for a particular purpose or in conjunction with list building.
ular appeal.

**Endorsement**  A show of support, a verification.

| | |
|---|---|
| **Endowment Campaign** | A campaign to obtain funds specifically to create or supplement an organization's endowment fund. |
| **Endowment (Pure)** | A fund that generates interest, which is available for use for grantmaking. Distribution for gift purposes coincides either with the donor's stipulation or, if there is no stipulation, at the discretion of an organization's board. |
| **Endowment (Quasi)** | A fund, the principal of which can be and often is invaded by a board in order to meet operating costs. Such endowments include gifts for which donors specify their use; they may also include gifts that are given for no specific purpose and that a board treats as endowment. |
| **Endowment Fund** | Funds an organization invests to produce income for operations and other approved purposes. |
| **Estate** | The legal status or position of an owner with respect to property and other assets; total assets of a deceased person. |
| **Estate Tax (Federal)** | A tax on the net value of the estate without regard to distributive shares. |
| **Executive Committee** | A formal group to which responsibility has been delegated by the board for direct operation and management of an organization between full board meetings. |
| **Executor** | A person identified in a will to administer the estate upon the death of the maker of the will and to dispose of it according to the wishes of same. |
| **Fair Market Value** | A value generally defined as the amount that a willing purchaser would pay in the normal market. The responsibility for determining this value generally is left to the donor. For gifts of commonly traded securities, the fair market value is the mean cost of the security on the day the securities are transferred to the institution. |

**Feasibility (or Development Planning) Study**  An objective survey of an organization's fund-raising potential that measure the strength of its case and the availability of its leaders, workers, and prospective donors. A written report includes the study findings, recommendations, and (when the goal is feasible) a campaign plan, timetable, and budget. The study is usually conducted by fund-raising counsel.

**Federated Campaign**  A joint fund-raising program that is administered by a 501(c)(3) organization and that distributes funds to other similar agencies. The Federation of Protestant Welfare Agencies, the United Negro College Fund, the United Way, and the Community Chests are all examples of federated campaigns.

**Foundation Profiles**  Background sheets on prospective foundation and corporation donors assembled and distributed by the Foundation Center Library.

**Friends**  A category of donors and prospective donors; also, an organized group that supports a specific project, e.g., "Friends of the Library."

**Fund-Raiser**  One who makes his or her living from working as a member of an organization's or institution's development department, as an independent fund-raising consultant or as a member of a fund-raising counseling firm; a volunteer who raises funds for a cause is also referred to as a fund-raiser; a fund-raising event has come to be called a fund-raiser.

**Fund-Raising Program**  An organization's or institution's strategy, tactics, objectives, case, and needs in their entirety; a campaign that is loosely defined in terms of time frame and specific funding opportunities; a campaign; a timetable for a campaign.

**General Purpose Foundation**  An independent private foundation that awards grants in many different fields.

**General Purpose Grant** A grant made to further the regular work of an organization, rather than for a specific purpose or project.

**Geographics** The study of markets by using geographic analysis, principally regions, states, counties, and localities. Specifically, geographics entails the study of markets by SMSA (standard metropolitan statistical area), zip code sectional center, or other territorial designation.

**Gift Range Table** A table of gifts that enables campaign leaders to know, in advance of a capital campaign, the size and number of gifts that are likely to be needed at each level in order to achieve the campaign goal. The table focuses the attention of campaign leaders on the sequence of gifts that will be needed.

**Giving Clubs** Categories of donors who are grouped and recognized by the recipient organization or institution on the basis of similar gift level.

**Goal** An all-embracing focus of accomplishment, supported by specific objectives that an organization is determined to achieve; the amount of money to be achieved by a fundraising campaign—that is, the dollar objective of the campaign.

**Grant** Generally an allocation from a foundation, corporation, or government agency.

**Grantor (or Grantmaker)** One who provides a grant or establishes a trust.

**Independent Sector (IS)** An organization composed of two types of member: corporations and foundations with national giving programs, and national organizations concerned with philanthropy. The purpose of IS is to further philanthropic endeavor in the United States.

**Independent Sector**   A term used to describe all not-for-profit organizations, as distinct from government and corporations formed to make a profit; not to be confused with the organization Independent Sector.

**In-Kind Contribution**   A contribution of equipment, supplies, or other property in lieu of money. Some corporations may also donate space or staff time as in-kind contributions. The donor may place a monetary value on in-kind gifts for tax purposes.

**Letter of Intent**   A letter that states a prospect's intention to make a specified gift or legacy; it is used when a prospect prefers to avoid making a pledge. Since it could possibly constitute a binding obligation under some circumstances, a prospective donor should consider seeking legal counsel before executing such a letter.

**Life Insurance Gifts**   The irrevocable assignment of a life insurance policy for a charitable disposition, for which the present value is fully tax-deductible, as are the premiums that are paid by the donor.

**List Broker**   A firm that maintains and rents mailing lists of prospect names. These names are usually maintained in a computer file to be reproduced in various formats. The lists are marketed by the broker.

**List Exchange**   The exchange of donor lists between two organizations or institutions on a name-for-name basis, to enable each organization to mail to the other's constituency.

**Lists**   A general term used in fund-raising to denote files and records pertaining to donors, prospects, and categories of constituencies in various stages of development and refinement, and to flat lists required for special purposes.

**Long-Range Development**  That aspect of development concerned with future goals.

**Mail Campaign**  A fund-raising campaign conducted by mail.

**Mailing List**  A list of names and addresses of people categorized according to one or more common interests used for mailing purposes and often computerized for quick availability.

**Major Brochure**  A campaign brochure that encompasses the generic case of support and is therefore applicable for use with all potential constituencies.

**Major Gifts**  Usually the third tier of giving to a campaign, inclusive of gifts of substantial magnitude.

**Market Value**  The current value of an asset if sold on the open market.

**Marketing**  Bringing an organization's product to the marketplace.

**Matching Gift**  A gift that is made on the condition that it be matched within a certain period, on a one-to-one, two-to-one, or three-to-one basis, or in accordance with some other formula. Also, a gift by a corporation matching a gift by one of its employees. Corporations match in response, i.e., matching one-to-one, two-to-one, or three-to-one, to the amount contributed by an employee in order to encourage employee giving.

**Memorial**  A gift to an organization commemorating either the donor or someone else, living or dead, designated by the donor, for whom a specific "memorial" will be set aside in accordance with the donor's wishes. Organizations often designate memorials and seek support from relatives and friends of the one being memorialized.

**Mission Statement**  A concise description of the purpose of an organization.

**Multiple Appeals**  The conduct by a single organization of several fund-raising appeals—either simultaneously or overlapping—with the consequence that the same constituencies are receiving more than one appeal from the same cause; multiple appeals to the same constituency for competing purposes.

**Named Gift Opportunity**  Name-bearing recognition of a gift for a specific purpose available to donors to a campaign. The "opportunity" is usually publicized prior to funding and serves as a special incentive for giving.

**Needs Assessment**  Analysis of a campaign's table of needs, which becomes the basis for explaining why each project is needed; provides a rationale that is persuasive for the funder's consideration.

**Nine Ninety (990)**  A report (information return) annually submitted by nearly all tax-exempt organizations and institutions (except religious) to the IRS, which includes financial information on income sources, expenditures, and activities.

**Nine Ninety-PF (990-PF)**  A report (information return) to the Internal Revenue Service annually submitted by private foundations. The 990-PF includes detailed information on the foundation's financial holdings, income, and activities. Filmed copies of these returns are also kept at Foundation Center libraries.

**Nonprofit Organization (or Nonprofit Institution)**  Any private organization that provides service of benefit to humankind without financial incentive and that can qualify as a 501(c)(3) organization.

**Nonprofit Postage**  A special, reduced postage rate accorded to qualifying nonprofit, tax-exempt organizations or institutions.

**Objectives**  The specific purposes for which a campaign is undertaken, encompassing the full scope of the needs.

**Operating Support Grant**  A grant to cover the day-to-day personnel, administrative, and other expenses for an organization's existing program or project.

**Pacesetting Gifts**  Those gifts received during a campaign that set the standard for all subsequent gifts; a category of gifts related to the gift range table of anticipated giving.

**Phase**  A specific stage of a campaign, often as determined by a feasibility study and built into a campaign schedule, e.g., initial phase, active phase, intensive phase, clean-up phase; also advance, major, special, and general gift phases.

**Philanthropic Dollar**  Generally, that portion of the Gross National Product allocated to support philanthropic causes.

**Philanthropic Foundation**  A corporation or trust that has been created with contributed funds, whether by an individual, family, corporation, or community, for support of 501(c)(3) organizations.

**Phonathon**  A fund-raising effort in which volunteers solicit gifts or pledges by telephone.

**Planned Giving**  The integration of sound personal, financial, and estate planning concepts with the individual donor's plans for lifetime or testamentary giving.

**Pledge**  A signed and dated legal commitment to make a gift to an organization over a specified period of time—generally three or more years—which is payable according to the terms that are set by the donor; or, the total value of such a commitment.

**Pre-Campaign**  That period preceding the launching of a fund-raising campaign during which preparations for the campaign must be completed.

**Private Foundation**    While there is a technical definition of "private foundation" in federal income tax law, the generic definition of the term is as follows. A private foundation is a 501(c)(3) organization that is originally funded from one source, that derives revenue from earnings on its investments, and that makes grants to other charitable organizations as opposed to administering its own programs.

**Pro Forma Gift Table (Chart)**    A table of gifts needed for a campaign to achieve a stated goal; based on experience in similar situations and accepted fund-raising principles.

**Prospect**    Any logical source of potential support, whether individual, corporate, foundation, organization, or government (at all levels).

**Prospect Profile (or Donor Profile)**    A research report detailing all other pertinent facts about a prospective donor, including resources, relationships, and past giving.

**Public Charity**    A 501(c)(3) organization that is not a private foundation, either because it is "publicly supported" (that is, it normally derives at least one-third of its support from gifts and other qualified sources) or because it functions as a "supporting organization" to other public charities. Some public charities engage in grantmaking activities, but most engage in direct service activities.

**Public Relations**    The practice of developing the reciprocal understanding and good will of an organization and opinion leaders and the general public.

**Response Device**    A form bearing the name and address of the prospective donor (coded by list), on which the donor indicates the size of his or her gift and returns it with a check in the reply envelope provided. The best response devices also restate the theme, offer, or appeal as a final "sell."

**Restricted Fund**  A fund in which the principal and earnings are bound by the donor's guidelines as they relate to investment and/or expenditure.

**RFP (Request for Proposal)**  When the government issues a new contract or grant program, it sends out RFPs to agencies that might be qualified to participate. The RFP lists project specifications and application procedures. Some foundations issue RFPs in specific fields, but most prefer to consider proposals that are initiated by applicants.

**Seed Money**  A substantial gift by a foundation, corporation, or individual to underwrite a fund-raising campaign, program, or project.

**Shotgun Approach**  Broad-scale and generally indiscriminate appeals for funds; the reverse of the "rifle-shot approach."

**Site Visit**  A visitation by a potential donor to inspect a project or review a program for which contributions are being sought; often, foundations and corporations will conduct one or more visitations after a grant has been made for the purpose of preparing a progress report.

**Solicitor(s)**  Volunteers and institutional staff who ask for contributions to a campaign or development program; professional solicitors are paid to solicit for programs or causes.

**Special Projects Campaign**  A fund-raising effort for one or more specific objectives such as programs or projects that do not comprise an organization's total fund-raising effort.

**Special Purpose Foundation**  A public foundation that focuses its grantmaking activities on one or a few special areas of interest, e.g., a foundation that makes grants only in the area of cancer research or child development.

**Sponsors**   Prominent individuals who allow the use of their names on letterheads and other campaign literature to convince prospects that the campaign or program has high-level endorsement; donors who assist in underwriting a campaign activity; a recognition category for donors who give a specified level.

**Subcontract**   To engage a third party to perform all or part of the work included in an original contract; a contract between a party to an original contract and a third party.

**Suspect**   A potential donor whose interests in an organization are in a embryonic state and who therefore cannot be considered a likely prospect.

**Target**   Any specific objective in a fund-raising program or campaign; a prospect; a campaign goal.

**Tax Benefits**   Savings in income, gift, and estate taxes brought about by giving to charitable institutions.

**Telemarketing**   Raising funds or selling products or services by telephone.

**Telethon**   A fund-raising program broadcast over a television station so that viewers call a telephone number and make pledges to support the charity for which the telethon is being conducted. Amounts of the pledges, names of the donors, and total commitments attained are often announced periodically during the course of the program, which is usually enhanced with personal appearances by celebrities from teams of solicitors working out of a central headquarters.

**Test Mailing**   A mailing in which a test of any nature is conducted.

**Testimonial**   An endorsement of an organization or its programs.

**Third Sector**   A term used to describe all not-for-profit organizations and institutions.

**Trust**    A fiduciary relationship with respect to property, subjecting the person by whom the title to property is held to equitable duties to deal with the property of the benefit of another person. For example: A gives property in trust, with A as trustee, to pay income to B for life and then to give property over to C free and clear.

**Trusts (Types)**    *Charitable Trust:* A trust established for the benefit of the public or some part of the public. *Inter Vivos Trust:* A trust entered into during the lifetime of the grantor. *Irrevocable Trust:* A trust that cannot be changed or terminated by the person creating it. *Revocable Trust:* A trust that may be changed or terminated by the person creating it. *Spendthrift Trust:* A trust protecting the beneficiary from creditors or his or her own imprudence. *Sprinkling or Spray Trust:* A trust that permits the trustee to distribute funds to the beneficiaries in proportion to their needs. *Testamentary Trust:* A trust created by a will that does not become effective until the trustor's death.

**Unrestricted Gift**    A gift made unconditionally; the reverse of a restricted gift.

**Upgrading**    The process of increasing the level of giving of donors of record.

**Value**    The worth of property, goods, or services.

**Voluntarism, Volunteerism**    The services of private citizens without compensation both in fund-raising campaigns and in other activities in behalf of philanthropic causes.

**Volunteer**    Any individual who works without compensation on behalf of a gift-supported organization on a temporary or a more or less continuous basis.

**Will(s)**  Normally a legally executed written instrument by which a person make disposition of his or her property to take effect after death. *Holographic Will:* A will entirely written and signed by the testator or maker in his or her own hand. *Nuncupative Will:* An oral will made by a person in his or her last illness or extremity before witnesses, often not honored in a court of law. *Pour-Over Will:* A will whereby assets controlled by the will are directed to be poured over into a trust. *Reciprocal Wills:* Wills made by two persons in which each leaves everything to the other.

**Worker**  Any individual who has volunteered his/her services or who has responded to a request to serve as a solicitor in a campaign.

# Index